STEPHEN GARR OSTRANDER & MARTHA ALADJEM BLOOMFIELD

THE SWEETNESS OF FREEDOM

STORIES OF IMMIGRANTS

Michigan State University Press · East Lansing

♾ The paper used in this publication meets the minimum requirements of
ANSI/NISO Z39.48-1992 (R 1997) (Permanence of Paper).

Michigan State University Press
East Lansing, Michigan 48823-5245

Printed and bound in the United States of America.

16 15 14 13 12 11 10   1 2 3 4 5 6 7 8 9 10

LIBRARY OF CONGRESS CATALOGING-IN-PUBLICATION DATA
Ostrander, Stephen Garr.
The sweetness of freedom : stories of immigrants / Stephen Garr Ostrander
and Martha Aladjem Bloomfield.
p. cm.
Includes bibliographical references.
ISBN 978-0-87013-977-2 (pbk. : alk. paper) 1. Immigrants—Michigan—History—19th century.
2. Immigrants—Michigan—History—20th century. 3. Oral history—Michigan. 4. Michigan—
History—19th century. 5. Michigan—History—20th century. I. Bloomfield, Martha Aladjem. II. Title.
F566.O78 2010
977.4'03—dc22
2010003504

Cover and book design by Sharp Designs, Lansing, Michigan
Cover art photo by E. Chris Dancisak from the Michigan Historical Museum exhibit
Movers and Seekers: Michigan Immigrants and Migrants

Michigan State University Press is a member of the Green Press Initiative and is
committed to developing and encouraging ecologically responsible publishing
practices. For more information about the Green Press Initiative and the use
of recycled paper in book publishing, please visit *www.greenpressinitiative.org*.

Visit Michigan State University Press on the World Wide Web at
www.msupress.msu.edu

In memory of my late husband, Jacob Joseph Climo, my parents and grandparents.

—Martha

To Jack W. Ostrander, veteran of World War II and Korea, father, teacher and friend; and to my grandparents and family who have immigrated to a new place, not on this earth.

—Steve

Contents

Acknowledgments

Many people participated professionally and personally with this project about Michigan's immigrants and migrants in a variety of ways and at different stages in the ten-year process from its inception as a research project, then a museum exhibit and now a book of narratives. We are grateful to all of them.

In 1999, Sandra S. Clark, Director, the Michigan Historical Center, asked a group of us, including Mary L. Ploor, E. Chris Dancisak, Saralee R. Howard, Scott Peters, Grant DeLong, Larry Griffin, Mary Patrick, Mark Harvey, and Martha Aladjem (Climo) Bloomfield, to do a research project about Michigan's immigrants and migrants based on oral histories and library and archival documents, artifacts, family photographs, family documents, recipes and maps to help tell the stories. Sandra launched a project scheduled for six months that stretched into ten years, culminating with the publication of this book. We thank her.

Realizing that we had wonderful materials for an exhibit, Martha Bloomfield talked with our museum director, Phil Kwiatkowski, and proposed an exhibit. Phil asked for a formal written proposal. A week later, he read and approved it. Phil also shared his thoughts about people's motivation to immigrate or migrate to another home. He believed that usually one family member has the vision and takes the lead to emigrate, or designates a family member to leave home to find a better life. This concept focused our thinking about the exhibit. He created an exhibit team that gave birth to a new partnership between Martha Bloomfield, the exhibit curator, and Steve Ostrander, the exhibit designer, as we had never worked on a project together.

After Steve conceptualized an exhibit plan, we revised it many times. As a Collections Specialist and Education Historian at the museum, Laurie Catherine Perkins helped select and gather artifacts for the exhibit and carefully and elegantly helped lay them out. She also worked on education and public programming. Rich Geer, Michigan Historical Museum artist, brainstormed with us about how we could effectively and safely use shattered glass in Bus Spaniola's father's store to help visitors visualize how the Ku Klux Klan had destroyed the store windows and display cases. Graphic designer Susan Cooper worked on exhibit labels, gleaning the essence of the stories from the interviews. Maria Quinlan Leiby, Historian and Education Coordinator for the Michigan Historical Center, conducted research on the history of immigration and migration to Michigan and the United States for the exhibit labels that also put each person's story in chronological context. We incorporated this information into the overall introduction to the book and in the introductions to each chapter. While Museum Educator and Web Curator Mary L. Ploor had researched migrants' and immigrants' journeys to Michigan before 1900, she provided much inspiration and support to the project and engaged in wonderful discussions about twentieth-century immigration issues. Grant DeLong, our audiovisual technician, recorded sound effects of a steamship whistle, seagulls cawing at the harbors of departure, the clip-clop of horse hooves, a jet plane taking off, trains speeding by, and automobiles chugging along.

Other museum staff also helped with the exhibit and/or education and public programs: Tami Averill, Cheryl Natzmer Valentine, JoAnne Arasim, Rose Victory, Eve Weipert, Lisa Konieczny, Rod Konieczny, Eric Perkins, JoAnn Carroll and Aaron Preston.

Michigan Historical Museum docents also helped develop and implement programs on immigration and migration to Michigan. Special thanks go to museum docents Marion Kennedy Heider, Joan Radashaw, Alice Hill, Terri Brantley, Gladys Wilson, Jim Groen, Mike LeMense and Sandy Frauenheim. Education Historian JoAnne Arasim also organized a Naturalization Ceremony at the Michigan Historical Museum, June 23, 2005. More than 225 individuals were sworn in.

Francis "Bus" Spaniola, President of the Friends of Michigan History, Michigan History Foundation Board Vice Chair, and Former State Representative from Shiawassee County, supported our endeavors, both personally and professionally throughout our journey. He willingly went on road trips with us to present talks on Michigan's immigrants and migrants and graciously accepted our invitation to write the foreword to this book.

Geneva Wiskemann, founder and secretary of the Michigan Oral History Association, believed in and supported this project and nurtured it all through the years. She validated our work and encouraged us to share our research at conferences, inviting us to present a paper at the Michigan Oral History Association Conference in 2005 and recommended that we give a presentation at the 2006 Michigan Women's Studies Association conference hosted by Delta College and Saginaw Valley State University. We gave presentations with Bus Spaniola at Macomb Community College's Lorenzo Cultural Center in conjunction with their exhibit "A Journey of Hope: Michigan's Immigrant Experience" and at the Chesterfield Township Library.

Once the exhibit was over, Steve realized it was not enough, that we shouldn't just put these documents on a shelf somewhere and that we needed to publish these immigrants' and migrants' stories in a book to preserve them in perpetuity.

The Michigan Historical Museum's Community Relations Director E. Chris Dancisak provided constant and long-term support of this never-ending project as we then began the long process of editing the transcribed interviews—without losing the immigrants' true voices—and searching for a publisher. Chris's perseverance, insight, editorial comments, and faith in the project cannot be measured. He has been invaluable and we are profoundly grateful to him for making this journey with us.

Laura Ashlee, Historian and Communications Coordinator, Michigan State Historic Preservation Office, believed in the necessity of publishing these immigrants' stories, encouraged, and supported us tirelessly throughout our journey, helped us find a publisher, and reviewed our final manuscript.

Mary Erwin, now retired editor, University of Michigan Press, guided us to edit the oral histories as narratives and recommended that we contact the Michigan State University Press to publish these stories, as they were seeking manuscripts related to Michigan's immigrants.

Steve Ferris, formerly with the Grand Rapids Art Museum, willingly and graciously shared his knowledge about Mathias J. Alten and introduced us to James "Jim" A. Straub, who patiently and consistently shared extensive knowledge about Mathias J. Alten. He, in turn, introduced us to Mathias Alten's granddaughters. As an independent art historian living in Grand Rapids, Jim has been documenting and compiling information on Alten's life and paintings since 1982. He has served on the Grand Rapids Art Museum's Collections Committee and wrote the artist's chronological biography for the museum's 1998 exhibition publication *Mathias J. Alten—Journey of An American Painter*. He is a member of the Catalogue Raisonné Scholars Association and recently published a catalogue of more than 1,700 authentic Alten paintings on the Internet at www.mathiasalten.com.

We also thank the following people who contributed in various ways to Gloria Gregory's remembrances of her grandfather, Mathias J. Alten: granddaughters Anita Gilleo and Carmen Corder; Celeste Adams, Director, Grand Rapids Art Museum; Kathleen Ferres, Registrar, Grand Rapids Art Museum; Henry Matthews, Director of Galleries and Collections, Grand Valley State University; Nancy Richard, University Archivist, Grand Valley State University; Nathan Kemler, Collections Manager, Art Gallery, Grand Valley State University; and Spectrum Health Foundation.

Carolyn Damstra, who works for the Michigan Council for

Arts and Cultural Affairs, and is a landscape artist, conducted oral history interviews with her Grandmother Trijntje (Tina Dam), her father Dick Damstra and her uncle Ted Damstra and wrote her family's story. She continued to support our endeavors.

Michelle S. Johnson, former Freedom Trail Coordinator for the State of Michigan, interviewed Carlean Gill. Michelle is currently Executive Director of Fire, a nonprofit Historical and Cultural Arts Collaborative in Kalamazoo. Olga E. Rojer, Department Chair and Affiliate Professor of Literature, Department of Language and Foreign Studies, American University, also helped with Carlean Gill's story.

Danielle Roth, a former student at Michigan State University's James Madison College, interned at the Michigan Historical Museum, conducted interviews with Marylou Olivarez Mason and Professor Deo Ngonyani, and helped organize other materials for this project. She went on to get a master's degree in history from Eastern Michigan University and a nursing degree from Michigan State University.

We thank Eric Byron, Ellis Island Emigration Museum of the National Park Service, for his enthusiasm and support in this project. Gary Boynton, Chuck Heiney, and Tom Sherry took some of the photographs of artifacts.

Patrice Apostel transcribed many of the oral histories.

A good friend, Marcia Horan, who worked for the Michigan Department of Environmental Quality, introduced us to her colleague Lance Truong, who had emigrated from Vietnam. Another good friend, former State Senator Burton Leland, helped us find Bernice Kutylowski. Another friend, Patti Roth, introduced us to Abraham Mach, a refugee from the Sudan, who had been one of her students in her English as a Second Language class at East Lansing High School.

So many immigrants and migrants and their extended families willingly and generously shared their stories, artifacts, documents and photographs with us for the exhibit and this book. Over a ten-year period, they answered questions and filled in the gaps for us. They graciously welcomed us into their homes and fed us on more than one occasion. We also thank them for traveling from all over the state with their extended family members to attend the opening of the Movers and Seekers: Michigan Immigrants and Migrants exhibit at the Michigan Historical Museum in February of 2005.

Approximately 300 visitors attended the opening, the largest attendance at any opening of a special exhibit at the Michigan Historical Museum. The multi-generational families who came that night or later included those of Mathias Alten, Louis Padnos, Haratoune Adrounie, Olga Honkala, Michal Skrzypek, Angeline Spadafore, Norman Gill, Marylou Olivarez Mason, Benno Levi, Trijntje (Tina) Dam, Iwao Ishino, Mary Kobayashi Ishino, Oh Ae Kyung (Jennifer Hanna Sochor), Sharkey S. Haddad, Lara Hamza, Abraham Mach, Lance Truong, and Deo Ngonyani. We thank graphic designer, Cathe Ishino, daughter of Iwao and Mary Ishino, for assisting us with the artistic and technological presentation of her parents' story in the exhibit. We thank them all for their support and participation and for traveling with us on our long journey.

We thank our editors at Michigan State University Press, Julie Loehr, Martha Bates, and Kristine Blakeslee, production manager Annette Tanner, marketing and sales manager Julie Reaume, and copyeditor Richard Isomaki, who realized the value of these stories and worked with us diligently, graciously, and patiently.

We are grateful for financial support for the exhibit from the following: a grant from the Michigan Humanities Council, funds from the Friends of Michigan History, and from private donors including the Louis and Helen Padnos Foundation, and the Esther and Seymour Padnos Fund of the Community Foundation of the Holland/Zeeland Area. We also had a grant from SBC, formerly Ameritech Corporation, secured by JoAnne Fritche, former director of the Michigan Historical Center Foundation (now the Michigan History Foundation.)

From Martha Aladjem Bloomfield: I would like to thank my late husband, Jacob Joseph Climo, for his support and engaging discussions, and for suggesting his colleague, Iwao Ishino, as an interviewee. I thank my two sons Avi Climo and Simi Climo for their support in this never-ending project and helping me have faith—they have been and continue to be two of my greatest fans! I am grateful to my current husband, Alan Jay Bloomfield, for his belief in me and empowering me to seek options and solutions and move forward with this project, and my terrific mother-in-law, Betty Bloomfield Soffin for her continuous, optimistic support. I also thank Patty A. Potter, my best high school friend, who, as editor of our high school literary magazine way back when, appointed me to its board.

From Stephen Garr Ostrander: I would like to thank my wife, Rhonda Ostrander, and my daughters Danielle and Andrea, for their love and support over the years. Also my extended family—parents and grandparents, aunts and uncles, all the way back to Pieter Pietersen Oostrander, an orphan who came to New Amsterdam in 1661 to begin a new life in America.

And to all the immigrants, thank you for sharing your stories.

Foreword

Francis "Bus" Spaniola

I first became involved with the authors and this project over ten years ago when it began as a series of interviews in preparation for a research project and then a museum exhibit entitled Movers and Seekers: Michigan Immigrants and Migrants. The authors chose to interview me and include my family's stories, photos and artifacts in the Movers and Seekers exhibit. The exhibit was one of the most popular shows at the Michigan Historical Museum in Lansing, Michigan, and I was proud that my family's history was included.

The authors interviewed more than eighteen different persons of various ethnic backgrounds, all of whom had immigrated or their families had immigrated to the United States. The information gathered was a collection of personal stories that touched the authors in a very profound manner. They believed in the value of these oral histories so much that they were determined to have them published. While it is true that those of us who were included in the project had personal reasons to support the publication of this book, its use as a tool to teach about America and Americans is far more important than relating my story or anyone else's.

The Sweetness of Freedom is an important contribution to United States and Michigan history. Our country is a land of immigrants, all of which, by their individual contributions, helped make the United States a world political and economic power. These personal stories are a testament to why we have, for the most part, been lauded for our high standards of social, political and economic justice. Each of these moving personal experiences is evidence that people were attracted to America because of the allure of fairness, common decency, opportunity and justice.

Many native-born, second generation Americans are unaware of the great sacrifices and risks that immigrants have taken to legally enter our country. Thirteen-year-old boys left their homes with little or no money in their pockets, traveling via steerage to enter the "golden door." Husbands left wives and children in the old world hoping to earn enough to pay for their family's passage to America. Many times, years would pass before the family could be happily reunited. Sadly, in some cases the families never were reunited. Whatever the case, the heart-tugging tales told in this book should make all of us aware of our nation's reputation and appeal throughout the world.

Bernice Skrzypek Kutylowski, a Polish immigrant, said during her interview, "The only thing I ever wanted was survival.... We didn't have enough food. We never had enough food." Her statement should enlighten the hardest heart about America's contributions to the cause of economic justice, as well as the necessity for America to continue to set an example for the world to emulate.

This work contains far more than a collection of inspirational stories. It is a larger story of what America is and what being an American truly means. It illustrates the genius of America and it teaches us in a positive way the peril of losing sight of that important part of our heritage.

The authors point out that even in this, the most just society in the world, there lurks a darker side that at times rears its ugly head. We experience periods that could, for want of better terms, be called anti-immigration frenzies. We are presently experiencing an anti-Hispanic era; there have also been anti-Italian and anti-Irish episodes throughout our history, to name a few.

Richard Gambino, writing in his book *Vendetta* says, "The political and economic motives behind [this approach] are exposed, and the consequences are laid out. In them one sees the uses that governments, institutions and individuals make of social violence, ethnic and racial hatred, propaganda and hypocrisy—and one sees the courage and the peril of the people who oppose such hell." *The Sweetness of Freedom* exposes the folly of this ethnic, racial and religious hatred in a thoughtful and reasonable fashion. Essentially, it tells us that we gain more from understanding other cultures than by the propagation of fear and hatred.

In this collection of stories it is evident that there is nothing un-American about being proud of your ethnic heritage. This was illustrated well by the comment of Marylou Olivarez Mason, a native born American citizen, when she said, "I feel more Mexican American now, but I'm still Mexican, that's something that never changes." Her comment reminded me of my dear mother, who was proud of her Italian heritage, who said, "I would love to visit Italy to see my relatives, but I love America so much, and I'm afraid I won't be able to come back home." In spite of our reasoned explanation that as an American citizen with a valid U.S. Passport, she would never encounter such a problem, we could not convince her to visit Italy as a tourist. In my opinion, these are the words of a true American patriot who never forgot her Italian roots.

If we were not already aware, these human-interest stories teach us that we are the sum of the experiences of our ancestors. Our perspectives are fashioned by the past, for good or for ill. Each immigrant came to America with a different identity, to confront essentially the same challenges.

This book, which includes experiences of immigrants and migrants from all over the world, is a timeless story. It would be timely had it been written one hundred years ago and it will be appropriate one hundred years from now. We all need to be reminded of the heroics of people yearning to be free.

Personally, I want to thank Martha Bloomfield and Steve Ostrander for recording my family's history, and for recognizing the desire of most people to learn as much about their family history as possible. I recall the emotion I felt on my first trip to Italy. On my arrival I understood more fully how Alex Halley felt when he discovered his roots.

This book and this entire experience is best summed up by this quotation, in part, from the words of Emma Lazarus inscribed on the Statue of Liberty:

> *Give me your tired, your poor,*
> *Your huddled masses yearning to be free,*
> *The wretched refuse of your teaming shore.*
> *Send these, the homeless, tempest tossed to me.*
> *I lift my lamp beside the golden door!*

Introduction

Without memory, the world would cease to exist in any meaning-
ful way, as it does for persons with amnesias or dementias that
make them forget the self through an inability to remember some
or all of their past . . . or to create new memories in their ongoing
life. Without memory, groups could not distinguish themselves
one from another, whether family, friends, governments, institutions, ethnic groups or any other collectivity, nor would they know
whether or how to negotiate, fight, or cooperate with each other.
From the simplest everyday task to the most complicated, we all
rely on memories to give meaning to our lives: to tell us who we
are, what we need to do, how to do it, where we belong, and how
to live with other people.

   —Maria G. Cattell and Jacob J. Climo, *Social Memory and*
   History: Anthropological Perspectives, 2002

E ach of us travels through life—literally and figuratively—
and has a memory of the journey tucked deep within us,
and a story to tell. Sometimes we emigrate from our homeland to get a better education or a more satisfying job, or to be
closer to (or further from) family, or for better health. Some of

us—refugees—flee our countries of origin to escape war, poverty, hunger, or ethnic or religious prejudice, discrimination and persecution, or political repression. Some of us migrate within our own countries to seek greater economic or educational opportunities or to escape racial prejudice. Our journeys are inspired by dreams, fears, freedom, survival, peace, greater opportunities, a better life, a better job, or better land. We make sacrifices and leave family and friends behind and never know for sure if we will see them again—a risk we take in choosing self-determination and self-actualization. Sometimes we send our children to a country thousands of miles away with hopes of a safer, more peaceful life (at least for them) and the hope that we will someday be reunited with them. Whether we are the travelers or those left behind to say good-bye, we can all appreciate the challenges and difficulties, the disruptions and changes, and the joys of reuniting. While people may destroy our homes, our possessions, our rights, and our physical beings, they cannot destroy or take away our stories or our spirits.

As human beings, we naturally want to choose our own destiny and make our own decisions. We want to do what *we* want to do, not what someone else wants us to do. We strive to better ourselves and improve our lives. America, and specifically Michigan, has been one of those special destinations where immigrants and migrants still come to realize their dreams or empower their children to realize their own.

This book presents an eclectic collection of oral histories and personal artifacts, documents, and photographs from twentieth- and late-nineteenth-century immigrants and migrants, or their children or grandchildren describing their ancestors' lives, experiences, and remembrances. Originally their stories were the foundation of a research project that evolved into an exhibit called Movers and Seekers: Michigan Immigrants and Migrants at the Michigan Historical Museum in Lansing in 2005. We now share their stories in this book. While we did not interview an individual from every single ethnic group who ever immigrated to the United States in the last century and a quarter, we researched the history and geography of the various waves of immigration and migration from all over the world to Michigan in the twentieth and late nineteenth centuries and then identified a select number of individuals whose stories were more or less representative of different time periods.

Some people shared their individual stories; others shared multigenerational stories. These future Michiganians came from Europe, the Middle East, Asia, Africa, Latin America, and Canada. Some came as part of immigration waves like the Great Migration of African Americans in the 1920s and 1930s or the more recent wave of Hispanic immigrants. Some came alone; others came with their families or sent for their families once established in their new homeland. They all came with a reason for leaving their birthplaces, and with a dream for the future.

While these immigrants and migrants had distinct ethnic and cultural identities, languages, and customs, they shared similar challenges. Some individuals actually walked out of their homelands on foot. Others traveled by ship, train, airplane, and automobiles. They settled all over Michigan, in both rural and urban areas. Each person had a vision, often revolving around an individual's or family's survival. Once here, many immigrants and migrants wanted to preserve their heritage, religion, traditions, and ethnic identity. Others wanted to forget their past conflicts and lost family members, so they adapted and assimilated. They all made contributions to Michigan society through their education and work, whether it be manual labor, military service, governmental service, or intellectual and artistic pursuits.

History and Memory

We can think of at least three different versions of our history: what we believe happened, what we tell people that happened, and what really happened. What we want to believe and what really happened may be different altogether. We can be guilty of sins of omission. Sometimes, we do not talk about events and memories that are too sad, painful, or embarrassing. Other times, we exaggerate our recollections because we want to give our past more importance and meaning. The stories in this book are presented as told to us, the interviewers, and it was not our intent to correct or otherwise influence the storytellers. We tried to remain as impartial as possible.

HISTORY

The earliest Michigan residents were Native American migrants who came here to live and hunt thousands of years ago. They were nomadic, moving about the landscape as the seasons changed, exploiting food sources, and following herd animals. Michigan was—and still is—a bountiful place to live.

The next wave of immigrants was European explorers, fur trappers, and traders who also came to exploit the natural resources of Michigan and perhaps convert the indigenous people to Christianity.

The completion of the Erie Canal in 1825 decreased the travel time from New York from a matter of weeks to a matter of days, and thus accelerated the populating of Michigan, leading to statehood in 1837.

Vast stands of three-hundred-year-old white pine attracted lumber barons from the east. Copper—first discovered and used by Native people—also attracted investors and laborers. Good soil, plenty of rain, and freshwater lakes and streams for transportation and power all created an environment ripe for agriculture and manufacturing.

The earliest inhabitants in the Upper Peninsula were the ancestors of today's Native Americans, who mined copper and fashioned it into tools. With the rediscovery of copper and iron riches in Michigan's Upper Peninsula in the mid-nineteenth century, came a need for laborers to work in the mines. Finns, Swedes, Irish, English, Italians, Cornish, Croats, French Canadians, Germans, Poles, Slovenes, and Chinese immigrated and settled in the iron and copper range towns in the Upper Peninsula.

In Europe, industrialization and rapid population growth changed Europe's economy, displacing small farmers and craftsmen. Political and religious oppression increased emigration, especially from Eastern Europe. Immigrants chose destinations that offered land, jobs, and greater freedom. Among the destinations was Michigan.

In the early twentieth century, rural southern African Americans began moving to northern industrial cities in an unprecedented "Great Migration." Facing poverty, indebtedness, racism, and crop failures, they moved north for better-paying factory jobs and greater freedom. Jobs in the fast-growing automobile industry attracted thousands of immigrants and migrants to Michigan, particularly to Detroit. When World War I cut off the supply of new immigrant workers from Europe, automobile companies sent recruiters south. African American newspapers and word of mouth also helped bring people north. Detroit was the primary destination in Michigan for migrating southerners. The city's African American population grew from about 5,700 in 1910 to 120,000 by 1930.

Immigration has always been a controversial topic in the United States. All of us are descended from immigrants—including Native Americans—and are now faced with the task of deciding who can and who cannot immigrate to this country. While the United States was once called "The Great Melting Pot," we have at times enacted laws that limited the numbers and selected the places of origin of immigrants.

During the 1920s, federal laws were passed severely restricting the number of immigrants admitted each year. These laws gave preference to people from the northern and western European countries that had supplied earlier immigrant streams. Immigration from East Asia was banned altogether. Legislation before 1920 focused on excluding certain categories of people: felons, prostitutes, those with contagious diseases or mental handicaps, and, in 1917, the illiterate.

Between 1940 and 1960, both African American and white migrants moved north to cities across the Lower Peninsula. Mexicans and Mexican Americans also continued to settle in Michigan, primarily working in the agricultural fields, moving around the state as different fruits and vegetables ripened at different times.

Provisions were made following World War II to admit war brides, refugees, and a limited number of Asians, excluding Nazis and Communists. But the quota system based on national origins remained in place.

In the mid-1960s, Congress restructured immigration policy. The Immigration Act of 1965 established a worldwide annual cap and a preference system favoring family unification, immigrants with certain skills, and refugees. The 1965 law transformed immigration. For the first time, Congress set limits on annual immigration from Canada and Latin America. By 2000, over half the country's foreign-born residents were from Latin America, and one-quarter were from Asia. Europeans only made up about 16 percent.

The Immigration and Nationality Act of 1990 is the most significant reform of immigration laws since 1965. As amended over the years, it provides the basic framework for the flow of visitors, workers, and immigrants to the United States. Since 2001, enforcement has tightened, and certain groups—Middle Easterners and Latinos—are especially subject to scrutiny, but Congress cannot agree on how to change the system. Immigration continues to be a major issue in the United States.

In the fall of 2001, in the aftermath of the attack on the World Trade Center, Michigan State University's Islamic Student Association organized a special public forum, "Women, Race, and Islam Before and After 9/11: Racial Profiling in Wartime and Peacetime." Anthropology Professor Emeritus Iwao Ishino from Michigan State University, who was on the panel and whose story is featured in this collection, said:

> Americans learned from the mistake of Executive Order 9066, 1942, which set into motion the racial profiling of all people of Japanese ancestry who were living on the Pacific Coast. I am persuaded that the wholesale racial profiling of Japanese Americans that took place in World War II will not happen again. I think we Americans have learned our lesson from the mistake of Executive Order 9066.

Ishino said that the fallout from 9/11 would have been far worse for the Arab American population in the United States had we not had the Japanese American internment camps in World War II. It was this comment that inspired us to organize an intergenerational symposium following the Movers and Seekers exhibit, entitled "Michigan's Immigrants and Migrants: Post 9/11," so that participants and their adult children had an additional opportunity to share their thoughts about immigration and to listen to each other reflect on their experiences. We understood more clearly than ever that the issues of immigration and migration are not past—that they are ever present in our lives and that we must confront them head-on if we are to learn how to live together in a peaceful, constructive way.

By understanding history, we hope not to repeat our errors from the past. While we have obviously not reached that goal, at least we can work towards it. By developing a greater understanding of other people's histories and discovering our own personal histories, we hope to better understand one another—and appreciate our similarities and differences.

Most Americans are citizens because they were born in the United States or were born to American parents abroad. Immigrants can become naturalized citizens if they meet certain requirements. They must be at least eighteen years old, have lived in the United States for at least five years, be of good moral character and loyal to the United States, be able to read, write, speak, and understand basic English, have a basic knowledge and understanding of United States history and government and the Constitution, and take an oath of allegiance to the United States. Immigrants who have applied and passed a multiple-choice civics test are interviewed to confirm their English skills and resolve any other questions about their qualifications. The final step to naturalization is promising to "support and defend the Constitution and laws of the United States of America against all enemies, domestic and foreign" in the Oath of Allegiance.

MEMORY

Our selves are the residue of all lived experience. By telling our stories, we create form and meaning, so memory can help locate us in the world. Being able to have a narrative of one's life is incredibly valuable for one's sense of cohesiveness and self.

—Patricia A. Potter, September 13, 2008

Knowing historical facts and events locally, nationally, and internationally is absolutely critical to our understanding of the past. However, we also strongly believe that people's personal stories about the past and, in this case, their narratives about immigration and migration to Michigan are essential to the full story. We asked Michigan immigrants and migrants to share stories from their memories—their own perspectives—about leaving their homelands, their journeys to America, arriving in the United States and Michigan, making Michigan home, and their dreams for their children and grandchildren and their future. We also asked them to share individual or family artifacts, documents, and photographs for the Movers and Seekers exhibit related to their immigration or migration story.

Historian Robert R. Archibald, president of the Missouri Historical Society, distinguishes between the significance of history and memory:

> History, relying on evidentiary rules, is factually more correct and thus more "true" while memory is suspect because it fails the test of evidence and accuracy and hence can be dismissed as unreliable. In a scientific age, anything that flunks the test is discarded. And memory often fails the test imposed by the mountains of historical evidence compiled and sorted in archives and libraries, stored on museum shelves, and interpreted by scholars concerned with the pursuit of a perfectly accurate memory: history. So individual and shared memory cave into history because they must. But memories and the traditions, habits and values they communicate are within the sacred and thus have authority. As many people now observe, our challenge is to define new relationships between memory and history.[1]

One of the most significantly universalistic statements in all of religious literature dating back almost 2000 years is that one human is as precious as an entire world because each single person is a world in miniature.[2] Our will to live usually dominates our fear of death, and our desire to preserve life is great. Unfortunately, not everyone desires to preserve life, and sometimes people choose to destroy other cultures and kill those who look or act or believe differently from them. Many of these immigrants not only saved their own lives from brutal enemies, but those of many of their relatives and friends.

Regardless of our life experiences—whether we have been blessed, injured, or imprisoned, or our homes and possessions kept safe, destroyed, or stolen, we all carry our memories deep within us. Sometimes they remain latent. Sometimes we are able to share them with others. When the memories became too painful for some of our contributors, as they told their stories, they broke down in tears and had to stop and collect themselves. But they all willingly moved forward. In telling and sharing their stories, people have the opportunity to heal themselves and others.

We were interested not only in the stories these people told, but also in artifacts they brought with them on their journeys. Artifacts are to historians simply "old stuff with a great story." Without a story, it is merely an object. A baseball is just a baseball, but if Babe Ruth—or Barry Bonds—hits it over the fence, it becomes an artifact. When we asked these immigrants and migrants about artifacts, the answer almost always was, "Artifacts? No, but I've got some old stuff that my great uncle Harry brought with him to America." And that's exactly what we wanted. People did not view these items as artifacts, but merely objects. We learned to phrase the question differently and ask them for heirlooms, antiques, or old stuff. It was our label applied by historians that confused the donors.

Most of them had carried suitcases and trunks that they had stored in their attics. They had carried their personal treasures in them on their journeys—three-dimensional objects that hold precious memories and meaning that complements their stories. They brought clothing and other personal possessions, such as jewelry, toys and games, kitchen and dining ware, religious items, books, art, and handmade goods that they often displayed or used in their homes to remind them of their native land and their past.

COURTESY OF THE MICHIGAN HISTORICAL MUSEUM. PHOTOGRAPH BY E. CHRIS DANCISAK.

Many immigrants brought their possessions to America in steamer trunks. Sometimes the trunks held everything the travelers owned. These are trunks from several immigrants from Europe who were featured in the Michigan Historical Museum's exhibit Movers and Seekers: Michigan Immigrants and Migrants.

The Hamza family brought kitchenware, games, traditional clothing, and religious books and objects from Lebanon that they either use or display now in their home in Dearborn, Michigan. While we visited and interviewed the Hamzas, they showed us many of their keepsakes. Insaf Hamza, Lara's mother, took great pride in having kept their belongings despite the many times that they had to move to different countries.

Lara showed us a pair of toddler red-and-white saddle shoes in the palm of her hands. She looked at them sadly and pointed to their soles. She had worn them when she went with her parents to the orchards to pick peaches in Libya. "You see the earth? My mom didn't want to clean them, because she just wanted to keep the memory of the region where I grew up. Even though I was born in Beirut, Lebanon in 1974, I wore these shoes on a family outing to pick peaches on a farm while living in Libya."

Others carried nothing except the clothes they wore and their memories. That tells a very different story. Either they did not own anything or were forced to leave quickly and could not take anything with them.

COURTESY OF THE HAMZA FAMILY. PHOTOGRAPH OF SHOES BY GARY BOYNTON.

Lara Hamza wore these shoes when she went with her parents to the orchards to pick peaches in Libya. Here she is with her father.

Robert R. Archibald wrote:

Emotion must be part of our work[,] for the most profound impact
of objects is emotional, their ability to make us feel what others
before us have felt, their power to inculcate habits of empathy and
sympathy for diverse points of view and make us feel part of the
human drama on this planet. . . .

    We know that objects, whether built environments or small
personal effects, are symbolic memory devices; that is, they
stimulate remembering. As public historians we understand that
memory is an ongoing process through which we create usable
narratives that explain the world in which we live, stories that
inevitably connect us to each other, history that builds community. . . . If the past has enduring meaning and implications, then
we as historians must become active conservators: of artifacts and
stories and community, of life on this earth and thus implicitly of
this earth that sustains life. As we face the past, we are also facing
the future.[3]

One of the most remarkable examples of a group of refugees
who fled their homeland without any possessions in the 1980s and
1990s and found their way to Kenya were the thousands of young
boys in the Sudan whose families had been separated from them
or killed. This happened as Sudan gained independence from the
British and the Egyptians in 1956, when long-standing cultural,
religious, and economic divisions between north and south pro-
duced decades of civil war. The effects of war were compounded
by widespread famine. Millions of people were displaced by these
disasters. About 4,000 of these boys, who became known as the
"Lost Boys," have come to the United States as refugees. By 2002,
120 Sudanese refugees settled in Lansing and 200 in the Grand
Rapids area, giving Michigan one of the largest concentrations of
Lost Boys in the country. The late Tom Luster, professor of Family
and Child Ecology at Michigan State University, said that a drive
for education, deep religious faith, and a brotherhood among the
Lost Boys are helping the refugees.

    Eight-year-old Abraham Mach and his brothers, David and

COURTESY OF AB. ABAM MACH

Abraham Mach, a refugee who came from the Sudan to East Lansing, ran in the Michigan High School Athletic Association 800 meters, Lower Peninsula Division Final, where he placed first. He still holds the record set on that day, June 5, 2004, at Rockford, Michigan. His time was 1:52.01.

Philip, walked to Kakuma, a refugee camp in northern Kenya. On November 15, 2000, the boys arrived in East Lansing, Michigan, as refugee foster sons of Yasmina Bouraoui. Abraham attended East Lansing High School, where he became a track and cross-country star. In June 2004, he set a meet record (1:52:01) in the 800 meters at the MHSAA Division 1 state track championships. He placed fifth at the elite Adidas Outdoor Track and Field Championships. He then went to Central Michigan University on a running scholarship and graduated in 2008 with a bachelor's degree. He became an All-American runner in 2008 in the 800, meaning he placed in the top eight in the country, and also qualified for the 2008 U.S. Olympic Trials.

At least a dozen pairs of sneakers filled the foyer of Abraham's home in East Lansing. We had identified Abraham as a good candidate for an interview because of the depth and breadth of the challenges he had encountered from the time he was a little boy. However, during the interview, Abraham was restless and seemingly impatient. The memories of leaving home were too close and frightening to share with a total stranger. While it was hard to complete the oral history and we did not include it in this book, we featured him in the exhibit along with the other immigrants because what we did learn about his story is so important. Abraham captured the essence of his escape from the Sudan so poignantly. When asked if he brought anything with him when he left, he said, "Only the shoes on my feet." He was running out of Sudan and he is running races in Michigan. His determination, tenacity, and goals were clear, and the motive was the same—to win, whether it was survival by escaping or winning a race.

We also asked these immigrants and migrants if they had family historical documents. Many had kept passports, identification cards, letters, journals, or school papers—primary documents that provide evidence, structure, and context for people's stories. These documents support their stories and provide an opportunity for us to get a glimpse of their lives when they were newcomers to Michigan.

Shirley Hanna wrote this in her journal about her adoptive daughter Oh Ae Kyung's arrival:

> We got to the gate and they landed at 4:05 P.M. About 4 babies and small children came through the door and escorts calling their names, then a stewardess with 2 girls—I was waiting for her to say a name and I turned to Dick and said, "That's her, isn't it?" And the next thing I remember is him holding her in his arms, her arms tightly clasped around his neck, unsmiling. She had on a beautiful long red silk traditional Korean dress.... the flight people remarked how lucky we were to be getting such a wonderful gift on Christmas Eve.

Photographs help preserve memory for us—the visual images of our relatives and friends. We asked the immigrants if they had photographs that could remind them of their loved ones and support their stories. Ever since photography came into being, people have been fascinated and even obsessed with taking pictures and sharing them. Looking at them helps us remember what family and friends and places looked like, what people were wearing, what they were doing at specific times in history. Photographs often trigger memories of our own stories from the past. Photographs comfort us when we are far away from our loved ones or if they have died. They also provide us with the opportunities to share memories with our children and grandchildren and friends. Sometimes they provide an opportunity for us to see our relatives whom we have never met. Other times, photographs allow us to see our parents and other relatives when they were children or at other periods in their lives, which gives us another perspective.

Mary Kobayashi Ishino, whose family had emigrated from Japan in the 1900s, told the story of how her cousin had renovated her mother's home in 1993 in Japan. While looking through the rafters of her house, he found several kimonos that Mary's mother, Misao Kitaya Kobayashi, who was a seamstress, had made—one of which was the first kimono she had sewn as an adolescent way back in 1903. When Mary shared this story during one of the interviews, she realized that in her living room she had a photograph of her mother as an adolescent wearing the same kimono.

Memories of Leaving Home

As these immigrants left their homelands and journeyed to Michigan, many of them risked their lives. Each had different thoughts and feelings about leaving home—some were sad, some were happy, some were excited, others were ambivalent—but all were motivated to create better lives for themselves and their families. They tell us why they left their homelands, what their challenges were, whom they left behind, what decisions and choices they made that significantly changed the course of their lives, what possessions they brought and those they could not take, what part of their journey was memorable, what was easy or difficult, why

Mary Ishino's mother, Misao Kitaya Kobayashi (*pictured to the right of her brother and sister*), made this black-and-gray striped linen kimono almost one hundred years ago. The kimono is the traditional dress of Japanese women.

they chose to settle in Michigan, and where they stopped along the way before they got here. The stories about leaving home are profound, touching, and inspirational. Each individual had dreams for the future; some were realized, others were not. After moving to Michigan, some yearned to visit their homelands. Some did; others could not.

On leaving their homelands, some immigrants realized they might never return home again. Ted Damstra came as a child with his family from the Netherlands in 1955 to escape poverty and find a better life. While Ted never went back to visit Holland, his parents did. When Carolyn, his daughter, was in college, she visited her family's homeland. When she entered a store in Friesland, her family's hometown, the storekeeper realized that she must be her father's daughter because they looked so much like each other.

These people were all profoundly motivated individuals. Their spirits were indomitable and absolutely resilient. Each of them had at least one defining moment in life, although they might not have realized it at the time. Their lives unfolded in ways that they could have never imagined.

Haratoune Adrounie traveled seventeen miles on horseback to get help from the British and Americans to save his fellow Christian Armenians from the Muslim Turks who were massacring them at the school compound, targets of economic jealousy and religious prejudice. This was the beginning of the Armenian genocide in Turkey that led to the ending of a million innocent lives. That action changed the course of his life. He had to flee for his life. He eventually realized his childhood dream and became a physician in Hastings, Michigan.

When Mathias Alten, an apprentice artist in Germany, was seventeen years old, he came with his family to Ferrysburg, Michigan, where they stayed with relatives for a few months and then moved to Grand Rapids. Alten's father wanted to provide his son the opportunity to become an artist. Mathias became one of the finest Michigan artists.

Iwao Ishino, who was born and raised in California of Japanese immigrant parents, was ordered to go into a U.S. government internment camp in Arizona during World War II. Little did he know that when he worked on a Bureau of Sociological Research Project there that one day he would receive his Ph.D. in anthropology from Harvard University and become a professor at Michigan State University.

Memories of the Journey

These immigrants and migrants traveled from their homelands by ship, train, automobile, and plane—from the east, the west, north, and south. They all shared different stories about their journeys to Michigan, depending on their mode of transportation, the era in which they lived, whether they came directly or made stops along with the way, whether they traveled alone or with other family members, and whether family members greeted them when they arrived in Michigan.

Some started their journeys on foot, such as Seymour Padnos's father, Louis Padnos, who walked out of Russia when he was thirteen years old. At the end of the nineteenth century, Louis and his parents decided he should move to the United States to escape the anti-Semitic Russian government and conscription into the Russian army. He walked many miles and rode in empty railroad cars until he got to the Netherlands, where he worked for a year to save enough money to pay for his boat trip to America.

After arriving on the east coast of the United States, Louis learned that he could get work on the railroads out west and got a free pass to Nebraska, Iowa, and the Dakotas. He also knew about horses from Europe and broke horses for agriculture. He learned to carry trade goods on his back as he traveled so that he would always have some income. He eventually went to Chicago, where his sister and brother-in-law had settled earlier. Some people told him that Dutch people had settled in Holland, Michigan. If he went there, he could converse with them—because he had learned the Dutch language when he lived in the Netherlands for a year—and perhaps could do business with them. He did just that.

Memories: Making Michigan Home

These people's lives in Michigan reflected their individual challenges, choices, and decisions. They endured homesickness and separation from family, adapted to their new homes, preserved their memories of the homes they left, continued some of their family social traditions, and faced problems similar to those they had hoped to leave behind. As you read their stories, try to think of them not only as immigrants and migrants but people with distinctive personalities and interests who worked hard to build new lives and contribute to the growth of Michigan.

While these immigrants and migrants have both individual and collective experiences, they all worked hard to help build Michigan's economy and society to make it what it is today. Many continue to do so. They made Michigan their new home and became citizens. They passed along their heritage to their children, grandchildren, and great-grandchildren. Most of them were not well-known people. Some became politicians, entertainers, executives, computer experts, professors, and more.

If they were lucky, they could continue in the professions they brought with them from their homelands, based on the skills they had carried with them. Mathias Alten had painted murals in cathedrals in Germany. He found similar work in Grand Rapids, decorated furniture, and became a prolific artist, with more than 3,700 paintings of Michigan, the southern, eastern, and western part of the United States, and northern and southern Europe.

Others who came to Michigan faced racism, bigotry, and confinement to second-class conditions and poverty, similar to that which they thought they had fled. Tony Spaniola's family left Italy and was persecuted by the Ku Klux Klan in Perry, Michigan. Marylou Olivarez Mason was not allowed to enroll in primary school until she was twelve years old, but had a will and a desire to learn. Her family encountered prejudice and racism. When they traveled by truck from Texas to Michigan, they could not use public restrooms in Michigan because they had signs that read "No Mexicans or Negroes Allowed."

Carlean Gill's parents raised six children in Ferndale, the segregated community that Ford built to house African American employees. The children attended an all-black elementary school and traveled by foot along dirt roads because the school system denied bus service to the children of African American descent.

Others had to abandon their professions from their countries of origin and find work in fields about which they had no prior knowledge and/or in which they had no interest. Wafic Hamza, who came with his wife, Insaf, and four children to Dearborn, where relatives had previously settled, had been an architect in Lebanon and Libya. He did not have the proper credentials to practice in the United States. Needing to support his family, he worked for the Wayne County Road Commission cutting and trimming trees, and he drove a bus at the Detroit Metro airport. Now he and two of his sons own two Italian restaurants, one son is a commercial airline pilot, and his daughter is pursuing a writing and teaching career. His wife, Insaf, keeps the home and the family together.

Dreams for the Future

All these people who left their homelands and came to Michigan had dreams for the future. Some dreamt of a better education, higher wages, and owning land. They passed on their dreams, legacies, and heritage to their children, grandchildren, and great-grandchildren. They all achieved personal goals. All of them have success stories to tell.

From a Research Project to an Exhibit to a Book

Martha Aladjem Bloomfield, Exhibit Curator

When we began this project, I was inspired to conduct the oral histories of those who came in the twentieth century or whose parents or grandparents had come then. I wanted to discover individual and family stories about people's journeys to Michigan as children or young adults or what they remembered about their parents' or grandparents' journeys.

I had a particular interest and passion for this project because even though I was not an actual immigrant, I was a migrant and my parents were both immigrants from Bulgaria. I had grown up in the Boston area. When I was twenty-one years old, I came to do an internship for Professor Leonard Kasdan in the Department of Anthropology at Michigan State University and eventually settled in East Lansing, where I have lived for over thirty-five years. Until that time, I could have never imagined the possibility of working on issues professionally about which I had so much passion and personal interest.

As the daughter of Jewish immigrants who came from Bulgaria just before the onset of World War II, and as a migrant to Michigan in 1974, I have always been intrigued with peoples' personal stories about immigration and migration.

My parents told me their story. My paternal grandfather—Tchelebi Aladjem—gave my family a gift. He inspired and financed my parents' trip to America before World War II. In 1937, Grandfather Tchelebi sent my uncle Nisso to study at the University of Illinois. In 1939, my grandfather came to visit him in Illinois and went to the World's Fair in New York City. When he returned to Europe and traveled by train from Paris to Sofia, he saw how terrible life was becoming for Europe's Jews. On return, he told my father, his son, Albert, to leave Bulgaria. My father was twenty-seven years old at the time and working in his father's haberdashery shop. My father did not want to leave. He had gone to a French high school and finally agreed to escape to France. My grandfather refused that solution. The story goes that he said, "You're going to America. While I was in Paris, I saw how bad life was getting for the Jews. I won a lottery ticket and I'm giving you that money for your trip to America."

Dr. Floyd H. Black, the president of the American College in Sofia, who had originally come from Illinois, had sponsored my uncle's trip to America and then my father's trip. My father left Sofia, Bulgaria, in 1939 just before the outbreak of World War II. He took a train to Italy and a boat to New York. When he arrived at Ellis Island, the immigration officials would not let him in, because of an issue with his visa and the quota system. They told him he had to go to Cuba or Canada for six months and then re-enter the United States. He opted for Cuba since, as a Sephardic Jew, he spoke Ladino and believed he would feel more at ease there.

My mother, Henrietta Hirsch, was born in Rumania in 1917 and spent several years of her childhood in Vienna before immigrating to Bulgaria, where she lived until she was twenty-four years old. She then followed my father, her fiancé, to America in March 1941. She had planned to take a train west from Sofia and then board a ship. But on the day she was scheduled to leave, the Germans entered Bulgaria, and canceled all trains west. Her only option then was to take the Trans-Siberian Railroad and go east through Russia, where she stopped in Vladivostok and Lake Baikal, then took a boat to Japan, Hawaii, and San Francisco. She entered San Francisco by way of the Golden Gate Bridge and took a train to New York.

When I visited San Francisco in the 1990s, I was mesmerized by the magnificent Golden Gate Bridge and marveled at my mother's courage coming alone at age twenty-four to the United States at the onset of World War II, more than fifty years before.

Our museum team realized we needed to have a geographical and historical representation of Michigan immigrants and migrants throughout the state. In 1999, I began the journey to find those people. While many of those featured lived in the greater Lansing area, I traveled all over the state in the Lower and Upper Peninsulas to discover people's stories, see their artifacts, read their personal historical documents, and look at family photographs. I traveled west to Grand Rapids and Holland, east to Dearborn, Southfield, and Redford, and north to the Upper Peninsula to Ishpeming and Negaunee. Everyone was hospitable and graciously shared stories and food with me.

I did not have a huge list of questions. Basically I wanted to know why and how each person or their family members decided to leave their home country, what inspired or motivated them or their families to leave home and go to America, what was difficult about leaving, what the journey was like and how they felt when they came to America and more specifically to Michigan. I wanted them to tell their stories the way they wanted to, the way they could make sense of them without much external direction.

Once they began to tell their stories, I said very little. Some cried as they got deeper into their stories. Some had to take a break for a few minutes to collect themselves. In some cases, more than one family member participated in the interviews. In others, family members translated the stories into English.

Phil Kwiatkowski, director of the Michigan Historical Museum, and I established goals for the Movers and Seekers exhibit, which carry over into this book: to help visitors and readers to understand their own migration and immigration stories and those of their families, the immigration and migrations stories of those who live in Michigan, and the connection between personal history and Michigan's social history. We recognized the need to inspire people to understand their personal, individual, and family histories, the local community's history, and their history and identity in relationship to their country and the world; to increase people's awareness of and sensitivity to others; to help develop tolerance towards others who are different; and to seek positive resolutions to conflict in our complex society.

Immigration and migration have always been important issues. However, in the light of such recent political and international crises as September 11, the wars in Afghanistan, Iraq, and the Sudan, and the current challenges our country faces with immigrants, it is increasingly important for people of all ages to understand our world. We have therefore seized the opportunity to explore and tell the stories of Michigan's immigrants and migrants. By understanding our individual and collective past, we can better understand our present and seek solutions to the issues that we must confront today and that our young people need to confront in the future.

Stephen Garr Ostrander, Historian and Exhibit Designer

In 2003, Martha Bloomfield suggested that the Michigan Historical Museum develop an exhibit based on the collected stories. I was asked to design the exhibit for the Michigan Historical Museum. Martha had already worked on the project for several years and had become quite acquainted with the interviewees. She asked me to accompany her as she went back to the interviewees to borrow artifacts, photos, and documents for the exhibit.

My first reaction was to say, "I don't normally do that. I'm a designer, not a collections specialist. I just take the artifacts and incorporate them into the exhibit." But Martha was insistent, "You have to meet these people," she urged. "You have to hear their stories." So I relented, and we embarked on a series of road

COURTESY OF THE HAMZA FAMILY

In 1995, Wafic Hamza decided to use his architectural skills to design and build a new home for his family.

trips across Michigan to visit the people whose stories appear in this book.

One of our first stops was Grand Rapids, where I met Anita Gilleo and Gloria Gregory, the granddaughters of German immigrant Mathias Alten. Then, we met another granddaughter Carmen Corder, in Jenison. They generously loaned paintings and told stories of their gentle but eccentric grandfather, the artist who loved painting west Michigan landscapes. Martha became enchanted with Alten's work and would often exclaim, "There's an Alten scene!" as we drove past a bucolic farm. (An Alten moment is like a Kodak moment, only instead of taking a photograph, he would have painted the moment.)

In Dearborn I met the Hamza family, who had come to Michigan after living for a few years in Libya. They were unable to return to their war-torn homeland of Lebanon. We sat in the house that Wafic Hamza had designed for his family's new home in Michigan. As they graciously offered us refreshments, we realized that it was

Today, Wafic Hamza and his two sons, Mahmoud and Toufic, own and run two Bellacino's restaurants in the Dearborn area.

Ramadan and they were themselves fasting. They also treated us to lunch at Bellacino's, one of their Italian restaurants.

We met the vivacious Carlean Gill in Saginaw, the former "Fiesta Doll," thoroughbred horse breeder, and beautician who grew up in a segregated neighborhood in Detroit. She told fascinating tales about Motown recording artists the Temptations, Della Reese, and the Four Tops, whom she had known while living and working at the Paradise Club at Idlewild.

In Corunna, I listened as former state representative Francis "Bus" Spaniola spoke lovingly of his Italian immigrant mother, his storekeeper father who longed to be a singer, and how his father stood up to the Ku Klux Klan. As a family they survived the depression in a small town in Michigan.

I met Lance Truong, who risked imprisonment by Communist authorities and drowning at the hands of pirates to escape from Vietnam. He made it to Thailand alive, but his journey wasn't over. He wanted to go to America.

As Martha and I drove the miles back to Lansing, we talked of what we had seen and heard. I was amazed at the determination, perseverance, and hopefulness of these people. Their stories moved and inspired me. Though they missed their family members and their homelands they had left behind, they all realized the promise of America, and they stayed. They represent the great cultural diversity that exists in Michigan. They overcame great odds and went on to contribute to Michigan society as artists, storekeepers, legislators, educators, and citizens of Michigan. Many came here with nothing, but they all had stories, and no one could take them away from these courageous individuals.

We talked about how I would design the exhibit. I realized it would be best to feature a handful of people and create vignettes of their home or their work life. Other shorter stories would introduce and conclude the exhibit. When we visited Marylou Olivarez Mason's home in Williamston, she had already spread out a collage of artifacts, photographs, and old family documents on blankets on her floors in her living and dining room. Marylou began working in the fields as soon as she could walk and lived in barns, tents, and in the back of a truck. Though she was denied primary education, she graduated from high school through sheer determination and later rose to head the Michigan Commission on Spanish Speaking Affairs where she helped other migrant workers find jobs, education, and health care.

As we sat on the floor reviewing Marylou's treasures, we struggled to determine how we would present her story. We had already figured out how to tell Bus Spaniola's story by creating a scene from his father's confectionary store. The Ishino story would be told by a scene in the Poston Internment camp fenced off with barbed wire. The Hamza story would be represented by a drawing board with plans for a new house, since Wafic Hamza was an architect. Then it came to me! Marylou had a photograph of the truck they used to ride in as they went from farm to farm. The women and children slept in the truck, the men slept underneath the truck. I would create a scene of their camp life and have a huge photomural made from the tiny two- by three-inch photograph for the backdrop of the vignette. Their truck was their home—a mobile home.

At the completion of creating the exhibit, which took nearly a year, we held an opening ceremony with many of the interviewees and their families present. Emotions ran high, with laughter and tears and a sense of accomplishment and relief on my part. When sadly, one of our participants, tripped and fell at the opening, Martha held her in her arms while others called an ambulance. She whispered to Martha quietly, "You should go and be with your people." Martha told her—"I *am* with my people."

Later, after the fanfare wound down, I began to reflect on the people I had met and friends made along the way. Although the exhibit was a success, something was missing. So much of the interviews had been whittled down to make abbreviated museum labels. So much was left unheard. I couldn't bear to see the interview tapes and transcripts stored away on some lonely shelf in the library or archives. I wanted these real people to continue to tell their true stories to those who had not or could not visit the exhibit, as well as students, historians, teachers, and future generations.

We could not listen to their stories and not be affected by them. We believed we needed to share their stories with more people and have them available indefinitely—not just in the confines of an exhibit in a museum for a few months. So we looked for an opportunity to publish them in a book. We believe that these immigrants' and migrants' memories and stories are important to preserve and hope that they will inspire you to discover your own history, realize your connections to Michigan history, and draw conclusions that produce new meaning and understanding in your life.

I suggested to Martha that we should publish the oral histories in book form. Martha, of course, thought it a wonderful idea. Though there were setbacks along the way, we both believed in the project, and it was Martha who was persistent and kept the project moving along when it looked like it was going to falter or die. We then found an excellent publisher at our alma mater, Michigan State University Press.

As Martha said to me, "You have to meet these people. You have to hear their stories." I wish you *could* meet and know the people as Martha and I have, to hear the emotion and passion in their voices when they told their stories and see the expressions on their faces. This book is as close as you will come to that. I hope you enjoy reading this book, and I hope you are as inspired as I was by these true stories. Their voices are louder now, because of this book. These are only a handful of their stories. Take your time now and travel with them on their journeys to Michigan.

NOTES

1. Robert R. Archibald, "A Personal History of Memory," in *Social Memory and History: Anthropological Perspectives*, edited by Jacob J. Climo and Maria G. Cattell (Walnut Creek, CA: AltaMira Press, 2002), 69–70.
2. Gilbert S. Rosenthal, "The Strange Tale of a Familiar Text," *Journal of the Academy for Jewish Religion* 3, no. 1 (2007): 57–67.
3. Robert R. Archibald, *A Place to Remember: Using History to Build Community* (Walnut Creek, CA: AltaMira Press, 1999), 23–24.

I Have a Beautiful Country to Work From

Almost one and half million people came from Germany to the United States in the 1880s, the peak decade of German immigration. Most settled in the Midwest. They sought economic opportunity as well as religious and political freedom. As a united Germany built up its army, large numbers of young men emigrated to avoid military service.

Mathias J. Alten was one of those immigrants. He was born in Gusenburg, Germany, in 1871. At the age of fourteen, he began working as an apprentice to an artist, painting decorations on ceilings and walls in churches and theaters.

When he was seventeen years old, he immigrated to Michigan with his family—his father, Michael, a schoolteacher, his mother, Maria, and his brother and sister. His father wanted him to have greater opportunities to become an artist. They sailed on the steamship *Pennland* from Antwerp, Belgium, to New York, arriving on January 25, 1889.

Mathias and his family first went to Ferrysburg, Michigan, where other relatives were already living. Then they moved to Grand Rapids, where many German, Polish, Irish, Dutch, and Scandinavian immigrants had settled.

Grand Rapids was a large center for manufacturing furniture,

Self-Portrait with Pallet and Brushes. Oil on canvas, 45 × 36 in. Alten painted this self-portrait on the porch of his home at 1593 Fulton Street in Grand Rapids. He painted self-portraits to experiment with lighting and brushwork.

and Alten easily found work using his artistic skills to decorate furniture. He also painted signs and decorated the walls of restaurants. He painted murals in churches and scenery for theaters. Today you can see many of Alten paintings in public buildings around Grand Rapids. Alten had numerous exhibits of his works in Grand Rapids and as far away as Los Angeles. He had his first exhibit at the Michigan State Fair in 1896.

After he married, he and his wife, Bertha Schwind, took over her father's business selling wallpaper, paint, artists' supplies, pictures frames, and window shades. Alten also opened a studio and art school at 66 Pearl Street in Grand Rapids.

Alten painted numerous portraits, landscapes, seascapes, and still lifes wherever he traveled—Florida, California, New Mexico, Connecticut, Massachusetts, and Maine. In Europe he painted in France, Spain, Holland, Germany, and Italy. He painted extensively in west Michigan and Grand Rapids, including many beautiful farm scenes. His children and grandchildren were frequent subjects for his paintings.

At one point Alten moved his family to New York, but after several months there, he realized it was not the place to raise his family. In an interview in the *Grand Rapids Post* in 1905, he said, "I have a beautiful country to work from . . . and there are no better cattle and horses in America I believe, than we have right here in Michigan. I feel I am . . . a better artist by staying here and working out my own ideas than if I were to pass my time in a luxurious studio in New York, with my fellow artists influencing my work."

Alten became a U.S. citizen in 1898. In 1899, he went to Paris to study at the Academie Julian and the Academie Colorossi. After studying there for almost a year, he returned to America, where he devoted the next forty years to serious painting. During the last years of his life, he stayed in Michigan and painted scenes in Grand Rapids, Ada, Saugatuck, and Leland, and several self-portraits.

Mathias J. Alten died in Grand Rapids in 1938.

Martha Aladjem (Climo) Bloomfield interviewed Mathias Alten's granddaughter Gloria Alten Gregory at her home in Grand Rapids on October 15, 2002, where Mrs. Gregory recalled her grandfather's life and work.

Early Memories of Grandfather Alten

I knew my grandfather personally for the first twelve years of my life and the last twelve years of his life until his death at the age of sixty-seven.

My memories are of my grandfather in his studio, smoking a

Alten painting in his Grand Rapids studio.

cigar. I didn't really know that he was an artist. I just knew that he worked in his studio all the time and that he was always busy painting pictures.

He definitely was a quiet man, yet things were always happening around him. However, he never liked being the center of attention. He had a wonderful wit and sense of humor. I can remember him thoroughly enjoying the company of others. Laughing and telling jokes, he seemed to be a very personable man. I know he had definite opinions about religion and politics.

My Grandmother, Bertha

My grandmother's name was Bertha Schwind, but grandfather called her Bert. She was born in 1898. She came to live with us before she died in 1945. Her father had a paint and wallpaper store and grandfather went there for supplies. He met her there and they later married.

Alten with his wife, Bertha Schwind Alten, and their three children. Clockwise beginning with Mathias Alten, Camelia, Bertha, Eleanore, and Viola.

She was Protestant, but he was Catholic at that time. The priest wouldn't marry them in the church, so he left the church. It's interesting that he always seemed to have a good rapport with the Catholic Church. The priest from St. Thomas who lived a mile down the street always was a very good friend and would often come on Sunday to visit.

Bertha's father died from diphtheria, and she and her mother took over the store. I have a ledger that my grandmother kept with beautiful handwriting, showing everything that was sold in the store, and to whom. All of the prominent citizens of Grand Rapids—all the names are there. They came to buy the materials to decorate their homes.

Bertha kept the books and paid the bills and kept everything going so that grandfather could do what he loved—which was paint.

My Mother, Camelia

Mathias and Bertha had three daughters—Eleanore, Camelia, and Viola. My mother was Camelia. I'm the oldest of her children.

They called my mother Cammy. It was her nickname. She died in 1999 at the age of one hundred.

She loved adventure. She tried everything. She was a women's-libber before her time. After she finished high school, and before she went to college, she spent a year in California with a friend. She kind of had that role in the family, of her trying new things.

Mother said that if she wanted a new dress, she would talk to her father and he would say, "Well, there's a new exhibit coming up," or, "I'm going to go to the fair and paint, so I think that we can manage that." She never could remember feeling that they didn't have enough money.

Everybody seemed to know that he was absentminded, but they seemed to accept it as the price he paid in order to produce his art. Mother told me about the many times grandfather would come home on the streetcar with only his left glove. He always read the evening newspaper on the way home. He would take off his right glove to turn the pages of the newspaper and leave it on the streetcar. The conductor made a habit of collecting all of the right-hand gloves and returning them.

There's a piece that Camelia wrote in her memoirs of her father. They were on their way to a picnic at Lake Michigan, but he saw a farm scene, and they had to stop so he could paint the picture. Often he would start off in the morning from his house with his equipment to go paint, and we wouldn't see him for hours. We don't even know where a lot of the paintings were done.

One time he was painting my mother's portrait. She was posed on a big white horse. Everything was going fine until the noon whistle blew, and the horse took off for the livery stable. She hung on for dear life, screaming at the top of her lungs with my

July Memories. 1917, oil on canvas, 50 × 42 in. Alten's daughter, Camelia, is the girl sitting sidesaddle on the white horse. Her friend, Lucile Cusick, stands next to the horse. Family lore says a whistle went off at a factory and startled the horse, which galloped off with Camelia on it. Alten ran off after the horse and his daughter.

grandfather running down the street after her. He finally got the horse stopped without her falling off.

There's another story she told about how he came upon these wonderful morel mushrooms that he loved. He started picking them, but he had an appointment to do a portrait of a lady in his studio. If he started on something, he forgot about everything. He would get so involved and so passionate about what he was doing, that time didn't mean anything. Finally, the lady gave up and left

Workers in a Field. 1916, oil on canvas, 26 × 32 in. This painting captures Alten's fondness for farm scenes, including fields, sunny skies, and reflections in the water. This one is a view of farmers in conversation.

because he didn't show up. That kind of thing happened a lot. He was a very absentminded professor type. But I don't ever remember hearing any complaints about it from anyone.

Grandfather's Work

When he was still in Germany, he apprenticed with an artist named Joseph Klein for three years. Klein did murals on walls and ceilings in churches. My grandfather came to America in 1889 when he was seventeen.

After he came here he started right in painting in churches. He had to do many things, whatever he could to earn money. He wasn't too proud. He earned his living by painting his entire life.

That was a big accomplishment for an artist. That was practically impossible in those days.

One of the things he said was so important to him were the fairs, especially the state fair. He would attend all of them. He sold a lot of paintings at the fairs. He was grateful for those fairs.

Except for formal portraits and still lifes, grandfather painted outdoors. If he wasn't getting the result he wanted, he would wipe the canvas off on the grass and start over. He didn't fuss over something if it wasn't going well. He never took work back to the studio to finish. He never went anywhere without a sketchpad or his sketch box.

He taught art in his studio for twenty-five years, so he had income from that. His classes were very quiet. It was all business. There was very little talking. They would work and he would come round and critique their work. One of his former students said this to me: "Mathias Alten was a born artist. His soul was in his art. He could see more things in one second than you or I

Alten loved painting at Laguna Beach, California.

Alten painting a portrait in his Grand Rapids studio.

could see in a week. He had a great respect for time. Every minute counted. He didn't want to waste time—his time or anyone who was not serious about learning. He advised us to 'go without food when you are painting. Don't stop to eat. You will never get those minutes back again!'"

The other way he earned money was doing portraits. The portraits and the classes were a constant source of income. The paintings were more sporadic. If he needed money, he would go to one of his benefactors and ask if there was anything that they needed. He had a couple of patrons who stood behind him. One was

Mrs. Wilcox, who had a very nice home on the corner of Fulton and College. He did a lot of murals of *Ivanhoe* for her in there.

He had art exhibits in his house and at St. Cecelia, and he was one of the charter members of the Grand Rapids Art Museum, so he had his works shown there. He had shows at the Grand Rapids Art Gallery. He had a show in Los Angeles. He exhibited at all the big museums—in Detroit, Cleveland, Chicago, and Toledo. That was always a big job for him—selecting the canvases, choosing the frames, crating the paintings, and shipping them.

There are a lot of stories about what happened to his paintings. Some are in private homes. Some are in a collection at Grand Valley State University. It's nice to see them in a place where they are well cared for.

There are two paintings by Alten at the Spectrum Health–Butterworth Hospital in Grand Rapids: *Hollyhocks* and *Boy Feeding Chickens*. My grandfather originally gave them to Grand Rapids

Boy Feeding Chickens. 1919, oil on canvas, 53½ × 72 in. Alten referred to this piece as an "exhibition work" because of its large size and impressive composition.

Junior College, which is now the Community College. In those days he would paint huge paintings because these institutions had such tall ceilings. The college had a new art instructor come in who had been schooled in modern art. She changed everything. They had *Boy Feeding Chickens* there and she told the custodian to get rid of it. It's very large and he couldn't throw it in the trash, but he did take the gold leaf frame and he chopped it up for kindling. He took the canvas home and put it in his garage.

At the time we lived across the street from the man who owned Lincoln Brick Company. He decided he was going to try to research what had happened to that painting. He found the custodian, and the custodian took him to his garage and there it was, nailed to some two-by-fours. He gave it to him and he had it restored and he hung it in his house. Then he sold it to a doctor and his wife who were pediatricians at Butterworth Hospital. They then donated it to Butterworth.

My grandmother gave a wonderful painting that grandfather did in Spain to the Detroit Institute of Arts in memory of my grandfather. Sometimes the curators of an art gallery can decide that they are going to de-acquisition some works because they need the money. They sent us a letter saying that they had some wonderful sculpture that they wanted to buy, and they were selling his painting to raise the money. You have no control over that. It is a dilemma for an artist when he gives things away.

I tried to call the Detroit Institute of Art and to buy back that painting, but they said they couldn't do that because it's against their rules. They have to put it on the auction block. They have a certain auction house that they use. It sold for about $8,000. If grandfather had known about merchandising and marketing, he could have sold his paintings for a lot more. But he didn't bother with that. He really was not a good businessperson. He loved to paint and that's what he did well.

I wondered how he could be so passionate about his painting. It was as if he were driven, and where did that energy come from? Was it the fear of not being able to earn a living that drove him so? That's what he loved to do, and he did it day and night. He was so grateful that he could paint full-time without having to work in some other kind of a job.

Grandfather's House

My grandparents lived at 1593 East Fulton. They have now renamed the cross street Alten Street, so it's now on the corner of Fulton and Alten. It's a large house and it was very comfortable.

We lived just a block away, so I went there all the time. I'd go over there and play with my cousins. We had the run of the house. Wherever we wanted to play, we did. I remember playing in the attic with the old clothes. That was so much fun! Getting dressed up in the hats and clothes. It was a wonderful place to play make-believe.

One time he was painting a nude upstairs in the bedroom. My grandmother made us lunch, and I sat there and ate lunch with the model! I really wasn't aware of anything being strange. He treated all his models with respect.

The Alten home at 1593 East Fulton in Grand Rapids is in the National Register of Historic Places and has a Michigan Historical Marker.

My grandmother worked very hard in her garden. She planted all the flowers in the side yard. It was a wonderful garden, and grandfather would go out and pick a bouquet of flowers to paint. One time my grandfather was painting my mother's portrait in the garden. It was a beautiful sunny day, but every once in a while there would be a cloud passing over the sun. Grandfather only painted when the sun was shining, so he told mother she could rest if there was a cloud. She looked up at a cloud and got lightheaded and fell over backwards, crushing the flowers in the garden!

He actually did a lot of beautiful art in their house. He did a beautiful stained glass window that would remind you of a Tiffany at their home on Hope Street. My mother said she sat and watched grandfather make that window. It was clearly inspired by the stained glass work of Louis Comfort Tiffany, with grapevines and a trellis. The Grand Rapids Art Museum now owns the window. He also did a tile floor with a large gold "A" in the center of the foyer. I wish that house could be made into a museum. That's been my dream.

German Food

Grandfather would be painting and my grandma would be cooking. I often stayed there for lunch.

My great-grandmother Schwind was a wonderful baker. She always made these baked goods that they had with coffee or tea, and baked goods for the open houses that they would have on Sundays. There were definitely family traditions in terms of cooking. Mother would make liver dumplings and *spaetzle*—homemade noodles, also, sauerkraut and *eirekuchen*—egg cakes. It's like a French crepe only it's German. They're real thin and you roll them in powdered sugar and put in jelly filling. I'd have a house party at the cottage and my mother would be at the stove cooking these *eirekuchen* and everybody was having a race to see who could eat the most. We'd count to see how many we ate.

House Parties

Other memories I have were of Christmas parties. They were wonderful! Traditionally they were on Christmas Eve at my grand-parents' house. They would always have a keg of beer. They had twelve-foot ceilings and they had a Christmas tree that went up to the ceiling. We would decorate it on Christmas Eve. Then the kids went to bed while the older folks stayed up late.

I think they always enjoyed their parties. My grandfather was very sociable—he enjoyed people. My mother said he was quite shy, but I don't remember that part. He had a wonderful sense of humor and he loved to tell jokes. You can see that sparkle in his eye in a lot of his self-portraits.

The Machine

Around 1914, grandfather bought a car. My mother, Camelia, and her older sister Eleanore went with him to the car dealer. They looked at different cars and they found one he liked. He said, "I think I like this one the best. I like the lines and the color." The sales-man asked if he wanted to look under the hood and grandfather said, "Whatever for? I don't know anything about machines. I just like the color."

They called it "the machine." He would take the machine downtown because he had a studio downtown as well as at home. Then he would forget and come home on the streetcar. When he got home my grandmother would say, "Well, Matt, where is the machine?" And he said, "Oh, did I take it? Well, don't worry, the police will call soon and tell me where I left it." And sure enough, they would call and he would have to go back downtown and get it.

He never really liked to drive it, but my mother loved to drive it. She had to jump on the hand crank to start it. Sometimes she would park it on a hill so she could roll it down the hill and it would start up that way. On Sundays she would take my grandparents to church, but she wasn't sure if she could get the machine started again, so she would drop them off at church and she would drive it around and around until it was time to pick them up!

Tending the Boats. 1935, oil on canvas, 26 × 32 in. Alten painted people with different ethnic backgrounds in many places in the United States. These fishermen are in Tarpon Springs, Florida.

Alten's Travels

My grandfather went to New York when the children were young. They sold the house on Hope Street. My grandmother really felt bad, because my they had put so much work into it. He had done the ceilings of the house in murals, and lots of stained glass windows. But he decided that for his career, he needed to be with other artists. So he went alone to New York. He stayed there three months and decided it was no placc to raise a family. He returned to Grand Rapids and he remained there the rest of his life.

Grandfather left to study in Paris for a year. He would bring us things from his trips abroad. He would bring back steamer trunks filled with all kinds of things that he wanted to bring home. He would bring things that he thought he would use in some way for his paintings, like satin material and hats that were picturesque, vases and statues and anything that appealed to him.

I remember being really excited when he came back from Florida. He was painting in Tarpon Springs, with the Greek fishermen in their colorful boats. They came over from Greece and had their boats painted up the way they painted them in Greece. They fished for sponges, and he brought back all these sponges for everybody.

He loved painting in Spain. He went there three times. They fished for sardines there. They would net them, and then these oxen would pull the fishing boats up on the shore. That is when he changed to the bright sunlit scenes. His paintings from there were very popular. They were a good source of income for him.

I think the longest he stayed in Spain was nine months. He painted all the time he was there. When he was there he lived with a bull-keeper, and he got malaria. He did not have wonderful accommodations.

He also painted at the North Sea. He took the whole family to Holland. The girls went to school there, although they couldn't

Bracing the Boats. 1922, oil on canvas, 40 × 50 in. Alten admired the works of Spanish painter Joaquin Sorolla. He traveled to Valencia, a sunny city along the Spanish Mediterranean where Sorolla had painted since the 1890s. Although Alten never met Sorolla, he painted the sunlit beaches he had seen in Sorolla's work. He spent a lot of time watching these fishermen and their oxen so that he could paint them accurately. The fishermen have a catch of sardines. They are securing the boat with large wooden braces so it does not drift back out to sea.

The Broken Mast. 1910–11, oil on canvas, 32 × 42 in. Alten spent a year in the Netherlands with his wife and three daughters. On this trip, Alten painted every day but one. In the Netherlands, three-horse teams were used to pull boats to shore, either for winter storage or for repair. In this scene, Alten captured both the strength of the horses working with the boat and a fisherman's sad story. The mast on the boat is broken, so the fisherman will not be able to fish for herring and sell his catch for several days.

speak Dutch. They were going to stay for about three years, but they only stayed a year because my grandfather felt like they weren't getting the schooling they should have.

That's where he painted all the pictures of the boats, and the fishermen going out, and again, they pulled all the boats in by horse. He liked painting the workhorses. That was so picturesque for him to paint. That was a favorite subject for him.

He was always glad to get home. I think it was a hardship for him having to be away from his family in order to earn a living. He enjoyed his children. He was a family man.

They had open houses on Sunday so people could come and see his latest work. He would have all these fresh canvases and there was all this flurry and excitement—"Matt is back with his latest paintings!" Everyone would come over and see the newest work. He stopped putting dates on paintings because everyone wanted

Gulls of Leland. 1936, 30 × 30 in. Alten painted these seagulls on one of his trips to the Leelanau Peninsula in northern Michigan.

to have the latest thing, and that was a detriment when trying to sell them.

Death of the Artist

Toward the end of his life, he painted up in Leland. We camped for the summer because Grandfather was painting there. I was probably ten or eleven years old then. That was a very picturesque place for an artist to paint—the seagulls and the fishing boats.

I can remember him perched way up in a little shed, looking out of a window to get just the right view that he wanted. It was very difficult for him to be in that position. It was extremely hot up there. But he said it was worth it to make the painting. Nothing was too much of a challenge. Nothing was too much for him to try.

When I was about twelve years old, I was over for a visit, and I remember grandfather saying, "Oh, I must paint your portrait!" I think I was just blooming, so to speak, becoming a teenager. He said, "As soon as I am well, I will paint your portrait." But he never got well. He was sick for two weeks and then he died. He was at the height of his painting career.

I remember that just before he died, they had put the bed down in the dining room because he had had a stroke and he couldn't go upstairs. I've often felt that now they have so much better medicine for strokes and heart patients. He definitely would have lived longer. In those days people didn't live as long. He did smoke a cigar constantly, but of course they didn't know then how damaging that was. And he liked beer.

I remember the funeral, because as a twelve-year-old girl, that made a big impression on me. They had the coffin in the living room and everybody was visiting. We were all upstairs—the family was separate when they did the service. There were pallbearers. They went down the long sidewalk and down the steps to the street then into the hearse.

He was buried in the mausoleum, partly because he did some sculpture work on the mausoleum. So I think that that's why he ended up there. In a way it doesn't seem real fitting, because it was stone and so cold. A more natural setting would seem more appropriate, because he loved nature.

That's my memory of the funeral. It was then that I realized that he was an important person. It was not until then that I realized that was not what all grandfathers did.

My Life

I'm seventy-six and going strong. And I don't intend to quit. There's just so much to do and see. I had a period where I was divorced and taking care of my four children, but I'm trying to make up for that in terms of traveling and doing a lot of things.

My life is filled with things about my parents and my grandparents. My father was an architect. He designed over two hundred homes. He also designed jewelry and I'm sure my father learned from my grandfather. He was sort of an amateur artist—just a pastime in his retirement years in Florida.

I have nine grandchildren. I had one grandson at Michigan State, and he called because he had to write a paper on his family history and how it changed his life. We talked, and some of these things become a part of you, and you don't even realize it until you start looking back at things, and see how that changed your life. Life goes on, and I'm very enriched by all this.

Where the Streets Were Paved with Gold

I n the late nineteenth century, Jews in Central and Eastern Europe suffered economic pressures and anti-Semitism. The hostility and discrimination they faced as Jews forced many of them to emigrate.

In the Russian Empire, which included Lithuania, Ukraine, and part of Poland, Jews could not live outside limited territories. Access to higher education and the professions was severely limited. Pogroms—organized attacks on Jewish communities encouraged by the government—killed thousands. Jewish emigration from Russia increased rapidly in the 1890s.

Louis Padnos was born in 1886 or 1887 in Byelorussia. When Louis turned thirteen, he decided to move to the United States to escape the anti-Semitic Russian government and conscription in the Russian army. He walked many miles and rode in empty railroad cars until he got to the Netherlands. There, he worked for a year to save enough money to pay for his trip to America.

After arriving in the United States, Louis learned that he could get employment working for the railroad and received a free pass to Nebraska, Iowa, and the Dakotas. From his prior knowledge, he knew about horses. In the west, he obtained wild horses and broke them to use in agriculture. Earning sufficient funds enabled him to carry trade goods on his back as he traveled so that he would always have some income.

Louis traveled to Chicago, where his sister and brother-in-law lived. He learned of the Dutch-speaking community in Holland, Michigan. Because he was fluent in the Dutch language, Louis believed he would have an advantage there. He settled in Holland in 1905 and started a business dealing in scrap metal and bones and furs.

Louis Padnos married Helen Kantor in 1919. Helen was born in 1902 in Warsaw, Poland, which was part of Russia then. Her stepfather immigrated to Michigan in 1906. She and the rest of her family followed in 1910.

Louis and Helen had two sons, Seymour and Stuart, who helped them develop the business into one of the largest scrap and waste recycling companies in Michigan.

In 1995, the enterprise that Louis Padnos started as a peddler shipped nearly one million tons of products, including recycled paper, plastics, iron, and other metals. Louis Padnos died in December 1962.

Martha Aladjem (Climo) Bloomfield interviewed Seymour Padnos at Holland, Michigan, on June 7, 2000.

Louis Padnos Comes to America

My father's family were timbering people and blacksmiths in Russia. My father Louis grew up with that background and started working when he was old enough to drive a team of horses. He used to tell us stories about how they went out in the forest and the workmen marked the trees. Then they felled the trees and he drove the team pulling the logs out.

I suspect they all left at that time because they viewed the United States as the golden world and where the streets were paved with gold. They had heard from relatives who preceded them to the United States—about their successes and substantially improved lifestyle. I don't think people necessarily yearn to leave everything they know and all of their family. They left because there was a perception of a better life.

COURTESY OF SEYMOUR PADNOS

Helen and Louis Padnos pose with their sons, Stuart and Seymour.

You have to understand that, as Jews, my father's people were serfs in Russia. They were beholden to the will of the barons and were chattels under his control. His only means of education as a Jew was parochial—learning Hebrew and religious responsibilities for his bar mitzvah at the age of thirteen.

Shortly after he was thirteen, it became clear that he was going to be subject to conscription in the Russian army for twenty years. He made a decision that the army wasn't for him. So he stole his way out of Russia—he wasn't free to just leave.

He went alone, working his way across Russia. He walked and rode under the railroad cars. He had to hide so he wouldn't be picked up and sent back.

He made it to the Netherlands. He always said that people treated him well along the way, so the Germans must have been kind to him, or maybe the Dutch were kind to him.

Once he made it to the Netherlands, he had to have money to cross the Atlantic. He had to stay there and work for a while. Having studied in the religious education, he had been taught Hebrew. He also knew Russian. The vernacular language was Yiddish—which is much like a Germanic language. German came easy to him, and the Dutch language is somewhat Germanic, so he picked up Dutch and became quite fluent in it.

He told me that one time in the Netherlands he was on the street and he was smoking. He must have been kind of conspicuous as a Russian Jew, because a woman came up to him and told him that it was the Sabbath and he shouldn't be smoking. Obviously, people seemed to care about that.

Louis knew that he had a sister in Chicago. He earned enough for steamship passage to the States. He came in steerage around 1898, when he was about fifteen years old.[1] Where he landed in the United States is a mystery. We should have asked him, but we didn't.

I've been to Ellis Island and searched the records and there's no record of his having arrived. Even though I wasn't able to find the record, I suspect that that's where he came through. He was a very able survivor. I'm sure he figured out some way of getting ashore without having documentation.[2]

If you see the movies and the pictures from that time, there were hoards of people arriving with countless numbers of kids, and I suspect that he just found his way in with another large family, and once he got in, he was gone.

He learned that there was employment out west, working on the railroads, so he was able to get a one-way ticket to go west, and he took that and ended up out in Iowa or Nebraska. He worked on the railroad for some time.

He told stories about the west—how he broke horses to sell as

COURTESY OF SEYMOUR PADNOS

Seymour Padnos comments, "The late 1930s and early 1940s were a tumultuous time for the junk business. It was a time when suddenly "junk" became "scrap," a vital raw material required by our nation's industry as it became the "arsenal of democracy." . . . The Louis Padnos Iron and Metal Company acquired its first real piece of mechanized scrap processing equipment in the late 1930s. . . . For the first time, Louis Padnos bought a new truck rather than someone else's cast-off."

draft animals. He knew about horses from his work in Russia. He told a story about how he traded with the Indians when he was up in the Dakota country. He had learned to carry some merchandise with him on his back. The Indians had nothing to trade with him but they received him openly. They shared what little they had.

They had no meat that day. Then the dog disappeared, and the next day they had meat. He knew very well what had happened to the dog. But that's not uncommon; Indians ate dogs. That was one of his stories, and the kids would just sit there wide-eyed and listen.

After a few years of bouncing around, he worked his way to Chicago. He learned that there were providers for peddlers who offered merchandise on consignment. Someone in Chicago told him about Holland, Michigan, and about all the Dutch people there who spoke the Dutch language. The fact that he was fluent in Dutch gave him a big advantage. So he boarded a boat in Chicago and came to Holland.

In Holland he saw a niche. He peddled clothing, tools, and utensils in Michigan and Wisconsin. He also bartered metal for animal skins. At that time, he wasn't dealing with the aristocrats—he was dealing with the man on the street. The people on the street in many cases were Dutch families who spoke Dutch in their homes. They called him "the little Dutch Jew"—that was an affectionate title.

Ben Van Raalte owned some vacant property on River Avenue. My father was walking down the street and he looked at this little empty store—kind of like a half-store. Van Raalte was watching him from the other side of the street, and it was obvious that he was some kind of a peddler. Van Raalte went across the street and asked my dad, "Is this something you're interested in?" My dad responded to him in Dutch that yes, he was looking for a place. He'd come to Holland to settle and open a business. Van Raalte said, "You can move in there. You can live there. You can have your store there. You can pay me when you can afford to."

In about 1916 my dad was drafted and served in the army, but he never left the United States. He was one of the last ones to go in for World War I.

He was single then. The telephone company had all these maiden ladies who were responsible for the day-to-day functions. When he went in the service, they sent him food and scarves and gloves and things like that. Later, my brother, Stuart, and I met these ladies, and they were always very sweet to us. We used to kid my dad—accuse him of having something going on with them!

He had his business and property in Holland. He had to go into the army, but he had no one to run his business while he was gone. My dad convinced his sister to let her son come to Holland and watch the store while he was gone. He was going to come back; there was no question about that. He said, "Just watch the place while I'm in the army." When he left, he requested that his many friends watch Joe. "Make sure he does the right thing here." While in the service, he wrote this postcard to his nephew: "Dear Joe, I'm getting used to army life. How's business? Please answer without fail." Not a word about "How are you?" or anything else!

In the winter, my dad bought muskrat and mink pelts from trappers and farmers. No one had any money then. It was a barter system. Anyway, these farmers brought in these animal skins to his nephew, Joe, and told him that they were mink. Joe didn't know a mink from anything else, and he bought them. He was so proud of himself that he went next door to one of Dad's friends, a barber, and the barber said, "Joe, they may be mink, but they have awfully long ears!" Of course, they were rabbit skins!

My dad came back from the service in 1917 and boarded in a number of homes. He lived with some very nice families. He visited local sawmills, creameries, and farms, trading his goods for old iron that he would ship to Chicago. He established a scrap metal business. In 1920 he bought a scrap yard on East Eighth Street in Holland. My dad married my mom, Helen Kantor, in 1919. I was born in 1920 and my brother, Stuart, was born two years later.

There's a very interesting story about my dad and Herman Miller, who was an established furniture manufacturer in Zeeland, told by Herman Miller's son to me. My dad borrowed some money from him, and as my dad was leaving, he said to Mr. Miller, "Don't you want me to sign something?" And Mr. Miller said, "No, Louis. Don't you realize that I would never have given it to you if I didn't think you were going to pay me back?"

Dad couldn't write well, so he had to draw when he wrote, really draw out the letters. He hadn't had any formal English education, but he could read perfectly. He depended upon his memory greatly, because he could not write out records. It was very laborious to do that.

Louis Padnos married immigrant Helen Kantor in November 1919. Helen left Warsaw, Poland, with her family when she was seven years old. The Padnos family lived above Louis's first shop and stored scrap metal in their side yard.

My father never went bankrupt in the Great Depression. Many of the people in the industry, our competitors, used the bankruptcy courts to reduce their debt. My father never did that. He paid off his debt. He survived the Depression with his good reputation intact, which served my brother and me very well in the subsequent years.

We used to live on East Eighth Street on the east side of the downtown, next to the scrap yard. During the Great Depression, we lived near the railroad tracks and all the hobos came through town. They always found us! Every poor person, every migrant that hit town found us. We always used to give my father a hard time.

We said, "The house must be marked or something!" My father explained, "I worked my way across Europe. I peddled goods across the United States. People always took care of me. They enabled me to survive, and if it's within my means, I'm going to do the same thing!"

About four doors away was a restaurant. My dad had a running tab there. Anyone that came to town that needed a meal, he sent them over to the East End Café. He wouldn't give them money necessarily, because some of them were hobos. He wasn't going to give them money to buy beer or wine, but he'd certainly always give them a meal. If there were any down-and-out people that hit town and, if they were Jewish, my father was the first person the police department would call. Not because they were felons. They came in at the bus depot, and they didn't have a ticket to go any place else.

Years later, I would get these Yiddish solicitors, but they were professional fund-raisers. It got to the point where I had to turn them away. Their standard argument was, "Your father always gave to us!" Some of these guys had chauffeurs! They were soliciting for charities in New York.

My father came to our home for dinner often. He liked our four children, and he felt quite at home with my wife—my wife's parents were also immigrants. He came to dinner and he sat and told my kids all these stories. I'm not so sure how many of them were fact, but they are stories we like to remember.

My Mother's Side of the Family

My mother's family lived in Warsaw. My grandfather—my mother's father—passed away in Poland in about 1903. My grandmother, Sophie, remarried David, a traditional Jewish scholar. He was a student at a yeshiva in Vilna. It was almost like being in a monastic order.[3]

My grandmother already had two children with her first husband. Unfortunately, he was a student and not a breadwinner. But fortunately, my mother's parents were quite wealthy. They had been umbrella manufacturers in Warsaw.

When she was a little girl she heard the Jewish old ladies talking in the meat market, and she put it together that David wasn't her real father, although she always respected him as her father. They never told her, and that's how she found out. Her real name was Helen; she never knew that until later.

Sophie's parents decided they should go live in the United States. They packed David off to the United States to establish a home. Sophie and the children followed later. I think it had something to do with being a Jew and being in Europe—the opportunities appeared to be in the United States. I still have her boarding pass. They sailed from Estonia in February 1910 for the United States. It doesn't say what class, but I'm sure they went first class. My mother was about seven or eight when they came here. They came through Ellis Island

I don't know what they thought the poor scholar, David, was going to do in the United States. He tried peddling and acting as a Hebrew instructor. They migrated to Kalamazoo, where David's brother-in-law, Avrom Hoffman, was a rabbi. Avrom Hoffman then moved from Kalamazoo to Cheyenne, Wyoming, where there was a vibrant Jewish community. Around 1920, Avrom wrote to David that the community needed a kosher butcher out there. My grandfather couldn't do anything else, but he knew kashrut[4] and slaughtering, so he became a butcher.

Later, I went out to Cheyenne and lived with my grandfather in 1932 for a year to study for my bar mitzvah.

After David moved to Cheyenne, my mother, Helen, remained

Helen Kantor's family just before their immigration to Michigan. (*Front row, left to right*): Helen Kantor, age four, her younger half-sister, Leah, and her older brother, Morris. (*Middle row: left to right*): Helen's mother, Sophie Brooke Kantor; Helen's stepfather, David Kantor, his mother and his father, Rabbi Jacob Kantor.

in Grand Rapids and began working for a department store. Mr. Herpolshimer, the owner, took a shine to her. She was his secretary. But the opportunity to be a telephone operator came up, and she thought that was a real profession. At about that time, that's how my father met her. He was introduced to my mother, who was living in Grand Rapids. She was seventeen when she met my dad. She was a very, very attractive lady.[5]

I have a postcard he wrote to my mother when he was courting her. He was in Chicago on a buying trip. "Regards from Louis Padnos." That was his love letter! They were married and they immediately moved to Holland. They bought a piece of property and built a home there.

I'm not sure that my father was such a great catch, but he had a business, and they did love each other. They moved to Holland and we lived upstairs at my father's scrap iron business.

My mother was only fifty-nine years old when she passed away. My father grieved greatly because they were truly in love. He really missed my mother.

My Life

My father-in-law came from Romania and my mother-in-law came from Poland. They met here in the United States. They had three children, two boys and a girl. My wife, Esther, was the youngest of the family. Her mother and father had a little delicatessen and grocery store in Grand Rapids. It was not an easy life.

My father-in-law passed away during World War II with two sons in the military. My mother-in-law was left with the store. It was their sole means of support. My wife had to quit high school and go to work with her mother in the store. My wife had worked in various department stores during high school.

I graduated from Hope College in 1943. Then I served in the army. My brother, Stuart, enlisted at the same time I did. He was captured at the Battle of the Bulge.

I came out of the service and I was committed to working in the family business. I had worked with my father before the war as a teenager, learning the business from him.

My wife was living in Grand Rapids when I met her. She is seven years younger than I am. I didn't think she would ever date me because I was an older man. I was afraid to call her for a date. I knew her older brothers, so I called her older brother first and I asked him, "Do you think your sister would go out with me?" It was a long-distant relationship. I lived in Holland and they lived in Grand Rapids. That wasn't easy, either.

The Next Generation

I try to be involved in the community. We have the Louis and Helen Padnos Foundation, trying to build bridges between business and education, and helping with health care issues, youth and social services, and the arts. We have formed a strong alliance with Grand

Valley State University with the Padnos College of Engineering and Computing, and the Padnos Hall of Science.

With our children, we now have a third generation of the Padnos family involved in the business that my father started over one hundred years ago. We believe that recycling is the key to solving many problems in the world for future generations—overflowing landfills, expensive and dwindling energy supplies, and environmental pollution, and we do these things profitably.

On the borders of the scrap yard, my brother, Stuart, has many sculptures on our premises. He has also done numerous commissioned pieces for the community and at Meijer Gardens. Stuart has maintained for many years that scrap is beautiful. He often tells this story: "My father was a 'junkman' who founded the family business. My brother and I followed into the business, but we were 'dealers in secondary materials.' Our children followed us and promptly became 'recyclers!' Now they say, 'Oh, you are the artist!'"

I think that's nice.

NOTES

1. "Steerage" refers to the practice of steamship companies selling budget fares for immigrants. The accommodations were in cargo holds and were very meager.
2. Between 1892 and 1954, the depot located on Ellis Island at the Port of New York processed the largest number of immigrants anywhere in the world, nearly 12 million people. The U.S. National Park Service now operates it as a national monument.
3. A yeshiva is a Jewish institution that teaches Torah, Mishnah, and Talmudic education.
4. *Kashrut* is a Hebrew word meaning "fit for consumption in accordance with Jewish dietary laws." In English it would be "kosher."
5. Herpolshimer's was a department store in downtown Grand Rapids founded in 1870 by William G. Herpolshimer and Carl Voight.

America Was the Best Country to Live In

Between 1894 and 1922, both the Ottoman Empire and its successor governments in Turkey attempted to eliminate the Armenian minority living in what is now central and western Turkey. Systematic campaigns of extermination, as well as mob violence, starvation, and disease resulted in the deaths of some 1.5 million Armenians. Survivors who were unable to escape the region by emigrating to the United States or Europe fled east into Russian Armenia, which is today an independent republic.

Haratoune Asadore Adrounie was born in 1882 in the mountain village of Zetoune, in the Ottoman Empire, which eventually became part of Turkey. When Haratoune was sixteen years old, he left home and went to St. Paul's Institute, an American school in Tarsus.

In 1909, just before he was to graduate, Muslim Turks rioted across the country. Many of them attacked Christian Armenians— targets of economic jealousy and religious prejudice. Thousands were killed as violence spread. When the Turks threatened to attack the American school in Tarsus, Adrounie dressed in Turkish clothes and rode seventeen miles on horseback to Mersina to request help from British troops.

Successful in his mission, Adrounie faced certain death if he returned to Tarsus. He fled to America. Once in the United States, Adrounie pursued his childhood dream of becoming a doctor. He wrote Dr. John H. Kellogg of the cereal company, who encouraged him to continue his education. Adrounie lived with the Kellogg family while studying at Battle Creek Medical College. In 1912 Adrounie graduated from the University of Illinois School of Medicine.

Haratoune Adrounie married Dirouhie (Dorothy) Kalaidian, the sister of a good friend from Turkey, in 1912. He received his medical license and set up his practice as a doctor in 1915 in Lacey, Michigan. In 1922 he became a United States citizen. In 1924, he moved to Hastings, Michigan. He and his wife had two children. He died in Ann Arbor in March 1936.

Martha Aladjem (Climo) Bloomfield interviewed his son, Dr. V. Harry Adrounie, on November 18, 1999. Dr. V. Harry Adrounie died on February 9, 2010, and was buried in Arlington Cemetery with a full military service.

Armenian Roots

My father, Harry Adrounie, was born in Zetoune, Turkey, which used to be Armenia at one time. Zetoune was way up in the mountains. To the Armenians, anybody from Zetoune was a warrior.

When some of the missionaries came through, they'd stop in the village. There were some physicians. So all of a sudden my father decided he wanted to become a physician. This was still when he was in his young teens, I guess.

So one day, he just up and left the mountains. He'd heard of this school in Tarsus called St. Paul's College, run by Americans. Dr. and Mrs. Thomas Christie were in charge of the school. So my father went down there. He was sixteen years old and big for his age. He said he wanted to start school there. They said, "Well, you can't just up and start school. You've got to know the language and a few other things." They turned him away two or three times.

One night, he climbed up the wall and went in a window under Dr. Christie's room and said, "I want to go to school." And

Haratoune married Dirouhie (Dorothy) Kalaidian in 1912. They are pictured here with their children, V. Harry and Zabelle.

Dr. Christie said, "Well, I guess you do." So he gave him a job with the horses and started him in the first grade. He said he felt kind of funny—a big kid with all these little kids.

Sometimes German and English people came around and wanted a guide or something. He took them where they wanted to go and translated for them, because he had learned German. He ended up knowing Turkish, Greek, German, French, Armenian, and English.

Then came the massacres in 1909. All the Armenians who were Christians were crammed into this college—it was like a compound. They had a wall around it. I drove up to Tarsus and visited it when I was teaching in Beirut. It's now a high school. But

Haratoune on a white Arabian in Turkey in 1909. He rode seventeen miles to bring British troops to save the school and people.

at that time, there were eight to ten thousand people crammed into this place so the Turks wouldn't get them. These were the young Turks doing this massacre. They sent word into this school to the officials that if they didn't turn out these people, regardless that it was an American school, they were going to storm it and knock it down and kill all the people.

So my dad dressed up like a Turk and got one of the horses, a white Arabian. He took off for seventeen miles to Mersina, where there happened to be some British warships in the harbor. He managed to get the British marines to come back up to Tarsus and save the school.

After the Turks found out he was the one who did it, they were after him. He had three months left to graduate to get his bachelor's degree, but the school gave him the bachelor's degree.

Escape to America

The teachers gave him twenty-five dollars and took him out to a freighter in a rowboat and sent him to the States. He came through Ellis Island. He had a letter that one of the teachers gave him—a letter of recommendation. He worked on a farm in New Jersey for one or two years. He paid the twenty-five dollars back.

```
                        Tarsus, Turkey,
                          May 7, 1909

To my friends in America:-
   The bearer of this letter, Haratoune A. Adrounie,
is a member of this year's Senior Class in St.
Paul's Institute. He has been advised by us all
to go to America, for the reason that there is no
safety for him in this country since the massacres.
We believe that he has a future before him, and
that he will become a good and useful man. His
ambition is to study medicine. I do hope that he
can attain to it.
   Mr. Adrounie is one of the very few Levantines
whom I could honestly counsel to go to America.
He has in him the elements of success. We have
tested him thoroughly and not found him wanting
Above all things, he has displayed two character-
istics, willingness to serve, and personal cour-
age.
   When Tarsus was invested on the dark night of
April 16th., Dr. Christie and I being absent in
Adana, he volunteered to carry a message to our
consul in Mersina - seventeen miles on horse thru
a hostile country. It was a dangerous undertak-
ing, and the chances were against his getting thru
alive. He was willing to run the risk, however,
in order to save Tarsus.
   I cannot too highly recommend him.
                  Faithfully yours,
                     Herbert Adams Gibbons
```

Herbert Gibbons was a teacher at Haratoune Adrounie's school in Turkey. He gave Haratoune this letter to serve as an introduction and recommendation to people in America.[1]

Then he heard about Dr. J. H. Kellogg in Michigan, who had a medical school in Battle Creek in conjunction with the sanitarium. A lot of people don't know there was a medical school there. So he came to Battle Creek. He had to go through the same sort of thing to get into the medical school here. He bugged Dr. Kellogg enough so that Dr. Kellogg took him into his home. He took care of the yard and the furnace for Dr. Kellogg. He started medical school and went to his freshman year of medical school there.

I don't know why they decided to close it, but they affiliated with the University of Illinois School of Medicine in Chicago. So he went to school there and graduated in 1912. I believe it was with his MD degree.

Then he came back to Battle Creek to intern at Dr. Kellogg's facility. That's where I was born. Nine months after I was born, he came on out to Lacey in Barry County. It was a four corners. He volunteered to go out there. He practiced in Lacy until I was seven or eight. I went to the country school out there. That's where I grew up, before I came to Hastings.

While he knew John Harvey Kellogg, he also met W. K. Kellogg. He talked W. K. into bringing Arabian horses here. W. K. had a ranch out in California. He started the Arabian horses there.

He got to be friends with both the Kelloggs. The brothers split up over the Kellogg's Corn Flakes deal.[2] They wouldn't even talk to each other. When one was at the house, the other went out the back door.

A Family Reunited

While my dad was still going to medical school, my mother, Dirouhie (Dorothy) Kalaidian, got out of Turkey. Her brother was already here. Between her brother and my dad, they fixed it so she could leave Turkey and immigrate to the United States. She came here before he graduated, so it had to be around 1910 or 1911. I was born in 1915.

He knew her from before, in Armenia. Her brother was in the school with my dad. Her brother brought her home with him once,

COURTESY OF H. MICHAEL ADROUNIE

The father of Haratoune Adrounie's wife, Dirouhie (Dorothy) Kalaidian, made this covered dish.

and my dad saw her that one time, and he said he wanted to marry her. He told her he was going to marry her. He had seen her once! He was kind of funny that way.

She had claustrophobia due to the fact that when the Turks were rampaging, her parents put her down under the floorboards so they wouldn't grab her and take her off and rape her. During one of these times, the Turks took her parents out and killed them. So she wasn't too happy about the Turks.

A Country Doctor

My dad was a general practitioner, one of the last of the ones who made house calls. That's the kind of guy he was. He taught me integrity. I still have people coming up to me and saying, "He delivered me!"

He was so good about taking care of people even though they couldn't pay. They were paying him in gasoline. One time he came home with an organ. That's one of the reasons I don't like chicken, because that's all I used to get to eat.

COURTESY OF THE ADROUNIE FAMILY

When his patients were sick, Dr. Adrounie made house calls. Sometimes he walked or rode a horse. Other times he drove this car. When they could not pay cash, he accepted gasoline for his car, food, or chickens.

Michigan Homes

We kept that house for over seventy years.[2] They named it Adrounie House Bed and Breakfast, on Adrounie Lane. They named a room after each one of us. I think after all these years my parents would be happy that there's an Adrounie Lane at Gun Lake and an Adrounie Bed and Breakfast. My mother died in 1988 when she was ninety-seven years old.

In those days there was no air conditioning, so people bought cottages because the lakes were cooler. My father went out around Gun Lake and he saw this cottage for sale. He bought it, and we still have it.

The George W. Lowry House is on the State Register of Historic sites and has a Michigan Historical Marker. Dr. George W. Lowry (1850–1922) was a mayor of Hastings and a local doctor. He purchased the land for his house and a medical practice from Dr. William A. Upjohn in 1887. In 1892–94 he built this house for his home and medical office. In 1922, Dr. Haratoune Adrounie purchased the house and brought his practice from Lacey. Dr. Adrounie's wife, Dorothy, lived in the house until her death in 1988. Today it is called the Adrounie House Bed and Breakfast. Each room is named after an Adrounie family member.

It had an artesian well. He liked the running water from where he came from in the mountains. I guess that's what reminded him of his home. I guess he liked Michigan because, in some respects, even though it wasn't like the mountains of his home, it reminded him of some of the areas of Turkey.

Family Connections

Eventually, I learned that the Turks killed my grandfather on my father's side. They took my grandmother and two of my cousins and threw them out into the Syrian Desert with hundreds of others and figured they would either starve or die of thirst. She managed to take her two boys and make it to Beirut. I remember my dad was

The Miami-Battle Creek

JOHN HARVEY KELLOGG, M.D., LL.D., F.A.C.S., MEDICAL DIRECTOR

MIAMI SPRINGS (MIAMI), FLORIDA

February 29, 1936.

I am deeply touched by the passing away of our dear friend, Dr. Adrounie. With him a hero, a man of the highest type has left us. By his courage he saved thousands and by his devotion to humanity he has helped multitudes.

Years ago I had the privilege of having him in my home for quite a long time and Mrs. Kellogg and I esteemed him greatly for he was so faithful and conscientious. We trusted him to the limit and missed him immensely when he left our home.

Just three weeks ago I received a communication from him asking if he could come here and rest and I answered promptly that he would be most welcome. But by the description of his symptoms I knew that he could not stand the trip any more and I was very grieved about it.

His life is ended and his works follow him. He rests in the Lord. His memory will always be blessed.

I send my profound sympathy to his dear wife and children and to the Hastings community as a whole.

J. N. Kellogg

Dr. J. H. Kellogg.

After Dr. Haratoune Adrounie died at University Hospital in Ann Arbor in March 1936, his mentor, Dr. John Harvey Kellogg, sent this condolence to his family.

sending money for her to get a house in Beirut, but he never did get over there to see her.

He had a sister, and the Turks took her and gave her to the Arabs. She disappeared to who knows where. She was very young, only twelve or thirteen years old. Two of his brothers escaped from Armenia. One of them became a photographer.

When the United States Department of Defense sent me to Beirut to teach, I met a graduate student with the last name of Adrounie. She was one of the daughters of one of those cousins. So I finally found that part of my family. She said my two cousins had made it to Beirut. She said their mother was a pretty tough gal. She now is a dentist practicing in Chicago.

My father always taught my sister and me that this was the best country to live in. And he taught us patriotism and love of country. He had nothing but good things to say about the United States.

NOTES

1. His wife, Helen Davenport Gibbons, an American journalist and author, wrote a book *The Red Rugs of Tarsis, A Woman's Record of the Armenian Massacre of 1909.* New York, The Century Co., 1917. She tells about Haratoune's heroic adventure. See http://armenianhouse.org/gibbons/Red-Rugs.html.
2. The feud began when Will Keith Kellogg acquired marketing rights to the Kellogg Toasted Corn Flake Co. Will Kellogg later bought out Dr. John Harvey Kellogg's interest in the company.

We Wanted to Be American

A wave of emigrants left Finland between 1870 and 1920, pushed by economic changes that left many rural people without land or jobs. Russia, which had ruled the country since 1809, provided another push as it tightened its control over government and language, and drafted Finns into the Russian army.

Nearly all the Finnish emigrants settled in the United States, where they clustered in the mining and farming regions of Michigan, Minnesota, Ohio, and New York.

Olga Koskela came to the United States from Perho, Finland, with her parents, Pietari and Anna Liisa Koskela, and her two brothers and three sisters when she was about two years old. After passing through immigration proceedings at Ellis Island, they took a train to Negaunee, Michigan. They arrived there on Christmas Eve, 1916.

Olga's family lived on a farm near Negaunee and her father worked in the iron mines. In 1930, he was working alongside his son in the Athens mine when he was killed by a falling rock.

Olga went to work in a clothing factory in Ishpeming when she was fifteen. When World War II began, she went to work at Ford Motor Company's Willow Run bomber plant. She married Oscar Honkala in 1937 in Laurium, Michigan, and had two children. Eventually she moved back to Negaunee.

Olga Koskela posed for this photo a few years after immigrating to Negaunee, Michigan.

COURTESY OF MAXINE HONKALA

Olga Honkala relates her experience of settling in the Upper Peninsula of Michigan, growing up Finnish American, and maintaining Finnish customs and traditions in an ethnically diverse Upper Peninsula community. Olga Honkala passed away on May 31, 2006 at the age of 91.

Martha Aladjem Climo Bloomfield interviewed Olga Honkala and her daughter Maxine Honkala in Negaunee on July 7, 1999.

Coming to America

MAXINE: It was hard to own land in Finland at that time. There was a famine in the province where my mother was from. The growing season was very short. My grandfather had a fear of being conscripted into the Russian army. That was prior to the Bolshevik revolution. Politically in Finland, times were not that good. It was hard times.

OLGA: My parents came here from Perho, Finland, to make a better living. It was very poor times in Finland. My father had already been to America for five years to earn passage. He had lived in Negaunee and worked in the mines to pay for us to come here.

It was a hard trip with so many children, with a small baby only three months old. I was two years old. It was during the time of World War I, in 1916. It was a rugged trip—my father was sick the whole time.

They came by boat to Ellis Island and took a train from New York to Negaunee. We arrived here on Christmas Eve.

Many Finnish people here in Negaunee came from the same place. Many people came from the same province that we did. I think they all tried to find the same kind of climate, the same kind of area as Finland.

After my parents arrived, the first thing they built was a sauna bath, and then they built the house.

Pietari and Anna Liisa Koskela posed for this photograph with their family around the time of their immigration.

The sauna was in an outside building. In the summer, we would use it as often as you felt like you needed to. You would heat up the water and wash up. It's a good place to go. We didn't have showers on the farm.

MAXINE: The typical Finnish sauna is in an outside building, and a wood stove heats it. In our home where I grew up, my father built one. It was an addition onto the garage. We always kept it going; there was always hot water.

Becoming American

OLGA: My mother never learned to speak English fluently. They spoke Finnish at home. My father learned a little English because he had been here before. He learned more English than my mother did.

Maxine Honkala took this photograph of the Statue of Liberty on a trip to New York.

It seemed like we tried to talk English and tried to be American. It just seemed like we didn't want to speak Finnish. We wanted to be Americanized. We didn't want to be Finnish at that time. It seemed like we were looked down on or something. We wanted to be American.

Now, everybody's trying to learn Finnish. I can speak it, and I certainly can understand it. Maxine is sorry that I didn't speak Finnish so she could have learned the language.

We never had any cousins here. They were all in Finland. No aunts and uncles, just our immediate family and friends. Only one cousin had come here for a visit through all those years.

My mother was rather lonesome the first years. She never had a chance to go back to Finland. My father never went back either.

In 1974 I went to Finland. I was anxious to see my kinfolk where I came from. We stayed with cousins and my uncle—blood relations. They were glad to see us. We had been gone a long time. They showed me where I was born. A man came up to me and told me he held me in his arms when I was a baby!

Life on an Upper Peninsula Farm

At first we lived in Negaunee in the Buffalo Hill location. A short time later we moved to a farm in Republic, about twenty-five miles from Negaunee. My father couldn't make a living there, so he had to get work elsewhere. He went to the mine in Republic and that was about five miles away, so he had to travel by horse every day.

Our neighbors were originally from Finland. They coaxed my father and mother to come out to this farm. It was all new land—the trees had to be cut down. Our home was built there. People helped us build the house.

It would have been better if they had found a place where there was really good farming, instead of that rocky area! When I was in seventh grade, we moved back to Negaunee and lived in town. My father got a job in the Athens mine.

My mother was a very clean woman. We had hardwood floors, and we had to scrub them. We had to start from the upstairs and work down.

Every morning we had to take all the carpets from every room and go out and shake them. We had to go through the whole house with the dust mop, and under the beds. We had to do it every day. That was the ritual.

Monday was washday. Tuesday was ironing day. Wednesday was baking day. Thursday was social day. Friday you start all over again cleaning. You go through that same ritual again.

Washday was a big day. We would put a copper boiler on the stove to heat up the water. Then we would slice up a bar of Fels Naptha soap and put that in there. We would boil the clothes. That was a big job to wash them by hand on the washboard. We had these two washtubs on the stand. You had to ring them out with the wringer. Then we had to hang them on the line. In the wintertime they would freeze. We used to have lines inside the house. Then the house would get really damp and cold.

We had two cows when we lived in Negaunee. The cow was used to having my mother milk her. If my mother would go away on a trip, my brother would have to wear her dress when he went to milk the cow, because the cow would sense that it wasn't her. Otherwise she'd hold her milk. I suppose my brother could have squeezed harder!

We had a pasture that we had to take the cows to, and then go get them at night. My younger sister had a lot of freckles on her face. My brother would tease her. He always told her that her freckles were from the cow going to the bathroom. The stuff would splash on her face, and that's how she got her freckles.

I used to help make hay. As young as I was, I still had to learn how to rake hay. We didn't have all the farm equipment that they have now.

My mother used to make carpets. I used to cut the rags for them. I'd get out the old clothes and cut the rags up. We used to have a loom for weaving the rugs. You put the rags on the spindles and you weave the carpets. Nobody has homemade rugs anymore.

We made paper dolls. We would cut the figures out of Sears or Montgomery Ward catalogues to make the paper dolls. We didn't buy paper dolls like you do now. We had to cut the figures and the clothes out from the catalogues.

We also had to use those catalogues for the outdoor toilets, because we didn't have toilet paper. It was very rugged! In the winter we had to go outdoors to the toilet. So there were two purposes for those catalogues!

My mother was the master. She kept tabs on us. She was very strict. She was very religious. We went to church a lot. I remember going to confirmation and Sunday school. My father was more easygoing with us.

Finnish Food

OLGA: My mother was not a gourmet cook. Mostly she made potatoes and meat, carrots and rutabaga—those were the things you could grow in a climate like Finland. Long winters and short summers, just like here.

We didn't have any cookbooks. My mother couldn't speak any English, so we didn't have any cookbooks in English.

In the summertime, we used to pick a lot of blueberries and raspberries whatever there was to pick. I remember picking bushels of blueberries. In those days, there were a lot of them. It wasn't like it is now, where you have to really look for them.

My mother would preserve them in jars so that in the winter we could have them. You could make what you wanted, sauce or pie or eat them as is. I think we mostly ate them as is.

We used to go for family picnics a lot, at a park near Champion. That was a tradition. My mother used to like to cook on the stove out on the picnic grounds. She used to cook a regular dinner, always had potatoes, meat, and carrots.

Custard pie was a typical Finnish desert. My sister and I often laugh about how we made it. Sometimes it turned out good and sometime it didn't, because we were just following what we thought it was. We really didn't know because we did not have a recipe. We just put eggs and milk together and sometimes it would set so that it was steady and firm. And sometimes it wasn't, because maybe we made a mistake and put in too much milk.

My mother-in-law was an excellent cook. She was more of a gourmet cook. She made prune tarts. It's a specialty in Finish culture.

I still make bread, whole wheat and rye mostly. Finnish people use a lot of rye. Sometimes flat bread, prune tarts, or coffee cake.

I still use all those spices—cardamom, caraway and fennel seed, and anise. I kind of mix them up.

MAXINE: There is a story about sourdough starter. When my grandparents left Finland, the sourdough starter remained there and the family kept it all those years, hoping that they would return. When my mother's sisters went back in the 1960s, they said, "Well, now you have returned." They kept it going for them all those years!

School Days

OLGA: I remember walking five miles to school. We wore little rubber boots. We packed our lunch in a pail. I went into the second grade when we moved to the farm near Republic. Miss Mudge was one of the teachers. I enjoyed writing. I had a certificate for the Palmer Method.

We were all in one schoolroom. My brother was in the same schoolroom, and he was much older than I was. It must have been kindergarten to eighth grade. You know what kind of teaching we got there. It wasn't much, I know that. I didn't know the language. I must have learned English while I was going to that school.

I remember my little brother misbehaved once, and the teacher took him by the shoulder and shook him and his coat ripped!

Factory Work

When my father was killed in the mine, I went to work at the Gossard factory in Ishpeming making bras and undergarments. I wasn't quite sixteen, but my sister took me there and told them I was sixteen. In those days, it wasn't that important. You could just get work. I remember that first day. I was sewing for nine hours and I thought my neck was going break!

I worked there for thirty years, but not continuously. I quit for a while and had children. Then I went to Detroit and worked at Willow Run before my husband went into the service.

Olga and Oscar Honkala posed outside their temporary housing at Willow Run. Ford Motor Company built the Willow Run factory near Ypsilanti, Michigan, during World War II to mass-produce B-24 Liberator bombers.

I was "Rosie the Riveter." I had to take a course in riveting. My husband said, "That's one job you shouldn't take because it's too hard." They examined me to see if my heart was okay when I got the job.

My husband was also working at Willow Run. He could have had a deferment. They told him when he got his 1-A card to come in and they would give him a deferment because he was working in a defense plant. He said "No way! I'm going to go in the service." He said that the rest of his family had gone in, and he was going in. He was very patriotic. He went into the navy.

I was married then. I was about twenty-nine or thirty. I was married for eight years, but we didn't have any children. I didn't have any kids until I was thirty years old. When my husband went in the service, that's when I found out I was pregnant.

I have two children, Maxine and Peter. When Peter was born, my husband was at the Great Lakes Naval Station near Chicago. My brother went down to the station to get him. He asked where I was. My brother said, "She's in the hospital!" They got back home just before Peter was born.

COURTESY OF MAXINE HONKALA

Olga holds her first baby son, Peter.

Olga and Maxine together in their traditional Finnish costumes.

COURTESY OF MAXINE HONKALA

I Have *Sisu*

I had heart surgery the other year. I had five bypasses. But I have that Finnish *sisu*, they call it.

MAXINE: It's like fortitude or strength, courage or guts. That's kind of the trademark of Finns. They like to say they have *sisu*.

Immigration Didn't Solve All Our Problems

From 1795 until 1918, Poland was divided among Germany, Russia, and Austria. The Russian and German governments, in particular, restricted the Polish language and the Catholic Church. However, economic circumstances in the Russian and Austrian regions provided the biggest push to Polish emigrants between 1900 and 1915.

Many Poles who came to Michigan for jobs in the auto industry had already worked for a few years in such industrial cities as Buffalo, Pittsburgh, and Chicago.

The Skrzypek family struggled to escape poverty by leaving Poland for America, and later moving from the Buffalo area to Detroit. Life was better, but it was still very hard.

Michal Skrzypek and Weronika Pezda were born in Janow Lubelski, in Poland, in the late 1800s. They married on July 21, 1903.

Life in Poland was very hard under Russian rule. Michal wanted to find a better life for his family than he could provide as a butler in Poland. Unable to find work on his first trip to America, he returned to Poland.

Skrzypek's second trip to America was more successful. In Lackawanna, New York, outside Buffalo, he found work in a steel

Weronika Skrzypek bought this brown-and-black *chustka*, or shawl, in Poland for just a few dollars. She wrapped it around herself and her babies in winter when walking to church or to the store in Detroit. Her daughter, Bernice Kutylowski, is wearing the *chustka* in this photo.

mill. He saved enough money to bring over his wife and three children. Three more children were born in Lackawanna.

A few years later, during a strike at the steel mill, the Skrzypeks received a letter from Weronika's sister and her husband, who lived in Detroit. They said that Henry Ford was paying autoworkers five dollars a day and suggested that the Skrzypeks come to Detroit.

In 1919, the family moved to Detroit. Hardship and deprivation continued to be part of their lives there, but it was still easier than living in Poland.

Martha Aladjem (Climo) Bloomfield interviewed Bernice Kutylowski, Michal Skrzypek's daughter, in August 1999. Bernice Kutylowski died on May 15, 2002.

In the Old Country

My father, Michal Skrzypek, and my mother, Weronika, were born in Janow Lubelski, Poland, in the late 1800s. When my mother was five, her mother died. When she was twelve, her father died. So her grandfather took care of her and her brother.

Her grandpa didn't like that because he didn't have enough food for himself. He'd hide the food in the closet, and the kids would break open the door and take all the food. They didn't have any water. Things were so bad for them.

My father, Michal, was a butler. He and my mother got married in 1903. They had my brother Michael and my sisters Cecelia, Julia, and Natalie (who died in infancy). On my father's first trip to America, he came alone on a freighter. He worked on the ship to help pay for his trip over. But he could not find work. So he returned to Poland.

Then he made another trip. He went to Lackawanna, New York. He found work in the steel mills. He saved enough money for my mother and my older siblings to come to America.

They took a horse and wagon from Poland to Antwerp, Holland. They then took a boat to America. While life was hard in Poland, it was also rough in America.

Mother also brought a shawl, a *chustka*, with her. In the

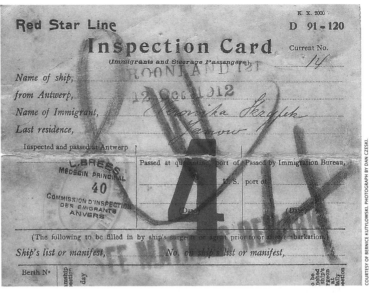

This card allowed Weronika Skrzypek to sail on the steamer *Kroonland* to America on October 12, 1912, with her three children a few months after her husband left.

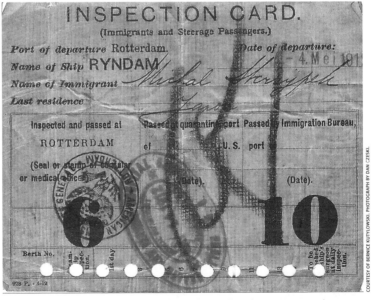

This inspection card allowed Michal Skrzypek to sail on the steamer *Ryndam* to America on May 3, 1912. Their cards assured immigration officials that they had no communicable disease or debilitating handicaps.

Weronika Skrzypek bought this silver soup spoon in Poland for her husband when they married. It was one of only a few things they brought to America in 1912.

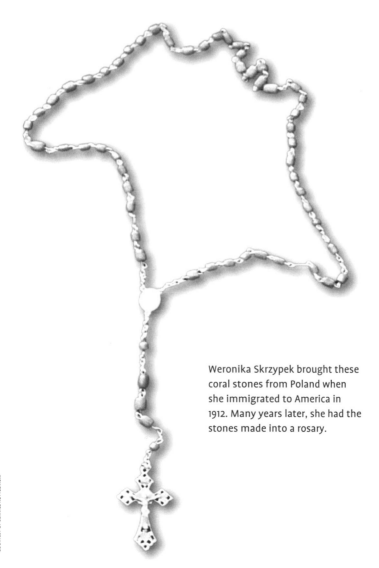

Weronika Skrzypek brought these coral stones from Poland when she immigrated to America in 1912. Many years later, she had the stones made into a rosary.

Weronika Skrzypek's husband, Michal, signed his name and date in the Polish Bible that the Skrzypeks brought to America from Poland in 1912. The Skrzypeks maintained a strong Catholic identity in their new home. The book helped them remember the words to familiar Polish songs and hymns.

wintertime, she wrapped herself and her babies in it when she went to church. She also brought a silver soupspoon. Mother brought amber necklaces with her. Later we attached crosses to them.

A New Life in America

Immigrating to American didn't solve all our family's problems.

I was born in Lackawanna, New York, on March 6, 1915. My father, Michal Skrzypek, worked in the steel plants in Buffalo, twelve hours a day, two dollars for twelve hours.

They went on a strike. My uncle in Detroit wrote a letter to my dad. He asked him, "Why don't you come to Detroit? Henry Ford is hiring people for five dollars a day. Forget about the steel mills!" So, my father took a boat ride—$1.50 round-trip to Detroit—for a visit. He came back home and told my mother, Weronika, "Get packing."

COURTESY OF BERNICE KITTLOWSKI

This family picture was taken in New York, a few years after the Skrzypek family immigrated from Poland. From left to right are Cecelia, Michal, Bernice, Weronika, Julia, and Michael Jr.

My father, my mother, my brother Michael, and my sisters and I took a train from Buffalo to Detroit.

When my brother Eddie was born—I was only about five then—my mother was going to send me to school. She didn't feel good, so I stayed home one whole year washing diapers by hand. Nobody had a wringer. She'd hang them behind the stove in the winter and they would dry.

My mother or my aunt sewed pillowcases. My dad and uncle used them to bring back cakes from the bakery. They were dry. They were hard. They weren't day old, they were two weeks old, or three. My mother would make coffee and we'd dip those cakes. Most of them were pound cakes. They had no frosting. We thought everybody ate cakes like that!

COURTESY OF BERNICE KUTYLOWSKI. PHOTOGRAPH BY DAN CZESKI.

Michal Skrzypek made this trunk from wood that fell off a train as it traveled past his house in Buffalo, New York. The Skrzypeks carried their household goods in the trunk when they moved from New York to Detroit in 1919.

We drank Pet Milk or Carnation milk. That was the best milk ever! We used that in our coffee.

My mother kept her own chickens. Before winter set in we had no place to keep them, so we had chicken soup starting in September. Every week she'd kill one of the chickens. And then she'd have one or two fresh eggs for the babies.

The only time we ate good food was in my aunt's house when

someone was baptized, christened, or a having first communion. Other than that I always had soup, soup, soup and day-old bread.

The only thing I ever wanted was survival. I wanted some food. We didn't have enough food. We never had enough food.

Donna Kutylowski (Bernice Kutylowski's daughter) and her husband, Dan Czeski, promote Polish culture by participating in an ancient Polish medieval feast called Staropolska Bleslada, hosted by the American Polish Cultural Center, Troy, Michigan. They are wearing traditional costumes that were hand-made in Poland. Donna Kutylowski was recently elected president of the Polish American Congress–Michigan Division (PAC-MI) Charitable Foundation. They are holding their daughter, Aurelia.

We Weren't Always Welcome in America

B etween 1900 and 1914, hundreds of thousands of Italians, mostly from southern provinces, came to the United States seeking jobs. Already accustomed to seasonal migrations to find work in Italy, southern Italians were among the immigrants most likely to return home. Italian immigration to Michigan before 1900 focused on the mining regions of the Upper Peninsula. The pattern shifted in the early twentieth century, and by 1930 about 73 percent of the state's Italian-born residents lived in Wayne County.

Francis "Bus" Spaniola comes from a long line of Italian store-keepers. His maternal grandfather, Andrew Spadafore, was an immigrant who owned two stores selling ice cream, candy, and tobacco in Corunna, Michigan. His paternal grandfather, Francis Spaniola, was a friend of Andrew Spadafore's and also emigrated from St. Ippolito, Italy. Bus's mother, Angeline Spadafore, was born in Italy and emigrated in 1919. His father, Anthony (Tony) Spaniola, made and sold his own brand of ice cream at his stores in Owosso, Corunna, Perry, and Lansing.

Following in the footsteps of his father and grandfather, Bus Spaniola owned and operated Anthony's Dairy Isle in Owosso for many years. He was teaching history at East Lansing High School when he decided to run for a seat in the Michigan House of Representatives. "It wasn't easy getting elected as a Democrat of Italian heritage in a predominately Republican district," he remembered about the 1974 election.

During his sixteen years in the statehouse, one of Spaniola's goals was to ensure that immigrants and migrants have an opportunity to share in the American Dream. "That's the way we fight the battle for decency and social justice and all those other high-sounding things that they taught us about in school—the things that my mother came to America for."

Pictures of his children and grandchildren, as well as his parents and grandparents, adorn the walls of his home and illustrate Spaniola's contention that "family is everything."

As a former state representative from Shiawassee County, Bus is president of Friends of Michigan History and the vice chair of the Michigan History Foundation Board.

Martha Aladjem (Climo) Bloomfield interviewed Bus Spaniola at his home in a quiet neighborhood in Corunna, Michigan on April 30, 1999. His mother, Angeline Spadafore Spaniola, died on October 3, 1998.

Passage to America

My maternal grandparents, Andrew and Rose Spadafore, were living in Corunna, Michigan, with their son, Carmine (Charles), when Rose became pregnant with their second child. She was a young girl, Old World, couldn't speak English and yearning to be with her mother and aunts for the birth. Somehow or another, my grandfather scraped together the money to send my grandmother and my uncle back to the little village of St. Ippolito in southern Italy.

In January 1909, my mom, Angeline Spadafore, was born in the old country in the home my grandfather had built and owned there. Of course, times were tough economically, and grandpa could not afford to bring them back right away. A number of years passed, and about the time he was getting the revenue together to bring them back, World War I broke out. There was a problem traveling

Angeline Spadafore, grandfather Palmer Dionese, and Carmine Spadafore. Andrew and Rose Spadafore were living in Corunna, Michigan, with their son, Carmine, when Rose became pregnant with their second child. Yearning to be with her mother and aunts for the birth, she went back to St. Ippolito, Italy, with her son. In January 1909, Angeline Spadafore was born. Andrew Spadafore began saving money for his wife and children to return to Michigan, but World War I made travel unsafe and they remained in Italy. After the war ended, Andrew's family rejoined him in 1919.

Angeline Spadafore sailed from Italy for the United States on the S.S. *America*. The ship was later used as a troop transport during World War II.

during wartime and I am certain he did not want them to. I don't know if it was not allowed, but I do know that during the war, they did not even think of coming.

Andrew Spadafore began saving money for his wife and children to return to Michigan. But World War I made travel unsafe and they remained in Italy. After the war ended, Andrew's family rejoined him in 1919. The war ended in November 1918 and my mother, who was then nine, and my uncle, who was about fourteen at the time, and my grandmother all got on the boat and came to the United States.

My paternal grandfather was in Owosso at the time. His name was Francis Spaniola, just like mine. Grandpa Spaniola and Grandpa Spadafore were great friends in the old country, and somehow or another they got together, settled in Corunna, and opened a business. My grandmother was here, and to be honest, I just don't know the details of her first entry into the United States. My grandma Spadafore, she came over earlier. She was here with my grandfather Andy, and whether she came when he came or came later, I don't know. My mother's older brother, who is named Carmine Spadafore, was in Lansing for years, and his family is still in business there. He was here as a little boy, and my grandmother was expecting my mom.

It's nice to be able to have an opportunity to talk about my mother's experience. She has only been gone about six months. We were all afraid that much of her wisdom and her experience would be lost, and much of it was. We have tried to keep as much of her experience in the family as possible, to talk to the kids about it.

She told an interesting story about leaving [Italy]. A number of people from her town all traveled together, so there were a lot of people who lived in central Michigan who were not only related to my mother but who were also friends from that little Italian town. They all had the same experience coming over on the ship together.

My mother told of leaving the little town and really wanting to see her dad. She had never seen her father, only in pictures. She was very excited by the prospect of coming to Michigan and seeing her dad. But she was also very sad to leave Italy. She said, "You know, it was almost like a funeral. People cried and went through all this emotion and many of them felt—and rightly so—that they would never see them again."

In many cases that was not true. People did go back and forth after a fashion, but most of the old-timers were not seen again—the grandpas and the grandmas. She said that her paternal grandfather was here in the United States but her maternal grandfather was over there, and he cried like a baby when they left. When they went from their little town to Naples, it was a bit of a trip for them in 1918.

She relates that they went north to Naples where they boarded the ship [S.S. America]. Of course they did not have much money, so they came steerage, as they called it then, or third class. They were separated. The men were in one area and the women in another. The sleeping arrangements were divided that way, but there was a central area where they all met, so it was sort of a family-friendly get-together. They didn't have staterooms. They had a great deal of fun coming over on the ship, I guess, other than the weather, which was pretty bad.

When they got to New York, it was quite impressive to come

COURTESY OF FRANCIS "BUS" SPANIOLA

Francis Spaniola, Bus Spaniola's grandfather, brought his possessions from Italy to America in this steamer trunk. It was lost for a time, but Bus reacquired it several years ago.

into the harbor and see the Statue of Liberty. Even as a girl of nine, it was a very emotional experience for her. She was trying like all of us are to sum up what it meant to come here. First of all, she was going to see her dad, and secondly, they all believed that life was wonderful here. The streets were paved with gold—you know, that sort of thing. They were looking forward to an easier existence, and they really did think they had a great deal of opportunity here. At least that was her impression—in spite of the fact that it was hard for people of southern European extraction to fit in, I suppose.

When they got to Ellis Island in New York they had to stay on the ship another night before they disembarked. My mother said the captain of the ship was very kind to them and let them occupy staterooms the last night they were on the ship. She said it was like living "high on the hog." It was impressive—nice beds and nice berths. It was higher quality than what they had been used to in the old county and of course, on the ship as well, coming steerage.

My grandmother apparently had citizenship at the time, if my mother's story is accurate. My grandfather was naturalized here, and if the husband was naturalized, then the wife was automatically a citizen, and the children would be as well. There shouldn't have been a problem at Ellis Island, but there was. They were detained there for two or three days.

My mother talked about nice people and bad people who worked for the immigration service or whatever they called it at that time. She said they were all very frightening to her and that they thought they were going to be turned back. It was a universal feeling that they were going to be turned back, and all of this hope that they had and joy that had swelled up in them when they came into New York harbor, was beginning to wane a bit because they were worried about it. Those who came steerage had to go through the island experience and have physical exams. Many people who were thin were so worried that they were going to be considered unacceptable that they would take newspapers and stuff their clothing to make themselves look heavier and more robust. Some of them were sent back. It was a very sad situation. If they weren't sent back, they were held back for a longer period of time. She didn't know what really happened to all of them.

She also said that when they would go through the lines as they were checking in, they would look their papers over and many times these immigration officers would change people's names. You want to talk about an insult—an absolute insult. My Uncle Charlie's real name was Carmine Spadafore. The immigration official told him that that was not a good American name and it had to be Charles Spadafore, not Carmine, and so my uncle became Charlie Spadafore. It bothers me that they would be so arrogant to tell him what his name was going to be. They changed the spelling of many people's names. That obviously bothered a number of people, and to this day, I am angry about it. It was not proper in any event. They had to face those kinds of difficulties.

My mother said she was introduced to cornflakes the first morning they were on the island. Of course they ate in a mess hall kind of setting. My uncle, mother, and grandmother had breakfast together. They sat down together at this table and they had cornflakes on the table. My grandmother, who had been here before, you would think she had known. My grandmother did not know what they were either. My mother says that Grandma—we called her Nonna, by the way—it is Italian for "grandma"—Nonna told her and my uncle, "Don't eat those things. Americans must be nuts. Those are dried potato peelings. What are they eating dried potato peelings for?"

My mother said that one of the problems that kept them on the island was that my grandmother was illiterate. I don't think that was unusual for women like my grandmother who came from this little town in southern Italy where men were macho and women of her age didn't have much of an education. She was illiterate, but she wasn't dumb by any means—she was a very bright lady. If my grandma had been a man, I think she would have been the CEO of General Motors or something. She was an astute, brilliant woman. In terms of her skills—reading and writing—they just weren't there. One of the things she apparently had to do in order not to raise suspicions when she came in (at least this is the way my mother related it, and I hope that this is accurate) was to sign in. My uncle and mother were going to school over there and they were both pretty bright people and they taught my grandmother how to write her name. When it came time for her to sign in, she froze, and they thought something was afoul. So that, and apparently some other things my mother was not aware of, kept them on the island for a couple, three days.

They had to communicate with the clerk here in Shiawassee County to find out if everything my grandma was telling them was true. I don't know if she had American papers that would show the fact that she not only had citizenship but also a husband or a relative who was waiting for her. I am not certain what the details were. They had to check back here in Corunna with the county clerk to find out if everything they said was accurate. When clarification came that my grandmother, mother, and my uncle were the people they presented themselves to be, they put a tag on them—of all things—giving instructions with their destination name and that sort of thing. They boarded the train and came from New York to Durand, Michigan, which is eight miles down the road [from Corunna].

Incidentally, I took my mother to Ellis Island in 1980. It was her first trip back to New York since 1919 and Ellis Island was open. The place had just opened and it was an absolute mess. It was an exciting emotional time for all of us. We got off the boat and went into the building. My mother was saying, "I remember that and I remember this." Things had not changed that much other than the building had deteriorated terribly. She pointed out the rooms that they had used for the examinations and that they used for sleeping.

A Department of Interior guide took us through Ellis Island. I believe he was a park ranger. He was telling us stories as we went through there and of course he finally asked if any of the people in the group, fifty or sixty of us, had come through Ellis Island. Two or three raised their hands, my mother included, and then he asked if any of them had been detained there. My mother said that she had and he asked her to relate her experiences. She told the story about the cornflakes. She also told a number of other situations that had occurred.

I sat there and I cried like a baby. Here's a grown man standing there, so emotionally overwhelmed. It was more than just a story. These are my roots. My people came through here and my mother came through. In the stories she related, some were funny and some were sad and some were the mechanics of what had happened there.

The ranger was taken by my mother's stories and he said, "I have heard all kinds of stories about people's introductions to different kinds of foodstuffs, but I have never heard the story about the cornflakes." Many people who came didn't know what a banana was. Many of them would start eating the banana by biting into the peeling. To us it seems funny and strange but it dawned on me, "How would anyone know, if they had never seen it before?" You can't call people dumb or stupid if they don't know what the food is. If they had never seen it before, how could you expect them to know how to eat it? I guess the immigration service had a great time laughing at these people. On the other hand, to those folks who were being laughed at, it wasn't terrible funny. At the time they felt embarrassed and inadequate.

Making Michigan Home

I don't really know why my grandfathers settled here. My paternal grandfather, Francis Spaniola, was in West Virginia before he came to Michigan, and he came to Lansing in 1901 or 1902. My dad (Anthony Spaniola) was born in Lansing in 1902. So Grandpa Spaniola had been in the Lansing area for at least a year, I would guess.

But a lot of these Italians in southern Italy from Calabria and our little town of St. Ippolito came to central Michigan communities. They opened stores. Of course, it was easy in those days to open a business. It's not as it is today where you have to have a half a million bucks to open the door. Back then, you could get a little stock, have a storefront, and you open the place. Most of them ran confectionery stores, or produce stores—fruits and vegetables. My mother's dad, Andrew Spadafore, ran a confectionery here in Corunna. Actually, he had two stores—a produce store and a confectionery where they sold candy and ice cream. He also had a restaurant with it as well where they sold food. My grandpa Spaniola had a fruit market and wholesale produce business. So anyway, they all settled here and pretty much went into the same business.

As my mother related to me, her dad, my grandpa Andy Spadafore, was a pretty genial guy and liked very much by his own people—I mean the people of Italian extraction who were here. He would leave his business and go stay with these people for a week or ten days and actually get their business started. People helped one another in those days. They weren't horribly jealous of one another, as some of us are today—jealous of our own siblings at times.

My mother came to Michigan and got off at the depot that I am presently working on as a board member to help restore and with the legislature to work to raise money to keep that building there. You know something, I never stopped to think about it that way, that she came to that building that now I am doing some work on to help restore.

She said that they were really excited about arriving here. It was in the wintertime. They came from the central part of Italy where

they had a very mild climate. She said my grandpa was there waiting for her when the train came in and some of her other relatives
were as well. A cousin, Paul Fortino, was there, who was in business
in Swartz Creek for years and married my dad's older sister. So we
were related to Uncle Paul and a number of Italian relatives who
lived in Durand. They came down to the train. My mother said
that as the train was coming to a stop, she recognized her dad from
pictures. They were jumping up to look in the windows to see if
they could see their family in there. That was her first sight of her
dad, jumping up and looking in the window. It was very emotional.

When they got off the train it was cold and the cars didn't have
heat, so eight or nine miles to Corunna was quite a ride. Apparently
they arrived later in the day. They went to a home, which was an
apartment above a store of one of the relatives who lived in Durand.
They stayed the night. They obviously reacquainted themselves
with one another. They had a wonderful time. The next day they
drove the distance here to Corunna. My grandfather had the stores
that I mentioned and he lived over the business, as most of my
people did, and as I did until I was twenty years old. No one knows
what it means to have a backyard when you live in an apartment
above a store. Not that it was bad. It was wonderful. To have a yard
now is nice.

They came and Mom said it was very cold in the car. My grandfather was a very kind man, empathetic and astute and recognized
right away that she was very, very cold. He told her, "You come and
sit by me and I will keep you warm. When we get to Corunna I will
give you some warm clothes." They went to the clothing store and
got her a nice coat with a fur collar on it and a muff. Until the day
she died she talked about that muff. She never had anything that
nice before. They didn't have much over there. Life was pretty hard,
and while it wasn't easy here, she had a nice coat and a nice muff.
I am not sure why the muff was so important, only she knows, but
I think I can understand it.

My mother would have been in fourth or fifth grade by American standards, and of course she couldn't speak any English. She
probably didn't start school for two or three weeks. She was probably getting accustomed to the area. She went to school and she

could not converse in English, so they put her in the first grade. So here is this big girl with these little kids and she said the teacher was just wonderful to her. She was a bright lady, extremely quick, and she picked up English rapidly. Before too many weeks went by she was with her own group.

She told me that she had really positive experiences in school. She spoke very kindly of the teachers that she had. Many of the people who taught her when she was in school here in Corunna also were teachers who my sister and I had as we came along—not just my older sister but my two younger sisters as well. We shared teachers. They always spoke kindly to me about my mom. She must have been a pretty personable young lady at the time. Being a foreigner in a white Anglo-Saxon Protestant milieu was probably not very easy. I feel good about the fact that she thought she had good experiences in the school, and as far as the people in the community were concerned, my grandfather was well liked as a businessman here. I think they were probably treated quite well. I think I shared the same kind of experience here. Italian Americans were not exactly on the top of the social ladder. I know that my mother always had a lot of anger about the fact that there was sort of a line drawn. It was sort of a love-hate relationship in terms of certain people in the community.

Silent Discrimination

My mother was never nasty to anybody. The way it manifested itself is that she taught us that we are what we are. We ought to be proud of that and not to deny the fact that you are of Italian extraction and that you happened to be a Catholic in a community in which Catholics were as scarce as hens' teeth, and that you had a little darker complexion than someone else.

I was never treated badly by anyone. You knew you were Catholic and a foreigner and you didn't run in the same social circles as others, but you know, I was a popular kid in school, treated well and liked by the people in the town. There were certain girls that you were in school with that you are kind of afraid to say anything to because you knew if there was anything there, it wouldn't go very far because their parents wouldn't want them to associate with a person like me. On the other hand, I am sure there were a whole lot of kids who felt the other way too, that there shouldn't be that imaginary line that is drawn, the glass curtain or whatever you want to call it.

I have great feelings about the town in spite of the couple of little stories I told you about—the social stratification and that sort of thing. Sure, its hurtful to say you didn't measure up, to be accepted in others people's eyes. On the other hand, it hurts, but it doesn't hurt. You understand this strange kind of attitude that one has and I don't really think I have ever spoken about this to anybody. It's one of those things you just kept inside of you.

Confronting the Klan

My father has some experiences with that, some interesting experiences. My dad was in Perry and he went over there in 1915. My grandpa opened a store over there and my dad was forced to leave school to go run the store at age thirteen. He was a really genial guy—much like my maternal grandfather. It is kind of strange. He was more like my maternal grandfather than he was his own father in his outgoing ways. I think that it is important to this story that you hear that. My grandpa Andy was just loved by everybody. My dad was well liked too—even though they were second-class citizens, if you can understand that kind of a dichotomy. Dad was in business there and had a little soda fountain and confectionery and sold tobacco and cigars. He was doing pretty well in the community, at least in terms of making friends with people.

I don't know what year this would have been—it was before my mom and dad were married. One night the KKK marched in front of his store and formed a semicircle in front of the place and burned a cross. One Klansman went into my dad's store and had either an ax handle or a baseball bat and proceeded to start breaking up the fixtures. My dad had just gone into debt for showcases to have the candy and everything else. They went in and destroyed the place. My dad was a very mild man. He wasn't weak. He was a gentle man and a gentleman.[1]

COURTESY OF FRANCIS "BUS" SPANIOLA

The Ku Klux Klan vandalized Tony Spaniola's store in Perry, Michigan. Tony "went into a rage and he picked the man up bodily and literally threw him through the plate glass window!"

He told me this story:

I went into a rage. I absolutely saw red. This was one of the few times in my life I couldn't control my temper. I said to myself, "To heck with it, they are going to do to me what they are going to do to me. By golly, I am going to protect my property." He said he did not know where he got the strength but he was so enraged that he went over and grabbed the guy and picked him up off the floor and apparently when he did, he ripped the sheet off of him and under the sheet was his best friend. He said he went into a double rage and he picked the man up bodily and literally threw him through the plate glass window! He said luckily that guy was not hurt that badly and it wasn't anything that serious. After he threw the guy out the window, they packed up and left.

He said, "Man, I was in a rage. My God, I hadn't even paid for these fixtures. I was in debt and I didn't know how in the world I was going to replace them." He probably didn't have any insurance. Who thought of insurance in those days? Foreigners wouldn't even think of insurance.

Couple, three days later, the guy came back in the store and Dad said, "I almost lost it again. I told him, 'You get out of here before I do something that I don't want to do!'"

The guy said to him, "Tony, you just don't understand . . . "

"What do you mean I don't understand? You wrecked my store! You—of all people! You knew that I went into debt for this, and I don't have the money to replace it."

The guy said again, "You just don't understand. You've got to know that it is very important for me to be a member of this group. All the guys like you, but I had to prove to them that the Klan meant more than your friendship, so this is why it happened."

My dad ripped off a badge from this guy that was in my mother's keepsakes. I saw it once and I have never seen it since. I was just a young boy—seventeen or eighteen years of age—when my dad told me this story. It enraged me so much that what was on it is burned into my mind like you would burn something on wood or a carbon granite. I read it once and I know it verbatim:

In 1924 the Ku Klux Klan held meetings and a parade in Owosso before the state elections in November.

I'd rather be a Klansman in my robes so snowy white,
Than to be a Catholic Priest in his robes so black as night,
For a Klansman is an American and America is his home,
But that Catholic owes his allegiance to that Dago pope in Rome.

I read that and I said to myself, "What are we, that we succumb to this kind of hate and insanity, to make light of people for what they are and what the color of their skin is, and where they come from, what religion they belong to? What kind of lunatic society do we live in that some people can buy that kind of stuff?"

I suppose it can be explained by people who do such crazy things, but it happens everywhere. It is still happening in the world. They are killing people in Kosovo because they are Albanians. They destroyed Jews. I guess who are we to cry—our store was destroyed? At least we are alive. At least they just terrorized us.

My mother or father never told me this story, but if you want another Klan story, if you find that interesting, an elderly gentleman used to come into my dad's store who was a dear friend of my grandpa Andy. This chap was a great friend of my grandpa's and his name was Al Weatherwax. He was known to people in town as "Weathy." He was a neat old guy. I used to love to talk to him. He would come in our store and weave stories about the old days, and he told this little caper that he and my grandpa were engaged in which made me rather proud of my grandfather. I was proud of him anyway—from what I had heard about him he was a pretty good guy.

He said, "You know your grandpa and I were talking one day and there was word out, in fact there was a notice given that there was going to be a big gathering of the Klan on the courthouse lawn. Your grandpa and me collected old rotten tomatoes and everything else for a week and put them on the roof of the building, and bombarded these dudes as they came prancing in their white sheets." I had a big belly laugh over this. That must have been a sight to see. To see these guys unloading on them. It was a wonder some of these guys didn't get hurt!

The kind of people whom I admire the most are those who stood up and said, "Look, do what you want. I am what I am, and you are

COURTESY OF FRANCIS "BUS" SPANIOLA

In 1926, Angeline married Anthony (Tony) Spaniola. They posed for this photograph on their wedding day.

not going to change it." My parents instilled in me, and in the entire family, this feeling that you are what you are. If the social elite in the community doesn't like what you are, that's too bad. You don't buckle under if you believe there is value to being yourself.

The experiences as you talk to these people are very similar.

Some were not as gutsy as others in terms of fighting that kind of insensitivity and hatred off, but others were not ashamed of who they were. I will be honest with you. Those are the kind of people that I admire the most—those who stood up and said, "Look, do what you want. I am what I am, and you are not going to change it." It's not that you can't improve yourself, that's not what I am saying. What I am saying is, you are what you are and you know you can't deny your roots and if you do, you are kidding yourself.

I always sit down and tell my children about this Klan kind of an attitude that also permeated other people in different ways, manifested in different ways. You had a dark complexion; you were a dago or a wop or whatever. They never felt any of that stuff and I would say, "You know, you've got to remember these things. It is important that you don't do anything to anyone else that would in any way hurt people's feelings the way our peoples' feelings were hurt. You just don't do that." I think they are all very socially aware. In their own way they are political activists.

Home Cooking

In the earlier days of my life back in the late 1930s and into the 1940s, my aunts and uncles came over, or we went to their house in Lansing. These were the most marvelous times I have ever had in my life. They cooked and they had all the good Italian foods you would think the southern Italian types would have. They made their own sausage at times. My grandmother and mother and my aunts would get together and make the sausage, and that was just great.

My family was not heavy into alcoholic beverages. Some of the relatives made their own wine. Even to a person like me who doesn't drink that much it was just really great stuff—when we got together and you didn't have a whole lot. It was just a joy being with your cousins and your aunts and your uncles. It was marvelous. Family was really something.

I was born in the middle of the Depression, in 1935. Things were tough. We were warm and we ate three meals a day. We were a heck of a lot better off than a lot of other people, but things were tough. You didn't have money to do a whole lot with, but I will tell you something. I had a mother who knew how to take inexpensive food and make it taste like it was gourmet. My mom would buy the cheap cuts of meat and they tasted better than steaks I have paid $100 a plate for! She made the best spaghetti sauce in the entire world. Of course that is one person's opinion! All the family thought my mother made the best sauce that was around. To eat a meal that my mother prepared was like going to a gourmet restaurant without all the fancy trimmings and all the other stuff.

She made omelets to die for. In Italian we call them a *frittata*. My mom would make whatever kind you wanted, but what I liked best was a plain one with two or three different kinds of cheese in it. She would put other things in it for other people, but for me that was like having a chateaubriand, like in the fanciest restaurant. We have tried over and over and over again to replicate that and we can't do it. We use the recipe that she gave orally, but she didn't have any recipes on paper. Everything was done with touch and sight—same with her spaghetti sauce. My wife is not Italian, but she makes pretty good spaghetti sauce. She can't reach that level. My sisters make good spaghetti sauce and they can't reach that level. I swear to God, she was so proud of her ability to get these compliments— "This is the best the best sauce, the best ravioli"—that she always held back when you asked her the recipe. I swear that she held back, but no matter what we did, we couldn't replicate it.

There were many American dishes that were marvelous. She made the best cream pies that I have had anywhere, wonderful cream pies. She would make a plain cream pie or banana cream pie. What a cook this women was! She would do it very frugally. Till the day she died she was always concerned about being economical about things. Tasted very good, but she never spent a lot of money. She was always worried that she would not have enough. I think it is probably because of her background.

Songs of Love

My dad couldn't afford a car and a truck as well, and he had to have a truck in order to conduct his business. So this was our car and in

Angeline, Francis "Bus," and Anthony "Tony" Spaniola pose with Tony's sedan delivery truck. "We'd get in there and we would love being together and we would sing and have a good time."

fact he got a new one in 1941 that was basically the same thing, a 1935 Ford sedan delivery. We didn't have a car as such with a real backseat until after World War II was over. When Dad had the money then, he couldn't buy a car except a used one, and he wasn't about to do that. We got our first automobile in my lifetime in 1947 when I was twelve years old. That old truck is where my heart is.

When we would go somewhere my dad had a studio couch that had this mattress on it that came off. It wasn't like a mattress on a bed; it was a kind of a decorative thing. He would slide it in the back of the truck. My sister and I would sit back there, and my dad had a wonderful voice, and he wanted to be an entertainer, but I think culturally, my grandfather thought it was a sissified business, not a man's business. My grandfather thought people had to work with their hands in their business. He thought it was kind of a flight of fancy that my father did sing on WJR back in the days of its infancy. The Arctic Dairy program—my grandfather kind of thought that was unacceptable. Dad also wrote some lyrics, published a tune with Leo Freidman, who wrote "Carolina Moon." Leo Freidman was a fairly well known composer. (Dad wrote the lyrics for others, too.) It was never published and didn't do anything. Somewhere in the archives we have a couple of pieces of sheet music with my dad's name on it.

We would get in that truck and we'd sing. Sometimes we would just sing with the radio. We would have a great time. You never know how good you have it until you don't have it anymore.

We got this other truck in 1941 and it was the same story. My entire family—I mean my sisters and brother—there were five of us altogether. My mother had six. She lost one at six months, before I was born. Two boys and three girls lived. We'd get in there and we would love being together and we would sing and have a good time. Then my dad was finally able to buy a car. Not because of money at the time, but you couldn't get them. We got this new car, 1947 Mercury. I can even remember the license number, LJ7676. I remember like it was yesterday. He brought that car home and I was twelve years old, and couldn't drive. Young boys were really impressed with cars. We had car with a real backseat. I would go

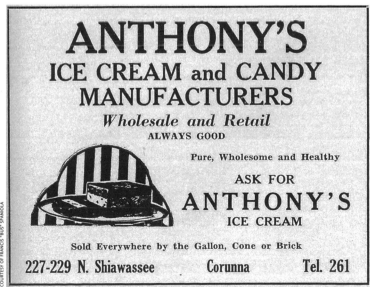

An ad from Anthony's ice cream store.

out there and sit in that thing. My dad would come out and say, "Come on, we have work to do." After a fashion I said to myself, "It's not the same. I like the old truck better."

I admit this to my children and my wife, but I don't think I have to admit it to anyone else. It had such an effect on me that for years I tried to recapture that. I bought station wagon after station wagon. It didn't dawn on me for a while that I was trying to recapture that. The station wagon was fancy and it wasn't the old truck and the feeling wasn't there, and I loved it so much that I was trying to recapture it. I finally grew up and realized I was never going to bring back the past. It was kind of nice to admit to myself that that was so important to me and that was such an important time in my life—that I was affected by that. I tell the kids that and they say, "Wow, Dad, you must have really liked that." I did, I really did.

This is what I called the old-fashioned foreign way. I liked it and I like it to this day. My kids kind of kid me sometimes. They say, "You know, Dad, you are an anachronism. You're a product of the fifties." In many ways they're right—I am.

I don't think I look backward. I don't think I am a backward-looking person. There were times, from the time I was born in 1935 until the mid-fifties when I was in college, that I, to this day, say these were great times, not just because of the heritage given to me by my parents but just the way times were and the way people got along. But anyway, the kids kid me about it and I say, "Well, you know, someday you are going to be looking back and saying our times together were basically the same." So you know we do talk a lot about the old times, and, I think, to them in some cases that is so distant that they don't think it is possible that things like that happen today.

Three-Time Loser

I am the first ethnic Catholic to be elected to the legislature from this area. I was a Democrat on top of that. I am a three-time loser in the eyes of the political public—being a Catholic, a Democrat, and a foreigner.

I was in office maybe a couple of months. They wanted to

build a senior center in Owosso. I got a call and they said, "We're going to take a trip and we are going to visit some senior citizen centers. You are our legislator and we would like to have you go." I said, "I would love to go. It is important to me that our seniors are taken care of."

So I get on this bus. I don't think anyone on the bus voted for me. If they did, they had to lie about it. They had to cover it up and say they voted for someone else. That circle just wasn't the kind of circle that someone like me would fit into. I know they were all jockeying around to see who wouldn't have to sit with me. I say this not in anger. It sort of amused me, to be honest with you. What happened next angered me, however.

I will not mention any names. This fellow was new to the area; he was an executive with one of the companies, so I guess he was designated to be the dummy who sat next to me. We were sitting there talking and he said something to the effect that "They are really frightened of you." I knew what he was saying, but I said, "I don't know why. I am a mild-mannered man. My girls call me a teddy bear."

"No, no, they think that you have ideas that are just unacceptable."

"Well, I guess that is their prerogative. They can think what they want to think. I am not going to get too concerned about that."

He said, "I told them, don't worry about him. He wants to be like us, so he is going to change his ways."

I told him. "I have news for you, mister. I don't have anything against you, nor do I have anything against the people on this bus—although I know they didn't vote for me. They have a right to their opinion, but I have a right to mine, and it will be a cold day in hell when I adjust to be accepted, so you are going to have to live with me the way I am."

What gave me the courage to do that, I'm sure, is the experience that I went through with my mom and dad. What kind of a person are you if you don't have the courage of your conviction? If you don't have any pride in your heritage? I had a great deal of that, a great deal of pride in my heritage, thanks to my mother and my dad and my grandparents.

Knocking on Doors

I was campaigning in a new district in 1982. The district was reapportioned and we had picked up part of Livingston County, Cohoctah Township, where a man well known for his racist activities operated. The guy, as I recollect, was involved with bombing school buses in the Detroit area. His name was well known but I won't mention it because I don't think that is terribly important. What is important is that we set the stage for this occurrence that opened my oldest daughter's eyes to the stories that Dad and Grandma and others told her.

We were in the little village of Cohoctah and I had no opponent, believe it or not. It was one of the few free rides that anyone like me ever had in their life. We were knocking on doors. I am on one side of the street and my daughter is on the other. I could see my daughter was getting very angry. I knew she knew how to handle herself, so I kind of laid back. She was red in the face. She stomped off this man's porch and she came across the street and I asked her what was the matter?

She said, "You will never believe what happened to me over there, Dad." I said, "I think I will. What happened?"

She said, "I knocked on the door and I told the man that I was your daughter and you were a state legislator and you were running for reelection and this was a new district. The guy said, 'Is your dad a Christian?'" She was kind of startled and said, 'Yes, sir.' To her it didn't matter what you were. He said, 'Does your father go to church?' She told him we belong to St. Joseph's Catholic parish in Owosso.

"I knew it!" he said. "This guy is not a Christian. He has got this foreign-sounding name; he's a Democrat and a Catholic! Get the hell off my porch!"

I told her, "You handled yourself okay. Never get huffy with people. What good does it do you? It only gives them the opportunity to say you're no good."

We went to the car and sat down and had a long talk. I said, "Angie, you learned a lesson today that you needed to learn. You wouldn't believe what I was telling you. Kids would say, 'Things aren't that way anymore.' You learned something. In some places, things are that way."

She was outraged. She recognized the fact that there is still some of that nastiness out there. She also recognized what I recognized, that those hatreds, even though they are submerged, they are linked. They are there and they are only waiting for another demagogue to bring them out. Hopefully that demagogue won't come along, but nonetheless, they are there to be manipulated and people are manipulated. We have learned, and if we learn well enough from the past, we know when someone is trying to use us.

The Feast of Ippolito

The old-timers are dying, but what I love is to sit down and talk with the old-timers. I just love to hear stories of the old country. I love to hear stories, particularly about my mother's town and my dad's community. Both families came from the same little town in the old country. I love to talk about what happened there, what life was like, the experiences that these people shared when they were there, the friendships and the connections. I love the culture and the heritage.

I think I told you how we have this feast day on the Sunday nearest the feast day of St. Ippolito, the patron saint of our town in Italy. If you go to Resurrection Parish in Lansing, they have a statue of St. Ippolito there, by the way. That was put there because of the large Italian community that settled in Lansing from the village of St. Ippolito.

When they started this festival, it must have been 1938 or '39. I was three or four years old. My uncle Charlie Spadafore and Emil [DeMarco] and a number of other men in Lansing decided this would be a nice thing to do. So they put this program together and we would meet out at Bunker Hill Township at this little church, and invite anyone who has any connection to St. Ippolito.

I remember the first year that they did this. The bishop of the diocese of Lansing was there and he gave a sermon about the importance of your ethnicity and the contribution of people of not only of Italian extraction but others made to the United States.

Then there would be a feast. You brought your own food and ate on the picnic table. Everything was al fresco, outdoors. You had everything laid out there, and if you didn't sample someone else's food, something was wrong. They wanted you to do that. People would sit around and talk about old times, and then we would play bocce and lawn bowling. The men always liked to play cards. I think that is universal. We had fireworks and a band. People would dance on the tennis courts. I wouldn't have missed those things for the world!

Native Tongues

That kind of brings me back to my grandparents and my parents.

Over the years you're in a different environment. There was a lot of conversation in Italian at home when I was a kid, and I will never forget the consternation I would feel when I didn't understand what they were saying. When I was real small I would get mad. I would tell them not to talk funny, so I could understand what was going on. Then, of course, later I decided that I wanted to pick some of this up. I thought it was kind of cool to learn the language. At the point I was developing some Italian language skills, my grandparents passed and I didn't hear much spoken Italian anymore. I remember I had to take a language at college and I signed up for Italian so I could feel that I was fairly articulate when it came to listening to conversations or even responding to conversation. I didn't take enough of it, and it wasn't this continual discussion. I lost it.

It is much like my wife. She spoke Czechoslovakian before she spoke English. She was born here and had the same type of experience as mine. People were kind of Old World. Her dad's family was abused here too, when they came to this area. We're different but we're much the same. She still has a great love for her heritage and I want my kids to know that too. I think it's important that they know both sides.

I used to kid around when I would go out here to the ZCBJ hall.[2] I was in office at the time. They used to make a big thing out of having me there and I'd say, "Well, we had an interesting kind of situation at our house. We have pasta and then we have *kolache* for desert. This is a United Nations table. There is sauerkraut and dumplings. There is a little bit of everything." They'd get a big chuckle out of that. They adopted me because I am ethnic. They had the same kind of experience that I did. My getting into public office—they thought that there was hope for all of them.

Ghosts of the Past

To tell you the truth, I love this town. My roots are here. I'll tell you how much I care about this town. I don't want you to misunderstand, because that wouldn't be fair to this community. When most of the stores burned downtown, of course my mother's place didn't get hit by it, but just about the entire block went up in smoke back in 1980, and I sat down there and cried like a baby.

An arsonist set fire to one of the buildings and it just destroyed about two-thirds of the entire block across from the courthouse. My mother's building was luckily not damaged, but it was a horrible thing. My wonderful memories of all the old guys who were in business on that street just went up in smoke. The good ghosts of the past that I used to remember as I walked down the street just went up in flames. It is different today. You don't get the same feeling. You go by the store and this was the shoe shop, and Dutch Bowersmith ran this place, and this guy and that guy and that place. You remember these people because they were just great folks. This is a nice town. I stood there on the courthouse lawn—of course, I guess you know I am an emotional Latin—I stood there and cried like a baby. I said to myself, "My God, what is wrong with you?—it's just a building. It's *not* just a building, it is part of me."

Sharing the Stories

I lost my dad in 1960. I was just a young man. Of course, I've had my mother around for a long period of time.

As I look back at all of my relatives, they all had so many neat things to share with the world. The sharing was there with their own family, and if their family didn't share it, it was lost. I am convinced that my grandchildren enjoy the stories that I tell them,

Bus Spaniola and his grandson, Nick, who wrote a report about his grandmother Angeline who had inspired him.

but I'm not certain I tell them the complete story. I give them bits and pieces, and there are other things that I should tell them.

When my aunts and uncles and grandparents passed, it was like someone took a part of you or your heart, and nobody can tell me there is a greater learning experience than that. I try very hard today to make my children understand the importance of being together. I think they do. You don't have to have a lot of money. You don't have to be wealthy in order to have this. I'm convinced that we had it all.

I don't think people really understand that today. As close as I am to my kids, I don't think they understand the depth of love that was there, and how you really needed one another. That was all you really had. You knew someone really loved you and it was beautiful. It was just beautiful!

My son's youngest boy wrote an article for the school project.

He lives down in the Troy area. He had to write about a hero, and interestingly enough, without any prodding, he wrote about his great-grandmother, my mother. He told in his own little way some of the stories I had shared with him and my mother had shared with him. It was really kind of cute to read. He relates some of the things she said, and how brave and frightening it would have been had he had to go through that experience. So maybe more sinks in with them, more than we think.

NOTES

1. In 1924 the Ku Klux Klan held meetings and a parade in Owosso before the state elections in November. The Ku Klux Klan was organized in 1865 in opposition to the Reconstruction policies of the federal government. It has disbanded and reformed several times since then. The height of Klan membership was from 1915 to 1933, when it boasted nearly 10 million members. There were at least ninety-three "Klaverns" chartered in Michigan. The Klan became known as the "Invisible Empire" because its meetings and membership list were secret. Originally opposed to civil rights for blacks, the Klan focused its hatred and violence on immigrants—especially Catholics and Jews—during its "Second Empire," beginning in 1915.

2. ZCBJ is an acronym for Zapadni Cesko Bratrske Jednota. In English: Western Bohemian Fraternal Association.

Anything That I've Set My Mind to, I Usually Accomplish

In the second decade of the twentieth century, rural southern blacks began moving to northern industrial cities in an unprecedented "Great Migration." Pushed by poverty, indebtedness, racism, and crop failures, they were also lured by the prospect of better-paying factory jobs and greater freedom in the North.

Michigan's burgeoning auto industry made the state a destination for migrants. When World War I cut off the supply of new immigrant workers from Europe, auto companies sent recruiters south. African American newspapers and word of mouth from earlier migrants also helped to bring people north.

Detroit was the primary destination in Michigan for migrating southerners. The city's black population grew from about 5,700 in 1910 to 120,000 in 1930.

Carlean Gill's father, Norman Gill, was born in St. Vincent in the Caribbean but left there after a volcanic eruption in 1902 killed over a thousand people. He went to work on the Panama Canal and then to British Columbia, where he worked in a coal mine. Gill then immigrated to the United States and settled in Michigan, working at the Ford Motor Company plant at River Rouge by day and building houses and farming in his spare time.

Elease Johnson came to Michigan from North Carolina and

married Norman Gill in 1925. They raised seven children in Ferndale, the segregated community that Ford built to house African American employees. The Gill children attended an all-black elementary school and traveled by foot along dirt roads because the school system denied bus service to the children of the African American community.

Carlean Gill is the youngest of the seven Gill children. After graduating from Lincoln High School, she attended Lewis Business College and worked as a model. She caught the eye of Arthur Braggs, who gave her a job as a "Fiesta Doll" in his "Idlewild Revue" at the famous Paradise Club in Idlewild along with famous black entertainers like Della Reese, the Four Tops, Sammy Davis, Jr., and the Temptations. Braggs managed the Paradise Club during the fifties and early sixties.

After her career at Idlewild, Carlean moved to Saginaw and attended All American Beauty College before opening Carlean's Beauty Salon. She then opened Saginaw Beauty Academy and Saginaw Barber College. She has won national and international acclaim for her hair-weaving technique, which she uses to help cancer patients who have lost their hair from chemotherapy.

Carlean Gill's list of honors and awards is extensive. The City of Saginaw, Saginaw County, the State of Michigan, and the U.S. Congress have all honored her as an outstanding African American businesswoman. The American Red Cross and Habitat for Humanity have honored her for work not only in the United States, but also in Ghana, Italy, Chile, and Zimbabwe. The Michigan State University Museum, the Michigan Historical Museum, and the Public Library of Saginaw have featured her in exhibits on Idlewild.

In addition to her modeling and business careers, she owned and operated a farm raising thoroughbred racing horses, and raised her daughter, Nichole.

Michelle Johnson, former Freedom Trail Coordinator for the State of Michigan, interviewed Carlean Gill at her home in Saginaw in 1999. There she recalled her parents' immigration to Michigan and her rise from a poor, segregated neighborhood of Detroit to her life in show business, cosmetology, and horse racing.

From an Island to a Peninsula

My father was from St. Vincent and he worked on the Panama Canal. Then he worked in Canada and years later came to Detroit. There he sent for the rest of his relatives, one at a time. Some ended up in Toronto and others in New York and Washington, D.C.

In St. Vincent, he came from a family of carpenters. My father was very skilled and could build houses. I remember him sitting down and talking to us about his homeland. We would say, "Daddy, what did they do, what did it look like over there?" And he would tell us about the mountains, and how they had to cut sugar cane with machetes. I remember him talking about ships coming over with slaves and how the slaves rioted and how he got to the Panama Canal, leaving the island to try to get a job. He told us about Ghana, Africa, where ships would pick up slaves and bring them down to the islands. And I believe that Ghana is where some of my ancestry comes from, and in fact, I know one of them was African, my great-great-grandmother.

My father passed away before he could return, but he often would talk about the island; and he sang songs from there and he had a Caribbean accent. A lot of people would say, "Your father talks funny!"

I went several years ago to the island of St. Vincent with two of my sisters and my sisters' husbands. And we met my cousins who live there. When I went to the island I could just feel my father's presence. I felt he was talking to me again, and it's a great feeling to travel to a land where your parents come from, because somehow you feel their spirit. It's so important to know your history; and what's been hidden from us often is our history, because it has not been documented properly. Like now, I believe what you're doing is great because you are documenting my history.

My father met my mother out in Ferndale. He was a young bachelor. They said at that time he was well off, I guess. He was much older than my mother. She came from North Carolina, from a rural area. I only went down there once. And I remember it was because of a death in the family.

I remember stopping at a restaurant. And the serving staff said

COURTESY OF CARLEAN GILL

Elease Johnson met immigrant Norman Gill after he came to Michigan from Toronto to work at Ford Motor Company's River Rouge factory. Elease and Norman Gill were married in 1925. Carlean was their seventh daughter, following Lillian, Christine, Jean, Sarah, Anne, and Elisa.

that they didn't serve colored people, so my sister said, "We don't eat colored people!" and walked out. So when we got in the car she said, "I'm not spending my money here." I remember my aunt hitting my sister on the head and telling her, "Girl, do you know where you are at?" So we stopped at another restaurant where we could get something to eat, but we had to go in through the back door. I had to be seven years old, eight, just old enough to know what was going on.

Life on a Small Farm in Ferndale

My father got a job at Ford Motor Company, and the money he saved he would send back to St. Vincent to get another family member to immigrate to the U.S. Still, he ended up buying a lot of property in Ferndale. He had land all over. And he had rental houses he had built.

My father also had cows and chickens, and we would kill pigs to eat, and we had honeybees to get honey. I remember him pulling a cap on his head so he could go out and smoke the bees to get the honey out of the beehives.

I remember him killing hogs, and my grandmother curing them. I remember feeding the pigs and a few cows. I remember killing the cows. We had roosters and chickens and you had to go to the back of the farm to collect eggs.

I remember my sister getting married, and the newlyweds couldn't afford to go anywhere else to live. My father refused to let them go elsewhere. So the chicken house we had in the backyard, out at the back of the house, was made into a house for them.

It was nothing but country life. We lived on a dirt road. But by the time I was a teenager, they had paved the streets.

We had an outside toilet, but after I was born, toilets became popular inside. As I grew up, though, I saw some neighbors still had outside toilets.

I remember making lye soap. It was made out of lye and hog fat. And they would cook it out in the backyard, and stir it, and then

The Gill family lived in this house that Norman Gill bought and moved to a segregated neighborhood in Ferndale, just north of Detroit.

they would pour it out on a sheet and let it harden. And then they would mark it off, and that's what you washed your clothes with.

My mother wanted a better house, so my father went and bought a house. The house that he bought was the biggest house on the block. He bought it from the highway department in Highland Park. They were moving the houses, so my father went down and bought a house on Davison and moved it out to Eight Mile. Had to be about fifteen miles. He moved it and put it on some land that he had bought, next door to a house that he owned.

He had a heart attack, so he retired from Ford. In order to keep our standard of living—and he refused for us to go on welfare—he had land, and he worked the land. When he got sick, rather than letting things go down, we went to a rummage sale every Saturday. Now he was picking up discarded food at the back of the grocery stores. Not all of our food came from there, but it was to supplement what we grew on the farm.

My mother would go out at night when my daddy was sleeping and kill a chicken, and say, "Now don't tell your daddy we just killed a chicken." It was a ritual. Mama killed a chicken, and she cooked it, and it was really great!

My father didn't want my mother to work, but she did, because she wanted to get away. And back then you either cleaned other people's homes or you sewed for them. But I believe she worked at a restaurant. It made us proud. Because my father kept telling us, "You are not going on welfare, no matter what!"

My father worked hard. He built an apartment onto the house for my sister Christine. He died building her a garage. I was out of town, over at one of my sisters and I came home and I remember them picking him up off the ground.

School Days

I went to Grant School, an all-black elementary school. Then I went to Lincoln High, a mainly white high school in Oak Park, and graduated in about 1956. Thereafter I attended Lewis College of Business.

They had buses for the white kids, but they didn't have buses for the black kids in the black neighborhoods. We had dirt streets. Once you hit the paved streets you knew you were in the white neighborhood. You walked to school and it was about a mile and a half to school and a mile and half to your home. Come rain or shine, you had to walk. Parents back then did not own many cars—you could hitch a ride with some other parent, but mainly you would just walk.

I will not forget how degrading it was for me at school to participate in swimming class. At that time in high school you couldn't wear your hair in an Afro. We had swimming class—I never had swimming before—and you had to get into the pool during the first class period. Before coming to school, you had pressed your hair, got yourself all shined up and ready to go to school, and then you had to go swimming. After coming out of the pool, your hair was all messed up. While combing your wet hair, the white girls would say, "What happened to your hair?"

And what would always get me peeved was the socks of white girls would always be white, and my socks, no matter what, my socks would be dingy, and I didn't like that. I wanted mine to be white. But that was because we were walking on that dirt road, and by the time we came back home we would be dusty, cars flying down the street and the dust going "whoosh!"

I was in modern dance, and then I belonged to a couple of clubs. But I was mainly by myself. I did have a couple of black girlfriends.

Of course, your parents don't know much about what classes you should take. So when I brought my report card home and I got a C and a B, my mother was just looking at those grades, she wasn't looking at what courses I should be taking to prepare me for college. And that's what a lot of parents did.

So what happened is, my sister—the one who went to college and then into bookkeeping—she came home and looked at my report card and said, "Look, this girl only has home economics, sewing, all these easy subjects. She will never make it in life." So she took it upon herself to go over and talk to the school counselor.

At that time the counselor had told her that all the other classes were full, it was too late. So my sister raised such heck that the counselor made me drop the easy courses and placed me in typing and bookkeeping classes instead. But my counselor did tell me, "You will never get a job in bookkeeping and typing." And when I went home and told my sister what he had told me, she really got upset.

But that's what they were doing to a lot of the black students. Preparing us for work such as sewing, cooking, or baking.

The only job I could get after high school was at a beauty shop, and I was the one picking up the dirty towels and dusting off the counter. The white girls I had graduated with would come in and get their hair done. I would see them come in, sit down, get their hair done, and say, "Hi Carlean, how are you?" And here I got a white apron on and I'm picking up the towels, and sweeping the floor. I swore that I would never do that again—unless I owned my own beauty shop. So that was motivating me. And the next job I had was being a fountain girl in a drugstore, fixing milk shakes and cheese sandwiches and serving people. My sister worked there too, so we were working together, and we both enjoyed it, somewhat. The shop was on Livernois where the rich used to live. And when we would drive through there my mother would say, "Black people will never live here. Look at those beautiful homes. We will never be able to live here." Now it's all black.

Then I had a job babysitting a white baby. I had just graduated from high school, and I said, "There's got to be something better!" That's the reason I started going to all these different schools and working part-time. I did a lot of different schools because my daddy always said as long as I worked, or I went to school, I wouldn't have to pay rent. So I was forever going to school, taking classes. It looked like every time he turned around I was trying to go to school!

The first school was downtown, off Woodward, it was a telephone school, where I learned how to be a switchboard operator. Got a certificate. Then I went to Lewis College of Business for shorthand and typing. I only lasted there for about five months.

The Missing Mink

I did some modeling. There was a club of girls in our community, and a lady would take us around and we would model. She would sew the clothes for us. That led to a beauty contest, "Ms. Bronze Beauty."

We, the participants, had to sell tickets to win. There were about fifteen girls in the contest and I won the contest! It was at the Latin Quarter, and all my family was there and everybody was excited. I was in a bathing suit and in a long gown—the whole bit, just like Miss America. Back in those times we had contests that were just as popular as Miss America, but blacks ran them all.

I won a mink! It was a mink stole. That was my prize. When I got the mink stole, I wore it and thought I was really sharp! I put it in storage at Hudson's Department Store in Detroit. When I returned home, I called and said, "This is Miss Gill calling, and I'd like to pick up my mink stole." The lady on the phone answered, "Wait just a minute," and she went in the back, came back and said, "Well, I'm sorry Miss Gill, we don't have a mink stole here for you, but we do have a dyed muskrat." I thought I had a mink on, and it was a dyed muskrat! I went and cried, "Mama, guess what, that lady told me I had a dyed muskrat!"

I was around people who knew furs. In show business, women dressed the best. They would wear their white fox furs and their mink coats, and I was wearing my little dyed muskrat, and I thought I was hanging in. I kept wondering why they kept saying, "Oh, that color is a little dark for you," or I would hear snide comments. I gave it away.

The Idlewild Revue

A friend of mine told me about Idlewild, that she was dancing there, and to come try out for the Idlewild show. I hadn't been up to Idlewild, but I had been to the shows when they came to the Flame Show Bar in Detroit.

At that time I ran into this same friend I later started the beauty school with. She lived on the same street I did. She had done some of the modeling shows with me while in the club. She was picked by Mr. Braggs to be in the show before I even knew about Mr. Braggs. She was tall and beautiful. More than six feet, real tall, and in heels she was even taller, a real showgirl.

Arthur "Daddy" Braggs was a Saginaw businessman and manager of the Paradise Club at Idlewild. He was responsible for recruiting the talent and producing the shows in the Fiesta Room. Braggs's dream was to create a high-class haven for black patrons who were barred from segregated clubs.

I went down to see her and it was a beautiful show. At that time I saw him [Arthur Braggs] off in the distance, but I didn't know him. He had just come back from Mexico. I was with my boyfriend, and I met my girlfriend and left after the show never thinking I would be a part of the show. One day she came home, called me up and said, "They got an opening for the show. Why don't you come and try out?" I went home and I told mama that they had asked me to come down for an interview to go into show business. I was going to college at the time.

I didn't think I was pretty enough. But I said, "Can I go try out?" My mother said, "Carlean, is this something you really want to do?" And she was explaining to me the pros and cons, and how people often thought performers and life in show business was for people on drugs. And the women were ladies of the night. So mama said, "If it is something you really want to do, you can go and try out." I went and tried out and Mr. Braggs called and said he accepted me!

Ziggy (Johnson) was in the office and he said, "Tell that girl to come back, I like her. Go home and talk it over with your mom."

So I went home and talked it over with my mom, and here's what my mama told me: "I trust you and I know whatever you do, you will try to be the best."

I couldn't disappoint her. My mother had this way of doing things. She didn't whip us, but she could talk to you and get you to come to some kind of sense of reality about something. And she didn't down you either.

I would still go to school, and I would go around to rehearsals,

COURTESY OF CARLEAN GILL

Joe "Ziggy" Johnson was a black dancer, choreographer, and instructor from Detroit. He was also master of ceremonies at the Fiesta Room in the Paradise Club. Johnson is second from the left and Arthur Braggs is second from the right.

COURTESY OF CARLEAN GILL

Lillian, Elisa, Carlean, and Anne Gill enjoy the water at Idlewild. Founded in 1912 near Baldwin, Michigan, Idlewild became a popular resort for African Americans seeking refuge from racist "Jim Crow" laws. At Idlewild, they could relax and enjoy the outdoors without the burden and humiliation of segregation.

and then finally I dropped out and I got ready to go on the road. We had to rehearse and exercise and dance and get fitted for our costumes. We went to Idlewild and that's where we did all of our rehearsing, over the first part of the summer, before the summer season opened.

Everybody who was going to be in the show would arrive, and Braggs would get cabins for us not far from the nightclub. And he would have to pay for those cabins, and then pay our salary too. I believe a month before Idlewild opened we were up there. The cooks would come in, and people from all over the country would come in. He would fly people in from Kansas City, the cooks, the waitresses, setting up for the club, get his bookings, and then getting people from New York to come in and fit us for the costumes.

Then in September it would close down. After Labor Day they would bury the show. "Burying the show" is where all the performers, singers and dancers, would exchange costumes and play a different role. If you were, for example, an exotic dancer, you would become a singer or comedian. Everybody would change roles. Men would put on women's costumes, and hats and gloves, and jewelry, and parade around the stage like the showgirls. Women would dress like men and imitate a male singer or do a comedy routine. The audience loved it!

Then Mr. Braggs would book shows all over the country. We might go to Kansas City or New York. We would leave here and go to Ohio, from Ohio to Chicago, from Chicago into Kansas City. From Kansas City to different places—New Jersey, Boston. We went to Canada. We would have a break in between to come home. He had a bus and we traveled by car and bus.

Mr. Braggs didn't have any trouble with the girls. Everybody had high respect for him. And there was no infighting, and I didn't see any drugs, even though at that time pot was popular. I didn't see anybody shooting up or using any other kind of drugs.

A small group of dancers were called The Braggettes after Mr. Braggs, and they were the ones doing the dancing. And we were the showgirls. We were the Fiesta Dolls. We were the ones that just walked around and pranced.

I couldn't sing, couldn't even walk that well, because I walked off time. But I always ended up where I was supposed to be on stage, on time. They said that they didn't know how I did that. I walk off time but I would end up at a certain spot at the right time, every time. They used to tease me about that. They called me "Nervous Nauseous" backstage, because my feathers would be shaking as I walked, because I was nervous at first!

At one time it was very popular to have an emcee come out and talk to the crowd. The emcee would say, "Ladies and gentlemen..." and introduce the show. It was, "Good afternoon ladies and gentlemen! Now the Idlewild Revue!" And then the show would hit, the girls would come out.

Then after that he would only say "Arthur Prysock" and he would come out. No more talking after that. Arthur Prysock would come up and sing, and then you would have us come back on the stage again. Then you would maybe have a comedian, and then you would have a tap dancer. Or you would have a shake dancer.

After auditions and rigorous training, Carlean became a "Fiesta Doll" in Arthur Braggs's Idlewild Revue of dancers, comedians, musicians, and singers.

A "shake dancer" was an exotic dancer and she would come out in beautiful costumes and shake. It wasn't a nasty act; it was with poise and grace.

Arthur Prysock was like Braggs's brother. He and Braggs were real close, and Braggs used to book him on the show and he would travel all over, and he would cook for the show. Arthur Prysock could cook! He would put the black-eyed peas on, and everybody would come over and eat. A lot of the entertainers cooked. We'd get tired of eating in the restaurants, so we would go and have a potluck. And then people would invite you over to their homes on the road. Chitlin' parties and stuff like that, and they would be so happy to see you. "The Idlewild Revue is in town!" We would go over to so-and-so's aunt's house, the whole busload of us. It was just great. There were about thirty-six of us in the Idlewild Revue, including the band.

COURTESY OF CARLEAN GILL

Popular black singers, dancers, and comedians performed in clubs like the Paradise and Flamingo Clubs. Idlewild declined after the Civil Rights Act of 1964 allowed blacks to frequent formerly segregated clubs and resorts.

People would come from all over the United States to watch the show. Chicago and Detroit, and they would come from Kansas City. You'd see the crowd coming in well dressed, best behavior, first class. There were all sorts of people from all walks of life, doctors, gamblers, teachers, lawyers, and racketeers, even pimps. It was just amazing.

They'd drive their cars up and the doorman would let them

into the club. So it was like being in a big city, yet country living, where you could wear shorts and people would invite you into their homes, or into their cottages, and have a party. If you didn't know anybody, you still felt safe, even going home with strangers. Laughing and talking and partying. It was like one big party. But everyone had respect for each another.

South of the Border

Braggs used to go to Acapulco every year. He ended up bringing back a troop from Acapulco, a whole revue. The band was from Cuba and the dancers were from Acapulco.

The Escobar Dancers was their name. At that time Acapulco was fabulous for shows.

Costumes were just gorgeous.

We first saw the Escobar Dancers in Mexico; they would come up on stage with live chickens. The club was high up in the mountains and they had fire all the way around the club. Seats were under an open sky. The club had no ceiling. It was really something to see.

The bongos and the drums would be playing and they would do a dancing ritual. They wouldn't kill the chickens, but they would take two chickens and fan them back and forth and make them fight, like you see in the movies. They were fantastic.

They performed in Idlewild, then we went to New York and we went to the Apollo Theater, Small's Paradise Club. We went to Boston, Basin Street East. People had never seen anything like that in the U.S.!

Mr. Braggs had to get temporary papers to bring them into the U.S., and when they arrived he had to house them, pay for their housing, and pay for their food. There was a lot of money involved.

The Final Act

Mr. Braggs was so far advanced in his ideas about musical shows. His dream at that time—he talked about having a nightclub with a round stage where the stage would be in the middle of the room and it would rotate around the audience. Behind that stage would be a second rotating stage. And behind the second stage there would be a third rotating stage. He would talk about how one stage would move off and then out would come the second stage with a different act. And then the second stage would move off and a third stage would appear with yet another act.

Mr. Braggs and I traveled a lot. We were in Montreal at one time and it was fabulous. The people there were fascinated with my color. I remember walking down the street and they would call me "Blackie." It was not facetious or anything, it was a compliment— they liked my black skin. Montreal was like being in Paris.

But after years of travel and promoting the Idlewild Revue, Mr. Braggs grew tired. One day he said, "You know what, honey, I'm going home, I'm closing the show down. This is my last time out on the road." He returned to Saginaw. He had a restaurant, the Hickory House. He started working in the restaurant. He was also doing numbers. But the profits in numbers dwindled in the early sixties. He never let me in on that part of the business too much. But, anyway, he returned to Saginaw. At the time I was in Detroit staying with my mother.

We had been together about two years. He said, "If you come up and stay with me, I will take care of you." So I talked to my mother and she said, "Carlean, I don't recommend it. It's your choice. I can't stop you. You know he's married, and I'm a little frightened for you to go and stay with someone like that. But don't have anybody pay for you, give you anything. Don't ask for handouts. Get an education and then people will respect you. You won't be beautiful all your life."

She was right. You won't be beautiful all your life. And when a person has to give money to you, then that's not the way to go. So I talked to Mr. Braggs, and I said, "I want to go to school to be a beautician." I had talked to my sisters and one was a nurse. And she said, "Be a nurse." I had another sister who was a beautician. So I wondered, "Well, which profession will it be? If I become a nurse then I have to work for somebody, and I won't be able to be free and do my own thing. But if I'm a beautician I can go as far as I want to in life." So, I said, "I'll be a beautician."

All American Beauty

So I came up to Saginaw and got in school here, on Lapeer at All American Beauty School. I explained to the instructor that I was in show business, and that sometimes I might need to miss class. She said, "No problem." Everybody in the show laughed and said, "Carlean, you will never be a beautician, because you like to sleep. You're used to partying all night and going out!" Nobody thought I was going to finish my studies. But Mr. Braggs said if I finished beauty school he would open up a shop for me. And if I moved here—to Saginaw—he would open it up for me in Saginaw.

I was in beauty school a year, a little over a year, because I had taken a leave of absence from school for a couple of months. Then I had to work for a while. At that time you had an apprenticeship for one year before you could open up your own shop. I did a one-year apprenticeship in Saginaw.

When I opened my beauty shop, I had a person who would check the patron's coats, and I had a receptionist to answer the phone. I had set it up like some of the shops I had seen on the road.

My mother had always instilled in me if you go into something, finish it, and then go in for the best of it. So I decided to also get my teacher's license. But in order to get my teacher's license, the same lady I had apprenticed with had to train me. I went to take the board exam twice and failed twice, mainly because I didn't know exactly what to study for and I didn't know how to make a lesson plan.

I found a beautician in Detroit who would tutor me on Mondays. My shop was closed on Monday, and I would go down and she tutored me in her salon over on Forest Street. She taught me how to make a lesson plan and told me what to study for my instructor's license. I went to take the board exam again and this time I passed it and got my instructor's license.

Then I wanted to work as a platform artist, so I talked Mr. Braggs into letting me learn this skill. A platform artist is someone who gets up on the stage and talks about hair products and sells the products. I worked for Summit Laboratories. Madam C. J. Walker and her nephews started Summit Laboratories. Summit Laboratories sold permanents and other hair products, and it was real popular back then. The laboratory is based in Indianapolis, Indiana.[1]

When I graduated from beauty school in 1989 I founded Saginaw Beauty Academy. I specialized in fly hairdos and haircuts. Then I changed my specialty. I changed the focus of my shop three times. I finally changed it to making black wigs; we did a lot of wigs.

I was also known for cuts and curls, wiglets and cluster curls. And then they came out with the Afro—"I'm black and I'm proud!" and the Afro hairdo was like a freedom. Before, we were always working at trying to look a different way. When Stokely Carmichael had an Afro and the riots happened, everybody wanted that Afro! In my salon we would take permed hair and put it on those thin, tiny rods, roll it up, let it dry and then take it out and pick it and clients would have an Afro.

When I was in Africa recently, I saw these young women, and you couldn't tell some of the young girls from the young boys. When I see that it makes me sad because I see a little girl in a dress and she has no hair. And she's playing with a little boy, and he has on boy clothes and she has on girl clothes, and you couldn't tell who was who.

That was an enlightening thing to see that at some of the schools in Africa, they don't allow the young women to get their hair relaxed and they make them cut it off. And a lot of times I thought that was just a fashion fad, but from being over there in this particular place I was visiting I realized they cut it off because they don't know what to do with it.

I've learned through a lot of mistakes. Looking back, I really didn't have to work that hard, but it was just a drive in me. I didn't ask anybody for anything. I worked for it. Everything I got I worked for. It made me feel good. I know that a lot of people have respect for me, for my accomplishments. And I guess that's what you work for, to a certain extent. Try to build a good reputation and be kind to people. And I've met a lot of people.

Horsing Around

About the same time I started with the shop, we bought a horse. Mr. Braggs called me and said, "Carlean, I bought a horse. You've got to fly down tomorrow and sign for it"—because everything was in my name. So I stopped what I was doing, got my things packed up, flew to—I can't remember where it was, but the horse's name was Marsha's Mistake. I go into the office at the track, and a white man, a horse trainer, said, "Where did this beautiful, young black woman get all this money from to buy a horse?" Someone answered, "Her grandfather died and left her very rich." I never really felt that I looked the part, but now that I look back at photographs from those days, I'm thinking, "Damn, I was good!" I looked nice!

It was raining that day and we couldn't tell who had won that race, and I believe we came in second. That was our first big race.

And then he bought another horse, and another, and by the time we had gotten this farm, we ended up with too many horses.

He bought my daughter two miniature horses, and I had a pony. He never wanted to sell any of the horses, and they were his true love. By the time he paid the vet bills those horses were living better than we were! But I loved the horses because I loved him. And I was behind him 100 percent, behind his plan to breed and race thoroughbred horses, and one day maybe even win the Kentucky Derby. He did not succeed, but not for a lack of trying.

Looking Forward, Looking Back

And so how do I feel today? I'm finally beginning to realize that I have accomplished a lot. Before I never gave myself any credit for anything, like there is always something better you can do or you are not good enough. But today I am beginning—just lately I am beginning—to say, "Carlean, you have done a whole lot and you have done it well."

I used to be very dedicated to my beauty business. And I still am. But I look at people, life, and work differently since my mother died. I would stay at that shop from sunup to sundown and be there for

In 2005, Carlean Gill posed in front of a photomural of herself at the opening reception for the exhibit Movers and Seekers: Michigan Immigrants and Migrants.

my clients. And I loved it. But after my mother died, I said, "I'm also going to do some of the things I like to do and not only work!" So I started to travel with my daughter and to volunteer with nonprofit organizations.

My mother taught me a whole lot—how to raise a child, how to be a good human being, how to have understanding. How she raised me, to try to do the best you can, is the way I raised my daughter. But I'm still not entirely satisfied with my life. Everyday is a challenge to me. But anything I've set my mind to, I usually accomplish.

NOTE

1. Sarah Breedlove, a.k.a. Madam C. J. Walker, was born in Delta, Louisiana, in 1867, the daughter of former slaves and sharecroppers. When she began losing her hair due to a scalp ailment, she experimented with herbal remedies and created a successful shampoo that she sold door-to-door. In 1910, Walker established a mail-order business and training school for her products in Indianapolis. At the time of her death in 1919, she was the most successful businesswoman and the first self-made African American millionaire in the United States.

No Mexicans Allowed!

Between 1900 and 1930, population growth, industrialization, and revolution dislocated millions of Mexicans. Many of them—about 1.5 million—migrated north to the United States.

During World War I, Michigan sugar companies began recruiting Mexican Americans from Texas as farmworkers. Families of migrants—parents, grandparents, and young children—spent long hours working in sugar beet fields.

In the 1920s Mexican Americans began harvesting other Michigan crops, including pickle cucumbers, berries, and other fruit. When they could find more stable, better-paying jobs in sugar plants or auto factories, farmworkers often became permanent Michigan residents.

Marylou Hernandez was born in San Antonio, Texas. In the late 1930s, when Marylou was three years old, the Michigan Sugar Company came to San Antonio to recruit migrant workers to work in sugar beet fields in Michigan.

For over twelve years, Marylou and her family traveled back and forth from Texas to Michigan, often living in the back of a truck. She worked in the farms and fields of Michigan, picking sugar beets, blueberries, cherries, cucumbers, strawberries, and potatoes. As a migrant worker, she was not enrolled in primary school, but she had a will and a desire to learn.

When Marylou was a teenager, her family finally settled in Michigan so that Marylou could get an education. She graduated from high school in Saginaw on schedule at age eighteen, even though she did not start attending school until she was nearly twelve years old.

After graduation, she married and started a family. After she divorced, for the next twenty-two years Marylou raised her five children on her own by working two jobs. One of her jobs was working in a doctor's office. The doctor encouraged her to enroll in college, where she received her nursing degree.

In 1981, she married George Mason. Like Marylou, he also had to struggle in order to succeed. He was the first quadriplegic to graduate from the University of Michigan Law School and was an assistant attorney general for the State of Michigan for thirty-five years.

In 1986 Marylou went to work for the Michigan Commission on Spanish-Speaking Affairs, where she is currently the director. She helped pass legislation protecting migrant workers and created educational and health programs for them.

Marylou has received numerous awards and honors for her work with the Hispanic community. She was awarded an honorary doctor of letters degree from Great Lakes Junior College. She has also served on the Lansing Community College Board of Trustees and is the co-founder of the first and only community college in Guadalajara, Mexico. She is on the Capital Area United Way Executive Committee and Board of Directors, the Greater Lansing Cesar Chavez Commission, and the Greater Lansing Hispanic Chamber of Commerce, and she is chairperson of the Cristo Rey Community Center Board of Directors.

Marylou no longer lives her life out of a truck or in a migrant camp. Her comfortable home sits on a wooded lot near the banks of the Red Cedar River. "I chose this property because of the trees," she admitted. "It reminds me of how I used to live. When my grandchildren come over, we make bonfires and cook outside, just like I used to do when I was growing up."

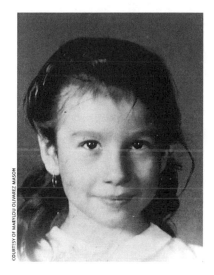

Marylou Hernandez as a child.

Danielle Roth, a student intern from Michigan State University's James Madison College, interviewed Marylou Olivarez Mason in Lansing on May 13, 2004. Danielle went on to earn a master's degree in history from Eastern Michigan University and a nursing degree from Michigan State University.

Leaving Home

The reason that we left Texas was because the Michigan Sugar Company came to San Antonio, Texas, and established an employment office there. They couldn't find people in Michigan to do agricultural work, and so they were there to set up the office to contract people to come to Michigan to work in the sugar beet fields. So when my father went to the unemployment office looking for work, they guided him to this new group that was there, finding people to come to Michigan to work on the sugar beets. My father signed a contract and that's how we came to Michigan.

There was no work in Texas—the only one that could work was my father. In Michigan, with all the agricultural work that there was and with nobody else who wanted to do it, and somebody had to do it.

COURTESY OF MARYLOU OLIVAREZ MASON

Marylou Hernandez, her sister, Benita, and brother, Joseph, dressed up for this family photograph.

I was about three and a half, four years old. I was walking, because if you could walk they would count you as a worker. If you were small and were not walking, then you would not be counted as a worker. You would get paid for every child who walked. That meant that the children would have to be out in the field working.

Every year we'd come back. We'd leave Texas like in March,

The Hernandez family used this beet knife to harvest sugar beets from the fields near Saginaw.

and then we wouldn't get back until like the end of November, first of December.

The first year that we came, of course, my father didn't know anything about sugar beets. He didn't know that you harvest the beets in the beginning but you don't get paid until the end of fall, when you finish harvesting them in November. And so, of course there was no money, because we didn't get paid. And so the farmer that we were working for took my dad to—not just my dad, but took the families—to the grocery store, where they would let us get the food on credit. And then the farmer took the responsibility at the end of the season. . . . They would come and find out and see if we owed anything and deduct all that and pay the grocery bill.

Of course, we quickly learned that we had to find something else to do between when you start planting the beets and when you finish harvesting them. So then, there are the other crops—blueberries, strawberries, cucumbers, potatoes, and cherries. In July, we'd know that—well we didn't know—but we found out that you go to Ludington, Hart, or Traverse City to pick cherries.

So we went to Traverse City and we started to work for a farmer there, on the Old Mission Peninsula, on Peninsula Drive. Then we knew that we had work there every year. So all the same families went to the same farmhouses. We had work. That was the main thing, that we had work. It didn't matter that we didn't have housing.

COURTESY OF MARYLOU OLIVAREZ MASON

"Wherever we were when it got dark, that was our home." Marylou Hernandez and her family traveled and slept in this stake rack truck.

They had a great big barn where they used to keep their animals. And they had built another barn, because they had more cows and things. So the old one, we used that for housing, but it was just one big huge barn. We had to use blankets or sheets or cardboard, then you kind of divided rooms. And then they had a couple of stoves, so we all took turns using the stoves.

But many times we lived under conditions where they didn't have housing and then we'd have to sleep in the cars and trucks. Then we'd go in the ditch and there'd be water and just bathe that way. Because it was all outhouses or the well, you know, get water from the well. Just warm the water up in this great big tub and then take turns going behind the outhouse to take a bath. A lot of the times that was how we took a bath. In Traverse City, we were lucky because the lake was across from the farm. So we would just go across the road to bathe in the lake and do our laundry.

The first year that we were contracted, we came on the train. They paid our transportation and everything. The second year, you know someone would have a truck, and you would come in the back of the truck. The trucker would bring many families, as many families as you could get in the back of the truck along with their belongings. It was just one great big truck that they would put wood rails on the side. The clothes and the trunks or suitcases would all be lined up all around the truck and they would put blankets or pillows on top and that's where you would sit. Then, in the center part, you would have boxes of food or formula or diapers.

And then, as far as bathroom facilities, you'd have to stop along the way on the roadside. They didn't have rest areas then. The men would wait until the women went to the bathroom, and then the men would go. We couldn't stop at a gas station to use the restrooms, because at most of the places we were prohibited from entering because they had signs—"No Mexicans or Negroes Allowed"—so we couldn't go into them.

In Traverse City there were no signs. You would enter a store and an employee would follow you around to see what it was that you wanted to buy. They'd follow you around, and then escort you out of the store.

It was very hard work—sunup to sundown—all day long, out in the sun. I mean there were no trees or anything in the middle of the field. It was just open fields. We hated those fields. We hated those fields with the long, long rows. It seemed like you would never see the end of the row. By the time we'd get to the end, it was great to see the end of the row. We were like, "Oh, we're almost there!" You'd sit in the middle of the row, and you'd look and you couldn't even see the end of it. That's how long the rows were!

We had to take water. The person that we went with, they would bring cans or containers of water out in the field for us. Of course, the water would be hot. There was no shade or trees around. I mean, the water was like soup. But at least it was water. That water kept us alive!

Of course, we had to take our own food, to make sure we had food during the day, because they wouldn't come back to get us until sundown.

"That water kept us alive!" Marylou and her family used this dipper to drink warm water from a lard can while working in the fields.

COURTESY OF MARYLOU OLIVAREZ MASON

When we were in Traverse City, we would have one day off, and they would take us into town—especially if it rained. We knew that we weren't going to work and they would take us to town. But that didn't necessarily mean that on Sundays we would be off. But Sunday was the day that they would take us to church. The trucker would take everybody to church and go to the grocery store and get some food and things like that.

We didn't have any transportation. There were nine of us. Nine families that came in the truck, and the men would get together and they would try to get an old car so that they could, between maybe, two or three families, they could buy an old junker. Just for around here, you know, when we were here—nothing that would take you anywhere further than fifty miles. But something that at least they would have so that if they wanted to go from field to field, or if they wanted to go from the field to the little grocery store to go get something.

If anybody got sick, you'd have to just wait until the truck came around. Or hopefully you could walk to a farmhouse if it was close by and someone could come help you—mostly sunstroke, because you were out there in the sun a lot. You had to be covered up really well. And then of course, with babies, the little ones out there, they'd sometimes start vomiting, they'd have diarrhea, and get dehydrated, and of course, we didn't know what was going on.

When we were in Texas, if you got sick, they would just boil some type of herb or tea or something and give it to you. They didn't take you to the doctor. One lady would tell the next lady what they thought you had and if they had any herbs with them, or any tea leaves they thought would help, they'd boil it and give it to the kid or the baby or whatever. So it wasn't a thing where we would nowadays go to the clinic. Now we have the health clinic, they have a migrant clinic that they go to. We didn't have any of those luxuries.

Making Michigan Home

When we started to stay here in Michigan, we still kept on traveling to go pick crops. We would go to whatever crops there were. My mom and my older sister still traveled. My older sister got married and her husband had a truck. So he became the person that was bringing people to the different places that you go to pick.

We all traveled together. We would go dig potatoes in Munger or Edmore. Linwood was cucumbers. Grand Haven and South Haven, you know those areas are known because of the resorts and the beaches and all that. Well, to me, when you say South Haven or Grand Haven, it's peaches, because that's where we went to pick peaches.

We used to pick tomatoes in the Blissfield area of Michigan. But we were like three miles away from Ohio, so we'd cross the border into Ohio. But in Ohio it was mostly tomatoes.

One year we went to Kokomo, Indiana, because there was a small factory there where they needed tomato pickers and also factory workers. So my dad worked in the factory and we picked the tomatoes.

Even when we were in Traverse City, it was like being in a city in Texas. I mean, you'd go downtown, the majority of the people that you would see there would be Mexican. Because during that certain time that's all there was, Mexicans there to pick cherries. Everybody came from all over to pick cherries. It was just for a certain period of time in July, from the beginning of July for four or five weeks. You started with the sweet cherries, you'd get those done, and then the sour cherries, and that was it. That was the end of the crop.

Kentucky would be the only place that we'd pick cotton. Sometimes in Texas there'd be a sign where they'd say, "Cotton Pickers Wanted." That was the worst thing—the worst work you could do is picking cotton. To get the cotton, it's all dried, and so your cuticles would always been bleeding. Because you didn't want to use gloves because you can't work as fast. The faster you work, the more money you make.

And then you pull this sack, and it gets heavy. You know, you're putting cotton in there and it gets heavy. Oh I used to hate that, because I was never a very large person. I was always skinny and I didn't weigh one hundred pounds, so it was a real struggle for me to pull that sack of cotton.

When I was twelve or thirteen, we were in Kentucky picking cotton, and the house we were living in—there were a couple of us families living in the same house—and the house burned to the ground. We lost everything! Money, everything, burned because they kept the money in the house. We were just left with the clothes on our backs.

It was a two-story house, and they said it was something electrical. They had taken us into town to go get groceries, and while we were gone, that's when it happened. Both our family and the other family lost everything. We had to start from scratch.

My uncle was very entrepreneurial. He had an old panel truck, and he would come out to the farms from Saginaw. He would bring baked goods and Mexican products and things they didn't have over there. He would go to the farms and sell to the people. He'd come once a week. Come from Saginaw to Traverse City because you wouldn't find any products like that at the grocery store.

My dad didn't know whether he wanted to stay in Texas or stay in Michigan. But then my uncle, as we were getting older, my uncle could see that we were not getting an education. We were going for a little bit here and a little bit there, and that we really weren't getting a formal education, so he told my dad he had to make up his mind if he was going to stay in Michigan or stay in Texas.

He owned a house in Texas, and he told my dad we could stay

there. Then, when we started to come to Michigan, my uncle sold the house to my dad. My dad was paying monthly rent. My uncle owned quite a few properties; that was a house that he owned and he let my dad live there for nothing for a long time, because my dad didn't have work, but then he sold it to him. My dad started to build to make the kitchen a little bit bigger. Inside, you could see the wood and you could see the metal, because if you didn't have wood to add on to a room you used metal.

There was a grocery store about a block away from our house. One day, I went to the grocery store, and the store owner, Mr. Tamez, was painting the walls in their house. I could smell the paint, so I asked him, "What is that smell?" He showed me that they were painting the walls in the house. I told him, "We don't have walls."

He said, "Well, you know, this is sheet rock. You could make walls out of cardboard boxes. You know, the big boxes that you get with supplies and things like that." He said, "I could save those and they would make a very good wall covering." So he started saving those boxes and I started to take them home. Then my mother and one of the neighbors came to help cover up the metal, and you couldn't see the metal anymore. Then he gave me the leftover paint, so my mother could paint the cardboard. So we had walls like the Tamezes.

I remember the first box that I took home, it was huge, but he had flattened it out. So I told my mother what Mr. Tamez had told me that you could do. She said, "How are you going to do it?" I said, "I don't know. The man next door, they're fixing their house. I'm sure that he knows how to do it." So my mother said, "Well, I'll ask him one of these days." I thought, "She'll forget. She won't do it." So I went next door and I asked him, "How did you do your walls? Because I brought some cardboard home from the grocery store." He said we could put it up on the wall, but my mother was afraid that my dad wouldn't like it.

Making Do

I didn't have the luxury of going to school and having nice clothes, and growing up with lots of food and toys and things like that. I didn't grow up like that. I didn't grow up with all those luxuries. I don't like ice cream. I don't like chocolate. I didn't grow up eating all those goodies. I can do without.

We only had an outhouse. We didn't have any bathroom in the house, or running water. We had a pump outside the house. When we washed our clothes, we would wash them by hand on a washboard. My mother had an old tub that she would put the clothes in—full of water, and then some kind of yellow soap that was really strong and the soap would melt in the water. Then they would boil the clothes. You just didn't wash clothes, you had to boil them, especially sheets and pillowcases and all that. All our clothes were boiled, and then we would hang them out on the clothesline. You'd have to get the clothes ready for the next day. Especially when you worked in the black dirt. You had to make sure you washed your clothes and got that dirt off your clothes.

I can remember my first dresses, during the war, when my father was in the military. We'd buy great big sacks of flour, like a hundred pounds. The flour would come in sacks of cloth, it wasn't paper bags, and it had different patterns. Some were little flowers; some were stripes. It was cotton. It was soft and it had pretty patterns. They were very colorful. My mother would save those and she would make our dresses out of that. And she would make my brother's shirts out of that.

My mother knew how to sew. We were little, small enough so she could do that. My brother's pants, they would be elastic on top just like little shorts. They would be a solid color. She'd get one of those stripes and always save those for shirts for him. But the little flowers would be for my dress. Sometimes I would see some flour sacks, and I would see some of those patterns and I would tell her, "Oh, they've got this real pretty color."

I remember when my father was in the military, my mother would get these boxes of cheese, and powdered milk, and I thought it was gross. I was the skinniest in the whole family. My other sisters were built a little bit bigger than me.

My father always worried that I was going to die of tuberculosis, because he had a younger brother who died of TB. He was afraid

COURTESY OF MARYLOU OLIVAREZ MASON

This photograph of Marylou's parents, Ricardo Duarte and Macedonia (Nonie) Bazan Hernandez, was taken while Ricardo served in the armed forces during World War II.

that I had been around that uncle when I was little and that the same thing was going to happen to me.

My father would make sure that we always had a case of cod liver oil. That was supposed to be some kind of a medicine with a vitamin. He didn't care if the other kids didn't take it, but he wanted to make sure I drank my cod liver oil. I used to hate that stuff. It tasted so awful. Whenever we could afford it he'd get oranges and make sure that they were kept just for me to drink the oil. He'd ask my mother, "Did she take her medicine today?" I can still picture my mother coming towards me with a great big spoon. I used to plug my nose and then take the spoon of stuff, and I would take like a quarter of the orange and stick it in mouth, and squeeze all the juice out trying to get that taste out.

Mexican Cuisine

In Texas, there was a slaughterhouse that was about a block and a half away from our house. There were certain days when they would slaughter the animals and they would have tripe, or liver and heart, and all the things that they were going to throw away that they would save and I would go pick them up.

We ate a lot of beans, tortillas, and hot sauce. That was our main meal. We ate beans every day, three times a day, and of course our flour tortillas and hot sauce. If you could afford it, you had, maybe, hamburger meat and potatoes that they would mix together.

It was called *carne con papas*, meat and potatoes. If we were sick, had a fever or something, my mother would take the hamburger meat and make it into a meatball and then roll it in rice and then boil it with spices. Everything we cooked we put spices in, and boiled it and then they would feed you the broth if you were sick, had a fever or something. That was supposed to be medicine.

I remember when I started to learn how to cook I was eight years old. The first time I tried to make rice we were working in Traverse City. I had watched one of the other ladies, so I thought I'd surprise my mother. So I fried the rice, like the lady did, and put the spices in it and then put water in it. I saw her put the water in it, but I didn't know you had to cook the rice. I thought after you put in the water, you just simmered it for little bit and it's done. Of course, it wasn't done. I did everything right except for that.

Then when I was learning how to make tortillas, I learned from the other ladies. When my baby sister was sick, they would leave me with the other ladies and I would take care of her. That's when I would try to learn how to cook. I would watch how they put the dough together, put the flour and the ingredients together, and then put in the lard and the water. But I could never get it to stick. I didn't know you were supposed to put real hot water in it, and then start kneading it. The more you knead, the more it sticks together. But I didn't know, so I was just throwing it away. The flour was going down. I didn't want to tell my mother because I was afraid she'd get after me that I was trying to make the dough. So I finally had to tell her that I was trying to learn how to make the tortillas and that I was just throwing it away, because we didn't waste any food at all. So one of the other ladies that always traveled with us, she finally showed me how to do it. From then on, I was making the tortillas all the time so I could help my mom. Because after you got home from work, you'd have to cook and feed everybody, and that's a lot of work, too.

Driving Miss Marylou

My uncle taught me how to drive when I was thirteen. He'd take me out to Caro, Michigan, or out to Quanicassee, because he liked to fish, and in those rural areas there were dirt roads where you could learn how to drive.

I was really little. I mean I was a skinny little girl—you know, I never gained weight. I would have to sit on top of a pillow and put pillows behind me to reach the foot pedals. He had a pickup truck and it had a clutch—it wasn't an automatic. I wanted to learn how to drive.

I already knew how to drive a tractor, because in Traverse City the farmer taught me how to drive a tractor. I was trying to get out of picking cherries, and I could see that if you drove the tractor, all you had to do was drive between the trees. I kept thinking, "I can do that." So I talked Bruce Lyon, one of the farmer's sons, into teaching me how to drive a tractor.

My mother never drove. I remember my dad trying to teach her how to drive when he had this 1930-something truck. He was trying to teach her out there in the field. It was not an automatic, and she couldn't do it. She felt that the ditches were too deep—she was afraid she was going to go into them. He was trying really hard to explain to her how important it was for her to learn how to drive. So that if he wasn't around, then she could still take us out to work and she could go to the store.

If you had an adult with you, even if you were not old enough, you could get a driver's license if a parent signed for you if it was for the purpose of agriculture, like when we were out there in the fields. So I got my driver's license when I was quite young, because my uncle took me and signed for me. I was the first woman in my family to get a driver's license.

Skipping School

We didn't go to school. I was almost twelve years old and had never been to school full-time because we didn't have the programs that we now have, like the Migrant Education Program or Head Start. So we were not obligated to go to school. They didn't have laws that state that you couldn't be out in the fields working. They wouldn't count you as a student because you weren't there long enough to be a full-time student, so it was like you didn't really belong.

The only education that you really received while you were out in the fields—the only people who came out to make sure you were getting an education—were the religious people. The priest and the nuns would come out and make sure that we knew our prayers and make our first Holy Communion. The kids were baptized, and confirmed for the Catholics—and most of us were Catholic.

My mother didn't have any education whatsoever. She never went, never set foot in a school at all. My dad went up to the fifth or sixth grade, so my dad knew how to speak some English. He could read and write English enough to at least know what he was writing—not everything, but at least he could get by. But my mother didn't know how to read or write English or Spanish. My mother didn't learn how to sign her name until she was over sixty years of age. After my dad passed away she learned how to sign her name, because she had to do things for herself. She learned how to speak some English. As we got older and got married and she was around the grandkids, she would speak English. The grandkids taught her English.

I was the only one in the family who spoke English. I was my mother's interpreter, so I never left my language. I never stopped speaking Spanish. I was the one in the family that translated for both of my parents whenever they needed me to.

I taught myself how to read. Some of the farmers had kids. They had books, and I would get with their kids, and they would teach me how to read whatever book they were reading.

Some of the farmer's wives would get books for us. I always had a desire to learn how to read. So I would borrow the books. I just picked it up on my own, with a farmer or the farmer's kids. And just being around people that spoke it.

I was very little when my dad was in the service. When my mother would get letters from my father, my mother would go to the neighbors so that they could read the letter for her. I would see my mother doing that, and I would tell her, "How come you had to do that?" She said she didn't know how to read the letter, so she had to go to the neighbors. So then I would take the letters and I would start going over the letters and trying to make out the words. And I would go to the neighbors and if I got stuck on a word I would ask them, "What does this mean?" or "What does this say?" and "How do you know what this word is?" Then one of the neighbors would take the time to kind of dissect the words.

I remember the very first time that I tried to write a letter. I took one of my dad's letters and tried to copy some of the words that I knew and answer for my mother so she wouldn't have to be going to the neighbors. My father carried that letter—the first letter that I wrote—in his wallet for many years.

After I started going to school, they told me the harder I worked, the faster they would move me up in the grades. So I worked hard. There were a couple of teachers who helped me. I worked hard so that I would get up to the grade level I was supposed to be.

If you spoke Spanish, you'd stay after school and they would punish you for speaking Spanish, because you were there to learn English. So if they caught you speaking Spanish, like if there were other kids and you were speaking Spanish, they would keep you after school—a whole hour after school! And punish you for speaking your own language.

Marylou's high school graduation photo.

COURTESY OF MARYLOU OLIVAREZ MASON

That was what we spoke at home, Spanish. Even in Texas, in school you were supposed to speak English and not Spanish. So it was very difficult because Spanish is our first language. But it was to get you to learn the language.

I graduated from high school in Saginaw. I was the first in the family to graduate from high school, on both sides on the family. When I graduated, it was as if I had accomplished something that I always wanted to. When I graduated I wanted to go to college. But, of course, I couldn't, because I had to go out and get a job and help my dad raise the family. Then I decided instead of continuing to work, if I got married, I probably could do something different. Well, I got married and had five kids—one right after the other.

He was a good person. He was a migrant, just like I was. We were very young, eighteen and nineteen. It wasn't what I thought it was going to be. We both were not ready for it. He was not ready to settle down. And then we had a family, one right after the other. He really didn't have a steady job, so it was one thing after another. It just didn't work out. We went our separate ways. I raised my kids by myself—four of them were in diapers. I worked two jobs, because I didn't want to be a welfare mother.

Seeing the Potential

I went to work as a receptionist for a doctor's office, Dr. Kirk and Barbara Herrick. They are the ones that inspired me. I've always had someone along the way who could see the potential that I could not see in myself. So this doctor and his wife could see that I had some potential.

They were educated. He was a doctor. She was a social worker. They helped me a lot with my kids. They taught me how to raise my family a different way. The way that I was brought up, in the migrant family, you were working out in the field and working day and night.

I started to work for him as a receptionist at his office. And then, as his practice grew, I became the office manager. I learned how to run the whole place. Then they encouraged me to go to nursing school and get my degree, so that someday I would have something to fall back on.

When I was going to nursing school for the first time, I felt as if I were different. I belonged to a different class. I was becoming a different type of person, because I was going to school. I was learning. I was going to be a nurse!

On the Road Again

The day that I went to court and got my divorce, I borrowed my dad's car, because I didn't have a car of my own. Dr. Herrick and some of his friends owned a resort up north in Indian River. So I went on our first vacation. We had never had a vacation before. Even when I was growing up we didn't know what vacation is. I took the kids up north and I told them, "From now on, every year we are going to take a vacation!" But I didn't have to pay for it because they owned the place.

After I was divorced and the kids were a little bit older, there were certain things I wanted them to see, places I wanted to take them. New York City was one of them. Washington, D.C., was another. Philadelphia. All the historical places: Washington, D.C., because it was the capital; New York City because of the Empire State Building.

Of course, I very quickly learned that it was going to cost quite a bit of money to go on vacation. When I took them to Washington, D.C., I pulled the camper and I found places where we could camp out and not have to worry about staying in a hotel.

The state parks and the campgrounds in those areas are nothing like ours here. It was kind of scary being in those places. For example, in the New York area, the campground was in New Jersey. So you had to take a bus to go into New York, and the campgrounds had no trees or anything. It was just a place to park your trailer. It was like out in the open. I mean, I expected it to be like Higgins Lake State Park, and then when we got there, it was like, "Is this is the campground?" I was even afraid to stay there.

It was the same thing when we went to D.C. It was in Maryland where the campgrounds were and the people were not friendly people like we have here.

I was used to going to Higgins Lake State Park where the conservation officers were, and I'd get there and I'd feel secure. And I didn't have to worry about my kids because I knew there were always conservation officers around, and I didn't have to worry about myself because they patrolled the area really well.

It was scary for me by myself with the kids. It was like, "What did I get myself into?" I was scared, but, of course, I didn't want to tell anybody because my father was very hesitant about me traveling like that with the kids. He thought that I should take one of my sisters with me. My dad said, "Are you sure you know what you are doing?" And I kept saying, "Yeah, Dad, don't worry about it. We're going to be just fine." Of course, I didn't tell him afterwards that I was really afraid.

He was afraid that the kids were going to get in the water and they might drown. He didn't think camping was a good idea. I kept telling him, "But, Dad, look, it's really inexpensive." I really had to talk him into getting that camper.

I said, "The officers are here, nobody can come into the camp-ground unless they go through that little house. They won't let them in. And then when they are closed, nobody can come in the park. The conservation officer has to check them in."

My father was really protective of us. He thought I was too daring, that my independence was getting to me, and I thought I could just go and do it and everything would be all right. But then once he came to see how it was, and the people around and the conservation officers, and how you go to the beach, and it is not like they were undersupervised. There were always adults there. The other families who were there would take turns to make sure we were supervising the kids. He saw that there were other people there, and they were good people.

To this day, I still miss going camping. My sons are all married. I don't think any of my daughters-in-law like to go camping. They say, "Yeah, we can go camping, I'll stay at the Holiday Inn, and you can go stay at the campground!"

Where the Roots Are

My son took his kids, about two or three years ago, to San Antonio, so I went with them, because he wanted me to show the grandkids where I was born and where our relatives—where the roots are—where we came from.

I took them to the neighborhood. There were some kids that were outside and didn't have shoes, and they were like, "How come they don't have shoes on?"

I said, "We went around barefoot because we didn't have shoes. We only had one pair of shoes and we had to save those to go to church on Sunday. Kids around here, they don't have to wear shoes, they go around barefoot." But they thought it was unusual that all those little kids were outside and that they didn't have shoes on. It was an eye-opener for them. I told them, "You don't know how lucky you are. You have anything and everything you want. You go to good schools. You have all the toys you want."

With the urban renewal and all, they had knocked all the old houses down. The street is still there, and the area where the house was is still there, but the house no longer stands. I was born in that house, 726 Carlos Street. So that's why some of the old pictures that my mom had of the old house are important to me, because that's the only picture I have of the old house.

Being in San Antonio was my comfort zone. My great-grandmother was there, my uncle, the neighbors. We lived in this neighborhood where the houses were right next to each other, so everybody knew everybody. I could walk all the way to the corner store, and didn't have to worry about it.

Education Is Important

I had a friend who was a farmer. I took my kids to work out in his field because I wanted them to see what it was like, what I had to go through and the kind of work that I did. I took them out there only so they could see how hard it was to work out in the fields, and that if they didn't stay in school, if they didn't get an education, this was the kind of work they were going to have to do.

They hated it. I didn't have to worry about them not staying in school. My goal was for them to at least graduate from high school—if I could help them, go to college.

Two of them have their B.A.s and one of them has a master's. The other one is working on their master's. The other one was in the air force twenty years. He retired a few years ago. The two oldest were the ones who were kind of left out because they were helping me with the others—putting the others through school. My oldest, he's telling his kids now—he has a son and daughter—he keeps telling them, "I didn't have a childhood. Grandma took that away from me. I had to help grandma all the time." And it is true. He did.

They were brought up differently. I haven't let them forget their roots, where they come from. They grew up around my parents. My dad always tried to tell them, "Education is very important to your mother." My dad couldn't be that way back then, but as he got older, he was.

Working for Change

When I became director of the Spanish-Speaking Commission in 1986, there were a lot of things that had not been done. For example, take the Field Sanitation Standard bill. The Field Sanitation Standard bill makes sure that there are bathroom facilities and water in the fields for the people who were working.

The pesticide issue was another one. We didn't have a pesticide bill. There were no laws or regulations that said you couldn't spray while the people were working in the fields. Of course, you didn't have to be certified to be spraying. We didn't know that all that stuff that was on the crops was harmful, that you should rinse them off before you ate them. I mean, we'd be hungry and we'd eat a tomato. We ate the cherries right from the tree. We never cleaned them—we'd just eat them like that.

We'd be working in one field and they'd be spraying the other field and all that stuff would be coming to where you were working. We didn't know that that was harmful.

Now you have to be certified to be able to spray. You can't spray while people are working on the fields. You have to post what kind of pesticides you use, and they have to be bilingual. You have to have them in different languages so people know what it is that's out there, so they know that it can harm them. Whatever crops you're working on, you have to rinse them off because they've got this pesticide on them. Also, now you have to be a certain age before you're out in the fields. You can't be out in the fields during school hours like I was when I was only three or four years old. My brother and I were out there in the fields just because we could walk. Now you can't do that.

And now we have the different health and educational programs. At Cristo Rey Community Center in Lansing they have a clinic and they go out to the migrant camps and take care of individuals who are sick. They'll do pap smears for the ladies, free of charge.

At least you can see the difference in how it was and how it is now. Even though they are still agricultural workers, at least there is housing. There has been money that has been allocated for migrant housing.

A Long Time Coming

One of the awards I received was in September of 2000. Then I received another one in October. Then I got the big award in November. I received five awards, one right after another.

The Hispanic Female of the Year I got in November of 2000. My parents had already passed away. I think they would have been very proud.

I kept telling my husband, "Honey, what's wrong with me? I mean, am I going to die, or something? Why am I getting all these awards? Why is this happening to me?" And he kept saying, "Well, it's been a long time coming. You deserve all this. Somebody just finally decided that you should get the recognition."

I received the Cesar Chavez Community Service Award from the National Hispana Leadership Institute in 2000. Then, I got inducted into the Hispanic Business Alliance Hall of Fame in Detroit. Then I got inducted into the Women's Hall of Fame here in Lansing. I received the Ordinary People Doing Extraordinary Things Award. Then I received the Mujer Award from the U.S. Hispana Leadership Institute in Washington, D.C., in November of 2000. It was in Orlando, Florida, and Walt Disney World hosted the event at the Epcot Center.

I knew Walt Disney World was hosting it, but I had no idea what a big event it was. It was at the Epcot Center. It was like VIP treatment from the moment I got off the plane! They had this great big sign welcoming me, and all that. The banquet was just so classy. It was a huge, huge event. There were hundreds of people. It was quite an experience.

I thought, "Wow! Here's this little migrant farmworker who is sitting in the middle of the field crying because I can see the school

Marylou Olivarez Mason meets former Mexican president Vicente Fox at a reception in Lansing, Michigan.

bus going by, and wondering if I'd ever be in the school bus." And here I am, standing in front of all those people from corporate America. Every corporation you can think of was there hosting this event, all these important people that I didn't even know. It brought back a lot of memories. I appreciate it.

I also work with national and international groups. I have a student exchange program with the University of Guadalajara and Lansing Community College. We're a sister city to Guadalajara. I was the co-founder of the first community college in Mexico, in Guadalajara. It originated with Lansing Community College.

The owner of the private university in Guadalajara came to sign the agreement for the student international program, the exchange program. So they learned the concept of a community college, and then as we got to work with the exchange program, he said, "How long does it take to build a community college?" This friend of mine and I said, "Well, it would probably take four or five years." Well, they built it in a year. It is a beautiful, beautiful college. Now they have satellite colleges, because the concept has grown tremendously. It is the only community college in Mexico. They have universities all over, but they don't have community colleges like we do.

The Person That I Have Become

I feel more Mexican American now, but I'm still a Mexican. That's something that never changes. I'll always be a Mexican American. I was born here in the Untied States. I was born a Mexican and I always will be.

My mother and my dad didn't live long enough to see me become the person I have become. He died in 1981. I had been working for the state. I was already making progress with my career, and I remember him coming over to the office one day and bringing me a briefcase with my name on it. My supervisor saw that my dad was in my office, so he said, "Oh! Mr. Hernandez, how are you?" He came to talk to him.

I told him, "See what my dad brought me?" So I showed him my briefcase, and then he said, "Oh, what did I miss? A birthday? An anniversary? What did I miss?" I said, "Oh, no. It's not a special day. It's not a special occasion."

Then he asked my dad, and my dad was not very expressive with words. He never said, "I love you" or anything like that. So he told my supervisor, "No, I brought her the briefcase just because I'm very proud of her. That's to show her how proud I am of her." For my dad to say that to someone he didn't know very well, I thought that was very nice.

Agricultural work is very hard work. No one wants to do it. It takes a special type of a person to do it. And once you start doing it, it is something you'll never forget. It made me a better person. I grew up appreciating a lot of things in life, maybe that I wouldn't have appreciated if I wouldn't have had to work as hard as I did.

The Trip Became a Great Adventure

In the late nineteenth century, Jews in Central and Eastern Europe suffered economic pressures and anti-Semitism. The hostility and discrimination they faced as Jews forced many of them to emigrate.

In the Russian Empire, which included Lithuania, Ukraine and part of Poland, Jews could not live outside limited territories. Access to higher education and professions was severely limited. Pogroms—organized attacks on Jewish communities encouraged by the government—killed thousands. Jewish emigration from Russia increased rapidly in the 1890s.

European Jews faced a new threat when Adolph Hitler and his Nazi Party came to power in 1933. The Nazi Party systematically deprived Jews of their civil rights, excluded them from social and cultural life, and took their land and possessions. Some Jewish families had the foresight to leave Germany or send their children to other countries, including the United States. By 1938, more than half of the 565,000 German Jews had emigrated. Over the next seven years, as Germany annexed most of Europe, nearly six million Jews were murdered in the Holocaust, as well as about four million other minorities.

Benno Levi was eleven years old when his father sent him along

On December 29, 1934, Benno Levi (*left*), along with his sister, Ruth, and brother, Ernest, left Germany for the United States. The German-Jewish Children's Aid Society sponsored the Levi children and arranged for them to live with a Jewish family in Detroit.

with his sister, Ruth, and brother, Ernest, to the United States. The German-Jewish Children's Aid Society sponsored their immigration and placed them with a foster family in Detroit. In 1938 his parents and a sister, Miriam, were able to join them here and their family was reunited.

During World War II, Levi served with the U.S. Army in the Pacific Theater. He was awarded the Silver Star and the Bronze Star for gallantry in action and heroism under fire. While in service, Levi maintained a detailed record of his army career in a daily journal. After his return to civilian life, he began to edit his notebooks and published several stories relating to the battles as the U.S. Army hopped from island to island towards Japan. On another theme, he wrote a story about his journey to America entitled "Escape from Nazi Germany" that appeared in *Michigan History* magazine in 1995. His story here includes material from that article.

After the war, Levi became chief fiscal officer of Sinai Hospital in Detroit, and later, treasurer and senior vice president of St. Joseph's Hospital in Mount Clemens, Michigan. He retired in 1985. He is a member of the Jewish Historical Society of Michigan and served as its treasurer for twenty-five years. He and his wife, Ruth, have six children and eighteen grandchildren.

Martha Aladjem (Climo) Bloomfield interviewed Benno Levi at his home in Oak Park, Michigan, on January 3, 2005.

Growing Up in Germany

I was born and raised in Germany, in the state of Hesse, in a town called Alsfeld. It had 5,000 inhabitants and survived World War II with one of the most spectacular examples of medieval European architecture fully intact. The city hall and many other buildings in the town center were built in the early fourteen hundreds.

Some of my ancestors had come to Hessen in the seventeenth century from France. Until 1933, I had the better of two worlds—a vibrant Jewish community and congenial, friendly gentile neighbors as well as many relatives in every village and town in the vicinity. There was no hint of the atrocities about to be unleashed.

In Alsfeld, Germany, the Levi family lived on the corner of Martin Luther Strasse, just two houses from the beautiful synagogue constructed by the Jewish community in 1915. Alsfeld is centrally located in Germany in the state of Hesse. It has remarkable examples of medieval architecture.

Our home was a comfortable three-story building that stood on the corner where three streets met: Alicestrasse, the main street, Martin Luther Strasse, where our magnificent synagogue stood just two doors from my home; and Bahnhofstrasse, which angled up to the railroad station. I woke up one morning in 1933 when I was nine years old and suddenly found that I was now living on the corner of Adolf Hitler Strasse, Hermann Goering Strasse, and Martin Luther Strasse.

In our building, my widowed aunt had a houseware store and comfortable living quarters on the first floor. The second floor was rented, and my family lived on the third level. My father had a mail-order business that was located in a small office building on the premises behind our home.

The children of our neighbors were my best friends. They were not Jewish. We played and went to school together and even shared our holidays. Their parents and mine were also best of friends.

Only Wilhelm, a dedicated longtime member of the Hitlerjugend, became vehemently anti-Semitic. He died on the Russian front. His brother, Horst, was a POW in Texas and we are still best of friends.

Since I came to America, hardly a week has gone by without one or two dreams about this little town. It is the foundation of my existence.

On a fateful day in January of 1933, everything changed. Adolph Hitler was suddenly made chancellor of Germany. It happened at a most unusual time. He was just coming out of a deep depression after having lost an important election in the previous month. In fact, Joseph Goebbels, his propaganda chief, had to talk him out of committing suicide at the time.

The Nationalists around President Hindenburg needed a strongman to bring order into the Reich. Hitler and his storm troopers could do it. They were confident that they could keep him in line to do their bidding. In the newsreels at the time, Hitler was so meek, humble, and obsequious with the German power brokers who had convinced President Hindenburg to make him his chancellor.

How wrong they were. Though the Nazis celebrated wildly, Hitler was still considered a bit of a joke as the combined membership in the Communists and Socialist parties greatly outnumbered the Nazi Party.

Then, on a night in February, that too changed quickly. The Reichstag[1] (Parliament) was burned to the ground. Abruptly, Hitler shed his sheep's clothing and assumed additional power closely resembling rule under martial law. He was no longer a laughing matter as he ruthlessly turned on the politicians who had brought him to power. A year later when, very conveniently, President Hindenburg died, Hitler added the title of "president" to "chancellor" and became the supreme ruler of Nazi Germany.

I was nine years old when Hitler was chosen to be chancellor. I was a child and loved the excitement—lots of flags and parades. I saw everything that was happening around me as a great adventure. Finally, when I wanted to join my schoolmates in the Nazi May Day parade, my father sat me down and explained it all to me. I understood and stayed home.

It was just before the High Holidays in 1934. My father met us as

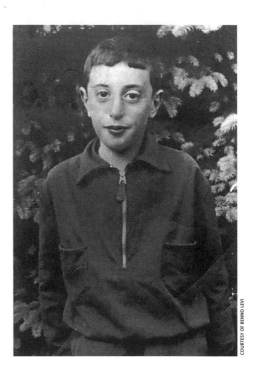

Benno Levi, about the time of his immigration to the United States.

COURTESY OF BENNO LEVI

we came home from school to warn us that the two spinster tenants who were renting our second-floor apartment had put up a picture of Hitler on their door facing the stairs. We could not miss it as we came up to our place. They, like most of the single German women, adored Adolph and were eager to harass us. My father warned, "Be careful when you come home. Don't react. Don't make a funny face or stick out your tongue at the photo of Hitler!"

Anti-Semitism

My parents were not physically harassed, but the mental harassment was everywhere. Many of my father's friends were beaten up. Some kids also picked on me simply because I was Jewish. We were no longer citizens even though our ancestors had been here for hundreds of years. We had no rights.

We anticipated some of this but certainly not the avalanche of evil that soon swept over most of Europe. Hitler was a loudmouthed rabble-rouser. His infuriating tirades to kill all Jews were too ridiculous to be taken seriously. Yet it did happen; that is the tragedy.

His theme was "The Jews are our misfortune." It was also the masthead on his propaganda sheet, *Der Sturmer:* "Die Juden sind unser Unglueck." They sang a song: "Wenn das Judenblut vom Messer spritzt dann geht's nochmal so gut."

Translated, it says, "When Jewish blood squirts from the knife, things will be twice as good." The words are tattooed in my mind. Everyone heard it. No one took it seriously, just a dumb song.

Unfortunately even in the United States there were many anti-Semitic newspapers in the 1930s. They were similar in many ways and took their cue from Hitler.

Roosevelt was a politician. He didn't want to show too much support for the immigration of Jewish victims of Nazism. There would be too much opposition. The population was not pro-Jewish in those days. A guy like Father Coughlin would bring together thousands of people and they were all anti-Semitic.[2]

In the summer of 1934 my father decided to submit our names to the German-Jewish Children's Aid Society in New York City, an organization that placed young children with Jewish families in America.[3] He did not inform us of his plans. His friends tried to persuade him to wait. "In six months Hitler will be gone." His answer: "Good, when he is gone, the children will be back. They will have learned English and broadened their horizons."

Sent to America

Word of the mission of the German-Jewish Children's Aid Society spread throughout Michigan by the *Detroit Jewish Chronicle.* Homes were needed in Detroit for children being rescued. It was a temporary arrangement until Hitler would be replaced.

All of my cousins over the age of sixteen were already gone, some to Palestine, others to South Africa and America. My father had cousins in Baltimore. They were very concerned and helped bring most of our relatives out. They were not too observant and my father wanted us to be raised in an Orthodox environment. That is how we ended up in Detroit.

Benno Levi's passport photograph.

He finally informed us of our pending departure just before we were to get our visa at the U.S. Consulate in Stuttgart. The trip there was made in early December of 1934. On our way home, we visited our grandparents and said good-bye to them. We never saw them again. They and twenty other relatives became victims of the Holocaust.

At school, I said goodbye to my best friend, Walter. He and I

Benno Levi saved this luggage tag from his voyage aboard the S.S. *New York*.

were the only Jews in our class. We had tears in our eyes. We didn't see each other again until 1992, when we visited Alsfeld together with our wives.

I went back to Alsfeld for the first time in 1963 and at least once every ten years thereafter. Where the magnificent synagogue had stood, only a marker memorialized both its existence and destruction by the "NATIONAL-SOZIALISTICHER TERROR." It had been burned and demolished in November of 1938. Not much else had changed.

Later in the 1990s I noticed that the buildings four to five hundred years old, in the town center, which, in the 1930s had been badly run down, now sparkled in their renovated ancient beauty. Alsfeld had become a major tourist attraction. It is now a beautiful little town, right out of Grimm's fairy tales and has been designated as a "model city of Europe." In fact, the old City Hall has been featured on a German postage stamp.

We came to America on the S.S. *New York*, of the Hamburg-America Line. The food aboard was strictly kosher. I've never tasted better food in my life! The most amazing thing was that I saw nothing that reminded me of the Nazi regime even though this was a German vessel.

I was homesick and seasick as I lay on a deck chair and imagined seeing the ancient tower that dominated Alsfeld, fading away on the distant horizon. Once I got rid of my seasickness, the trip became a great adventure. It was fantastic. I will never forget it.

Our arrival on January 8, 1935, in New York, the most exciting city in the world, was an event that we had eagerly anticipated and fully satisfied all of our expectations. There was no time for homesickness. We lived at the Jewish orphanage on Amsterdam Avenue. They treated us like royalty. Every day we went on tours and were invited for dinners in the homes of the committee members of the organization that made all this possible.

On the evening of our arrival, our first tour took us by subway downtown. In awe I gazed at the skyscrapers and all the cars and people. I remember seeing the word *restaurant*—it was the same word in German. Now I knew another English word to go with *yes* and *no*.

One night in early February, we boarded a train at the New York Central Station and slept in the Pullman car. The following morning, looking out of the big window, my eyes surveyed a scene of what seemed to be the snow-covered Wild West. I had just finished a book about a little American boy who was captured by the Indians. I scanned the horizon for hostile natives. Thank heavens it was only western Ontario.

We arrived at the Michigan Central Depot to be met by our new family. I had heard the name Detroit for the first time only a couple of days before and still had difficulty pronouncing it. As we drove down Fourteenth Street, the city looked like a small town. I was so disappointed. Then, a month or so later, we drove downtown and I saw the high buildings, the gigantic department stores—J. L. Hudson and Kerns, Tiger Stadium, and all of the magnificent movie houses. This was Detroit, the fourth largest city in America. I suddenly was proud and happy to be a part of it.

Benno Levi (*front row, second from left*) with his foster family, the Rosenbergs, in Detroit.

A New Home and Family

A new family, the Rosenbergs, embraced us and became Uncle Robert and Aunt Ella. We instantly acquired dozens of relatives, two sisters, aunts, uncles, cousins, and grandparents.

Ernest and I were enrolled at Roosevelt Elementary School, where we became instant celebrities as the first Jewish child refugees from the Nazis.

At the time I knew only four words of English, but three months later I was able to speak fluently. I was given special lessons. I had one teacher named Mrs. Snow. She took me out in the hall and taught me English. She could also speak German.

During the summer of my first year I avidly followed the Detroit Tigers as Hank Greenberg paced them into the World Series. At the time, the State of Israel was just a distant dream, but Hank Greenberg was the symbol for the Detroit Jewish community. Can you imagine old ladies who never knew what baseball was? Suddenly they were glued to their radios, listening to the ball game. It was amazing. He was my hero.

I wrote to my parents every week in German. I got letters back and I saved most of them. I have difficulty reading them today. In

COURTESY OF BENNO LEVI

On June 14, 1936, Benno Levi celebrated his bar mitzvah with a children's party at the home of Robert and Ella Rosenberg, his new American family in Detroit.

the summer of 1938 my parents and sister, Miriam, joined Ruth, Ernest, and me in Detroit. Once more we became a whole family.

In the Army

When war came in 1941 I was about to graduate from Detroit Central High. My first job was with the newly created *Detroit Jewish News*. I expected to be drafted and when a year went by without a word from my draft board, I called them up. "Hey, all my friends are going in the army. How come you're not calling me?" They said, "The FBI is checking you out." After all, I was an enemy alien.

I was finally drafted in June of 1943. I could speak fluent German and I was sent to the Pacific! The captain who inducted me looked at my name—"Benno Levi, born in Germany." He quickly stamped my file "Not recommended for European Theater." He never asked me, "Are you Jewish? Are you a Nazi?" I was too scared to protest and very disappointed that I would not be able to come back to Alsfeld with a gun in my hand.

A couple of weeks later, the *Detroit Jewish News* ran a story about my departure from the paper. They made it sound as if I were a very important employee. I was just the copy boy. But I did write some stories about my friends as they entered the army.

My first permanent assignment was to Camp McCoy, Wisconsin. Everything was great, the climate, the entertainment, and I made a lot of good friends. Only one very disturbing event marred my stay.

I had been deeply impacted by the racial bias of the Nazis and was aware of the presence of similar hatreds against Jews and Afro-Americans here in my new homeland. The race riots in Detroit in the summer of '43 shocked me.

In the army, where there should have been equality through common purpose, race-based hatred still persisted. In my barrack at the time, a group of enlisted men from my town was discussing the subject in the barracks. They were unaware that I was lying on my cot. I was shocked as one of them blurted out, "After they beat the hell out of the niggers, they should clean up Twelfth Street [the Jewish section of Detroit]." There was no hint of dissent from his pals. I felt crushed. Later during basic training in the South, I found conditions that made me realize that we had a long way to go, and I was determined to make a difference.

Six months later, I was assigned to Company A of the Seventy-seventh Statue of Liberty Division. The following month we made our way across the country to Camp Stoneman, port of debarkation in Pittsburg, California, near San Francisco and right on the Bay. Here we relaxed for almost two weeks as we waited for our ship to take us to an unknown destination. It was a gorgeous camp. Sunny spring weather prevailed. Lush green hills surrounded it. The distant mountains clustered on the horizon and we all fell in love with California. Early on a Saturday morning a ferry finally took us from there to our ship in Frisco. A week later we were in Hawaii after zigzagging across the Pacific to avoid the stalking Japanese submarines. We underwent some tough amphibious and jungle training. Finally, on July 1st, 1944, we headed out for our first battle. As General Andrew Bruce, our commander, put it on the day before our landing, "Here today, Guam tomorrow."

Fighting on Guam

After a successful landing on July 21, our initial mission was to seal off Orote Peninsula to Japanese reinforcements. The marines were fighting there to recapture their former U.S. Naval Air Station. We accomplished that objective, and then waited at the base of Mt. Tenjo, the highest mountain on Guam, to close a pincer movement with another marine division making its way from the northern beachhead. Unfortunately, heavy Japanese resistance held them up, so we waited for a couple of days. At this point, our brave commander, General Bruce, offered to take the mountain. The assignment, a "reconnaissance in force," fell on Company A, my unit. Signals were arranged with our support that included a marine fighter squadron. A red flare from us—we need help. A green one—success, mission accomplished.

It was a tough climb as Company A, with my third platoon in the lead, straggled up the steep mountain in single file against scattered mortar and sniper fire.

My job as platoon runner placed me just behind the lead scout and in front of our platoon leader, Lt. Scullen. As we reached the summit, our objective, there was a big explosion followed by another. What was it? The lieutenant assumed that it was friendly artillery fire targeting us. He ran down from the top a short distance calling out, "Artillery fire! Send up a flare!" The guys with the flares were at the bottom. What he really meant to say was, "Send up a *green* flare" meaning, "We're okay—don't shoot at us." Instead, the guys at the bottom set off a red flare. So these six fighter planes, they saw a red flare from the bottom, and they saw these soldiers on top of the mountain, and they think, "Japanese." So they attack—friendly fire. Unfortunately, it was the proper response to a red flare.

Machine-gun fire suddenly sputtered out of the sky from planes diving down at us. I recognize them immediately as being our own marine fighter squadron that had been designated as one of our support teams. Simple solution: pick up a signal panel and wave it at one of the diving pilots. I grabbed a panel, ran to the tip of Mt. Tenjo, and waved as the next attack came in. I was sure this would end our problem. No way, the pilot continued his descent towards a soldier waving a Japanese flag—me. I, on the other hand, see a small dot leave the belly of the plane growing larger and larger falling at an angle—a bomb with me as the target. I dropped the panel and ran like hell to the opposite side of Mt. Tenjo. Big explosion, covered with dirt—no harm. *Wow!* Now it hit me, if I am unable to properly identify our unit quickly, they will request all the battleships and cruisers offshore to zero in on us, and that will be the end of the Third Platoon.

While the pilots got ready for another run, I got hold of a second panel and raced to the summit once more, this time pointing both in the form of an arrow to the Japanese positions. That did it. They continued their dives once more but this time recognized the proper signal, tipped their wings, "So sorry!" and were gone.

Six weeks later I got the Silver Star, first one in Company A. I couldn't get over it. Here I was always so afraid that I would be the first one to run in the face of fire, and now a big hero. I sure needed it to build up my image.

Raising the Flag

One of the most memorable scenes on Guam was one that I happen to witness by chance on July 29, 1944, as the Third Platoon relaxed on top of a mountain. I had borrowed my platoon leader Lt. Scullen's binoculars to look for something of interest. It was the day after we had captured Mt. Tenjo. Below us, just a couple of miles away, was Orote Peninsula. The battle there that had lasted a week had been drawing to a close all morning. The big guns and mortars were finally silent and the constant chatter of rifle and automatic fire had faded away. Only the echoes of scattered, isolated shots reached my ears, while wisps of smoke marked the dying flames. Suddenly I heard something most unusual. Was it real or was it my imagination? The faint whisper of a bugle floated up from Orote. Impossible, it only happens in the movies. Once more I swept the scene with my borrowed binoculars. Sure enough, there it was. On a flagpole, in front of the remnants of the shattered old marine barracks, a flag was slowly rising. I was awestruck. Nobody else in the Third Platoon was aware. I was looking at the culmination of a long battle that began on December 10, 1941, when the invaders raised the Japanese flag on this very same pole as the island of Guam became the first American possession ever to be lost in battle. Now, with the flag waving proudly over the ruins of what had been the United States Naval Air Station, we were back. Soon all of Guam would be ours once more.

Since my schooldays in Alsfeld, Germany, under Hitler, I had learned to abhor the daily Nazi deluge of patriotic bullshit that poured out of the school radio as we stood at attention in the hall outside our classrooms. They were just tools used by opportunist Nazi politicians. Since then, I have looked upon all such displays, both over there and in the United States, with extreme skepticism. But this was genuine. I felt a surge of patriotic pride, proud to be a participant. Without a doubt this moment would remain in my memory as one of the most outstanding episodes of World War II.

History was being made and I was present. I called Homer [Quintern], Wiley P. [Turner], and Pete [S/Sgt. Garrilli], standing nearby, and passed the binoculars around.

Happy Days Are Here Again

A few days later we headed east across Guam in pursuit of the enemy. The road had turned into a very narrow path, forcing us to abandon our vehicles. As a result, in addition to the heavy combat load, I was now carrying shells for our mortars. It turned into a real hell as we headed down into one valley through heavy brush and across a small stream, then up the other side and down and up again and again.

It was around 17:00 in the afternoon. We were on the verge of collapse from exhaustion and hunger when we saw a sight that I will never forget.

Coming towards us was a long line of civilians guided by a small group of GIs. It really got to us as we realized these were citizens of the first American territory to be recaptured from the enemy.

Forgotten was my own misery and we all felt rewarded for

all our efforts. These people had just been freed from a Japanese concentration camp. Men, women, and children of all ages, and even a few animals, were all carrying whatever they could, and walking to freedom.

Some hobbled along on crutches. Others had to be carried, and many had bandages. One old man with bleeding feet was carrying an old woman whose feet also were badly festered. We directed the couple to an aid man, who bandaged their wounds. Most of these people were sickly and exhausted but all seemed very happy to be liberated, wearing big smiles from ear to ear.

The phrase "Happy days are here again" was heard over and over again, and "We've waited for a long time but knew you'd come back." We were all thrilled at the scene as it unfolded. We eagerly shared our K rations, cigarettes, and candy and were thanked profusely. Most greeted us in English, but some in a very strange manner, as they bowed their heads deeply with foreboding, fear, and deep anxiety clearly reflected in their faces. This was how they were forced to greet their Japanese conquerors. I was not the only one with tears in my eyes.

Rest and Rehab

After Guam we were off for R & R in New Caledonia. We never made it. MacArthur was having trouble on Leyte in the Philippines. I'll always remember Saturday, November 11, 1944. I was sitting on deck with one of my buddies when suddenly we noticed the whole convoy change course with a sharp U-turn. We had heard the news reports from Leyte; the battle was stalemated and enemy resistance stiffening. We also recalled the words of General Andrew Bruce, our brave commander, and knew that he was pulling strings for an opportunity to flaunt his martial prowess. Confirmation came as we made a quick stop at Manus Island in the Bismarck Archipelago, northeast of New Guinea. We reloaded for combat. We were given a half-day break on a "recreation island" where we went swimming and were handed a bottle of beer and a can of nuts—our rest and rehabilitation.

Leyte, Philippine Islands

On Thursday, December 7th, the Seventy-seventh Division entered the battle for the Philippine island of Leyte with a landing behind the enemy lines in a spectacular effort to end the existing stalemate. We accomplished it by capturing the big supply port of Ormoc. General Bruce didn't make the cover of *Time*, but the magazine quoted his triumphant message to Higher Headquarters in the vernacular of the GI crapshooter: "Rolled two 7s into Ormoc, come 7, come 11." The two 7s pertained to our Seventy-seventh Division. The Seventh and Eleventh divisions were on their way over the mountains supposedly to help us capture Ormoc. By the time the three divisions made contact with us, we had taken our objective without their help.

The Battle for the Ryukyu Islands

In March '45, the Seventy-seventh Division was included in the greatest invasion armada of the Pacific War heading north toward Japan—the objective the Ryukyu Islands, which included Okinawa, the largest and most strategic island in the chain. Its capture would give us the key to the inner ring of Japanese defenses, within easy striking range of the industrial heart of the enemy. On March 26, six days before the assault on the beaches of Okinawa, our battalion landed about fifteen miles to the west, on Zamami Shima, the largest of the Kerama Islands. The conquest was completed in three days. Luck was with us—just a few casualties for Company A. For the vast fleet of warships taking part in the operation there now was a safe anchorage and, for the artillery, a strategic site to support the landings on D-day, if necessary.

Death on Okinawa

Back aboard our LST [landing ship, tank], we watched anxiously from the rail as four divisions assaulted the western beaches of Okinawa. Paradoxically, it was Easter Sunday and April Fool's Day. We fooled ourselves into believing this would be a pushover.

Opposition was light, and, incredibly, by the end of the third day our troops had advanced across the island to the eastern shore.

Our fleet of LSTs, troop carriers, and protective warships, with most of the Seventy-seventh Division aboard and now in reserve status, began to circle the islands waiting for our next assignment.

On a Saturday afternoon, two days before our next action, Captain Barron called us together on the deck of our LST with the devastating news that on Monday, April 2nd, the day after the invasion of Okinawa, our highly regarded and beloved regimental commander, Colonel Vincent J. Tanzola, was killed with seven other members of his staff, four officers and three enlisted men. Other fatalities included the ship's captain and a number of crew members. The U.S.S. *Henrico*, the regimental flagship, carrying, among others, the entire staff of regimental HQ, was attacked by eight kamikazes. One of the suicide planes went straight for the superstructure, destroying meeting rooms and most of the officer sleeping quarters. Also lost were important documents, records, and maps relative to future operations.

We all were deeply shocked by this great loss. The colonel was a much admired and respected CO. He was short and always struck me as rather jovial. He was a fellow Michigander, a native from Battle Creek.

Our battalion CO, Colonel James Landrum, has been assigned to regimental HQ. His departure added to the tragedy since he was very well liked and an especially competent leader. The men had a great deal of faith in him and would follow him through hell and high water.

Ernie Pyle Killed

On April 16, the Seventy-seventh Division made its next move against the southern beaches of Ie Shima, five miles west of Okinawa's Motobu Peninsula.

It was Wednesday, April 18; we were just moving out for an attack when my buddy Biciolis stopped me. He knew that I had just finished one of Ernie Pyle's books and was one of his great admirers. "Levi," he said, "Did you know that Ernie Pyle was killed?" "No, I did not; He's in Italy, isn't he?" He then quickly filled me in with the facts. Ernie had been right here on Ie Shima with our regimental commander, Lt. Colonel Coolidge, in a jeep, on their way to visit some of the First Battalion units when he was killed. A couple of hours ago, not knowing who the occupants were, I had seen the jeep just as it had passed in front of our foxholes and just as the machine gun which had been harassing us all morning, started to traverse our area once more. I got in my hole and waited for it to pass. The sudden call for litter bearers, coming from the area where the jeep had stopped and its passengers had jumped into a ditch, indicated trouble. Evidently Pyle raised his head to get a look at what was happening and a sniper with the machine-gun nest got him. What a sad story. He chose to be here just to write stories about us. He was not ordered here. What a terrible loss. He was the infantryman's advocate, our hero.

Loss of a Buddy

Two days later, another loss, my buddy Charles Peterson. Friday morning, April 20, 1945, we began the final assault on Iegusugu Yama, the pinnacle that dominated Ie Shima. Its conquest would end the campaign. The Third Platoon led the attack up the steep path towards the summit. Peterson, the scout, was just in front and Quintern behind me. We were making good progress when suddenly, the screaming face of a Japanese man popped up in front of us, like a jack-in-the-box and I heard the explosion of a grenade. Peterson went down in front of me as another grenade hit my foot. I grabbed it and lobbed it down the mountainside. It did not explode. It was a dud! *Wow!* Quintern and I were already removing Peterson's pack and dragging him down to one of the medics. He was drowning in his own blood. Shrapnel had cut his jugular vein. He died at the aid station.

It was exactly one week ago, aboard LST #946 just a few miles off the coast of Okinawa. Peterson and I had been lying on our cots next to each other under a spectacular star-studded sky. That morning the news of the sudden death of President Roosevelt had shocked every one of us. The Allies in Germany were closing the noose on Berlin, and the end of Nazi Germany was just around the corner. We talked all about that and the shift that was to come quickly to end the war with Japan. He told me about his wife and how wonderful she was. "How do you know when you're in love?" I had asked. He put his chin on his elbow and said, "Well, Levi it's like this. In bed, looking down at my wife fast asleep next to me, I hear myself begging God: *Take me first.* That's love. Then, abruptly he said, pointing in the direction of Ie Shima, "You know, Levi, I'm not leaving that island." Startled, my response was, "Don't be ridiculous." He was not the type to be melodramatic. His statement bothered me. I went to sleep.

A Close Call

A few days after the battle of Ie Shima ended, the Third Platoon was ordered on a patrol to bring in some of the remaining Japanese soldiers hiding on the island. We had a Japanese lieutenant who had been captured a few days earlier. His English was pretty good and he had a sister living in Hawaii. He was very pleasant and eager to bring back some of his comrades. When we asked him what he thought of the Americans, he said, "Very strong—I like."

After about an hour of fruitless searching, our Japanese lieutenant finally led us to two soldiers in a cave. A brief conversation with them and they came out to surrender. A little later they pointed away from the rocky cliffs overlooking the ocean. We followed their instructions and headed a short distance inland to some other caves hidden under heavy growth. After some shouting in Japanese by our escorts, a couple of civilians came out. They were followed by a group of about 50 men, women, and children.

They had been living in these caves with all their possessions for quite some time. In spite of the fact that our interpreter and the Japanese lieutenant assured them that we were only interested in their safety and well being, fear and apprehension was reflected in their faces as they were about to confront the "Barbarian Americans."

One of the children, a little boy, had a head wound and our medic immediately bandaged him. After he was all finished and his head was encircled with a very large white bandage, all the little kids surrounded him to admire the handiwork of our medic. The little boy basked in the glory of being the center of attraction. We handed out some candy and food and soon everyone was talking and the kids ran around and played. I could sense the skepticism on the part of the adults begin to vanish.

A couple of our men, standing a short distance from us at the edge of the cliff leading down to the water, suddenly spotted some more Japanese below. Again our interpreter and the Japanese Lt. went to work. There were eight soldiers and a nurse. Slowly but somewhat reluctantly they came towards us.

One of the men leading the group had his right hand deep in his pocket. I motioned him to put his hands up. He wouldn't do it. So, I walked up to him, took his hand out of his pocket and pulled out a grenade. I threw it over the rocks into the ocean where it exploded harmlessly.

At this point we ordered all of the men to strip to the waist and searched them for additional weapons. We found a few more grenades but nothing else. We then took them up to the plateau where the civilians were gathered.

The soldiers were now in a separate group and guards placed around them. We still had some food left that we now distributed among them. Where needed, our medics supplied first aid.

The civilians and soldiers now spoke freely among themselves and plied the Japanese Lieutenant with lots of questions. A more relaxed atmosphere prevailed. When I took pictures, the soldiers smiled broadly. The fear and apprehension that had clouded their faces had vanished. I'm sure they had expected to be cruelly tortured and even killed upon being captured. As I looked at them, I could imagine their thoughts—these Americans aren't so bad, those horrible stories we heard were all a bunch of B S. I was happy for them; the war was over, they were alive and, eventually, would make it home in good health. I envied them.

After about an hour the military police came and took the group to the camps set up for civilians and Prisoners of War near Ie Town.

Fourteen Days on Okinawa

On Monday, May 7, after a short trip on an LST from Ie Shima, we entered the biggest battle of the Pacific War, for the most strategic island, Okinawa. Our troops had reached the major Japanese defense lines and the worst of the fighting was now in progress. The Third Platoon came with a full complement of forty-three men. Exactly two weeks later we came back—just eleven of us.

The toughest battle of this two-week engagement took place on Friday and Saturday, May 11 and 12. During those two days we had a casualty rate close to 75 percent. It culminated on May 12 with a failed attack as we walked into a trap. That morning our company with three others had attempted to take a heavily defended position without success. We of the Third Platoon were fortunate since we were in reserve and stayed behind to mop up. In the afternoon the Third was assigned to probe once more a small ravine in the area where this morning's attack had been thwarted. We packed up and headed down to the company command post. Satchel charges to blow up caves were immediately distributed. One was handed to me.

As he gave platoon leader Sgt. Walter Gibbs his final instruction, I noticed that Captain Barron's face was masked in worry. I was aware of this morning's heavy losses in the same area, a fact I instinctively pushed aside as we piled through an opening into a narrow valley. A hill at the end of the gorge was probably this morning's failed objective. The steep slopes to our right and to our left were like everything else here—naked, covered with shell holes of every size. The dark entrances of a number of caves loomed ominously, daring us to advance.

In two columns, one on each side of this narrow passage, a heavy tank between us, we headed in. The satchel charge on my back was a burden on top of everything I already carried. About one hundred yards into the draw, a small bend halted us for only a moment. We headed on a short distance. Suddenly, there was chaos as bullets zipped in from all directions and mortar shells blossomed in our midst. One landed near our supporting tank. It turned around, back to the safety of the line of departure. We felt abandoned. There was no cover. Tom Chambers, next to me, suddenly stiffened. His hands clawed the side of the hill. He must have died instantly. I looked at Bloechil. He shook his head. There was nothing we could do. Marucci and four others were also hit in the barrage but they were able to make it without help as the order came to end the attack. In a flash we headed around the bend and to the line of departure. Captain Barron was waiting, relief on his face: only one fatality.

Once more we settled down in our old holes. I kept thinking of Chambers. That rough-and-tough southerner always protective of me. He had shared his last drop of water when I was so thirsty on Guam. In his own endearing way he used vulgar language to prod me through the perils of life in this army jungle. He was regular army, dating back to the years before the war, and had been up the scale to top staff sergeant, then down to buck private a couple of times. The point system that went into effect on V-E Day, about ten days ago, placed him in the number one spot to be shipped home for Company A as soon as we came back from the front. Unfortunately, he was a big man and made an inviting target. Next to him, I was insignificant—I think that saved me. One bullet into my satchel charge and we would both have been blown to shreds. Bloechil thought Tom was hit by at least ten bullets.

This day, Saturday, May 12, 1945, was a very bad day here on Okinawa. Almost four months later I found out how much worse it really had been.

It was just after V-J Day; the euphoria of peace was shattered when the chaplain called me and handed me a letter from my father. The news was devastating. My dear mother had passed away in the hospital after a short illness on May 12 at the age of fifty nine. I could still see her standing by the front door on Collingwood Avenue waving good-bye to me, a sad smile on her face. One bullet into my satchel charge that Saturday afternoon and we would have died together.

Saving a Buddy

The day before we were to return from the front, Company A was assigned to take a group of heavily fortified hills. Attempts by other units to do the job had been repulsed with stiff losses during the last two days. At around 11 A.M. we headed out.

The Third Platoon with only eleven men left out of the forty-three that started out just two weeks ago was in reserve and waiting in the company command post.

Fifteen minutes after the attack began, word came back that devastating fire from a pillbox and surrounding caves had forced a quick withdrawal and that the platoon leader, Sgt. Blevins, had been killed. Ten minutes later came a revision—he was wounded, lying fully exposed in the middle of a field. Continued heavy fire kept would-be rescuers at bay.

A little later, Staff Sergeant Coolter of the First Platoon sent a message; a satchel charge was needed to blow up a cave. I got the job and cautiously made my way back to him. His platoon was sheltered behind cover, facing our objective. I crouched next to him behind a mound of earth. In front of us was an open area surrounded by a series of small hills. Commanding the battleground, and sitting like a stage in a theater, was a large pillbox at the furthest edge of this half circle directly to our front. It had the support of a series of caves set into the flanking hills, their dark entrances like eyes staring at us. The ground was pocketed with craters of every size and shape. Devastating fire from these positions had halted the platoon in its tracks.

"Where is Blevins?" Coolter pointed to a shell hole maybe 400 or 500 feet from us. I could barely make out his crumpled body lying in it. He turned to me. "What do you think, Levi, should we try it?" I was ready to blurt out, "Are you kidding? A bunch of fanatic Japanese are holed out there just waiting to cut us down. You saw what happened to Blevins and his platoon." Why me? He had been sitting here for over half an hour with the platoon he commanded. Now, with me here, he comes up with a rescue attempt.

How much longer do I need to disprove the vicious stereotyping that has haunted me all my life? This was suicide, but as defender of my Jewish faith, there was only one answer. He may not have expected my affirmative reply, and I was surprised to hear myself say it as I envisioned that fatal bullet tearing through my body.

Without another word, we took off our packs and raced across

PHOTOGRAPH BY DR. JOEL WEINBERG, BENNO LEVI'S SON-IN-LAW, COURTESY OF BENNO LEVI.

Benno Levi earned a Silver Star for gallantry (*left*) and a Bronze Star for heroic action (*right*).

the field. Before I knew it, we were crouching in the hole at Blevins's side. I could see that he had a chest wound through which air was sucked every time he took a breath. We quickly got rid of his field pack and lifted him out of the crater. Coolter was a powerful guy; I helped him hoist Blevins over his shoulder. We dashed back.

The medic, waiting for us, went right to work while Coolter and I collapsed on the ground. We looked at each other with a thin smile of satisfaction and relief. We were alive—unhurt. I was almost sure that no one had fired in our direction, though only if I had been hit would I have noticed. Was it the supportive fire from the rest of the company blazing over our heads into the Japanese positions that saved us, or was it a miracle?

Ten months later, when I was a civilian once more, a Bronze Star arrived in the mail as the army's appreciation for this episode. Later, a Christmas card came from Blevins. He thanked me for joining Coolter in saving his life. This I treasured even more than the medal.

War Is Over

We were getting ready for the invasion of the Japanese mainland. We had all kinds of materials, descriptions of the areas that we were supposed to hit. Indications were that all the civilians were being trained to be fanatic fighters and were ready and willing to sacrifice everything for their emperor. The landings were planned for November.

It was Friday, August 10, 1945. We had been on pass in Cebu City and had a great time. I came home with a headache and tried to go to sleep early, at around 8:00 P.M. About fifteen minutes after I had hit the sack, I heard some shouting and cheering coming from the direction of the open-air movie area. Like a wave, the cheering seemed to be coming closer. Suddenly someone came running down the company street yelling, "The war is over!" My first thought was a drunk home from his sojourn in Cebu City. Wilson, who had also retired early, got up to investigate. He returned with word that there had been some news on the radio. With that, I rushed down to the mess hall, where a small group was gathered. I was just in time to hear the announcer repeat the report of an intercepted *Domai News* dispatch indicating that Japan had requested Sweden and Switzerland to inform the Big Four that it was ready to accept the Potsdam Ultimatum but with the proviso that Emperor Hirohito remain as sovereign ruler. The announcer then urged that we stay tuned to our Armed Forces Radio Station for additional news as it was received.

Wow! What sensational news. I rushed to my tent to spread the news to the returnees from Cebu City who, like me, has been too pooped to participate in any activity. This news spurred them to jump out of bed and search for the ingredients for an immediate celebration. Sheldon came in and offered to get me a couple of aspirins. In no time at all I felt fine and was ready to join my buddies. But first I stopped at the tent of our mailman, John Kerrigan, who had a radio. The news was repeated as it had been originally reported and nothing new was available.

By the time I returned to my tent, I found a very large celebration in progress there. At 01:00 the news reported that the White

House had confirmed the Japanese offer. The only concern was the proviso that the emperor continue on the throne. To me that did not seem to be an issue since he was only a figurehead. As sovereign ruler he could greatly facilitate the peace process. Still, it was an issue that needed full consent from the Allies. How long would that take?

Feeling fully confident that this was it, I decided to go to sleep as the celebrants continued to sing and make merry all night long. At around 3:00 A.M. the Officer of the Day came in to request a little quiet. I finally fell asleep with that pleasant feeling: our dream has come true, and the war is over. It was not until the morning of Wednesday August 15 that President Truman announced the acceptance by all parties of the surrender terms, and V-J Day was finally a reality.

NOTES

1. On the night of February 27, 1933, the Reichstag building—home of the German Parliament—was destroyed by fire. While the Nazi Party accused the Communist Party of arson, it is widely believed that the Nazis set the fire to delay elections that were scheduled for early March. Declaring the fire a national emergency, Hitler used it as an excuse to suspend certain freedoms and rights of German citizens.

2. Father Charles Coughlin was a Catholic priest at the Shrine of the Little Flower Church in Royal Oak, Michigan. He was one of the first clergymen to use radio to preach his doctrine. Coughlin broadcast weekly radio shows to over 40 million listeners. Coughlin was an anti-Semite who was sympathetic to the policies of the Nazi Party. He was also critical of Franklin Roosevelt and his New Deal policies.

3. The German-Jewish Children's Aid Society was formed in New York in 1934 to aid in the emigration of German children and orphans. The society provided funds and located foster families in the United States.

The Promise
of a Better Future

D uring World War II, a quarter of a million people—half of them Jewish—were killed in the Netherlands. Many more died of starvation during the four-year-long German occupation. The war left Holland's countryside flooded with salt water from broken dikes; buildings and factories were stripped or destroyed; and there was little wood left with which to rebuild.

To help the country get back on its feet, church officials and the Netherlands government set up emigration offices in poor areas. Their goal was to decrease unemployment and reduce overpopulation. Travel expenses were subsidized and people were assisted in making arrangements and contacts overseas.

Between 1948 and 1953, nearly a million people left the Netherlands. One hundred thousand went to the United States; many others went to Australia and Canada. Most grew up during the Depression of the 1930s and had experienced hardship for a long time and now had large families when jobs and farmland were scarce. Some emigrants resided in Indonesia, but were forced to leave when the country separated from the Netherlands. Since there wasn't room in their homeland, they had to go elsewhere.

In Michigan, many descendants of earlier Dutch settlers welcomed and sponsored the new immigrants, making sure jobs were lined up for the newcomers. A key person in organizing sponsorship was Willard "Bill" C. Wichers. Among other accomplishments, the "Father of Holland" brought the De Zwaan Windmill to Holland, Michigan, from the Netherlands for visitors to enjoy. He served on the Michigan Historical Commission and was the Tulip Time Festival director from 1946 to 1952.

Wichers became involved with the Netherlands government in 1941 when Princess Juliana visited Hope College. In 1953 the U.S. Refugee Relief Act was passed, which allowed 17,000 Dutch individuals or family units to come to the United States. Wichers and his wife, Nell, helped find sponsors and jobs for immigrants in the Holland and Grand Rapids area. They also personally sponsored 1,000 immigrants who couldn't secure sponsors. Wichers recalled, "We didn't have to spend a cent on any of them. They all made it in this country."

Friesland is a northern province of the Netherlands, but its citizens consider it almost a separate country, as most people speak Friesian as their primary language. In 1955, Carolyn Damstra's grandparents, Tys and Trijntje (Tina) (nee van der Velde) Dam decided to move with their five children, Durk (Dick), Trijntje (Terri), Tjitze (Ted), Lammert (Bert), and Allert (Al), to Grand Rapids from Friesland. After coming to the United States the family name, Dam, was changed to Damstra.

Today, all but one of the children of Tys and Tina live in or near Grand Rapids. Tys passed away in 1994, Tina in 2005. Dick and Bert are retired from T. Damstra and Sons painting business, Terri (who lives in Chapel Hill, N.C.) worked for the World Health Organization and passed away in 2009, Ted is a retired Amway executive, and Al is a bartender. Two of Tys's granddaughters (Dick's daughters) follow in his footsteps as artists: Emily does freelance work in scientific illustration, and Carolyn is a landscape painter and works for the Michigan Council for Arts and Cultural Affairs.

In 2004, Carolyn Damstra interviewed her grandmother Tina, her uncle Ted, and her father, Dick. Sadly, her grandmother died in 2005 shortly before the Movers and Seekers: Michigan Immigrants and Migrants exhibit opened at the Michigan Historical Museum. The following includes excerpts of an article she wrote

Tys Damstra made these toys for his grandchildren in his workshop.

that appeared in the January–February 2005 issue of *Michigan History* magazine in conjunction with the exhibit.

Childhood Memories

My favorite childhood memories of my grandpa are quiet afternoons working together in his basement woodshop, the smell of sawdust, paint, and turpentine hovering in the air. After a lifetime of working ten-plus hours a day, often six days a week, his hands did not know how to be still. In 1955 his tireless spirit motivated Tys to bring his wife and their five young children to the United States from the Netherland's rural northern province of Friesland.

My grandma was my favorite person on the planet, and food had a lot to do with that. She often made toast with butter and De Ruijter sprinkles: orange-, pink-, and yellow-colored sugar, or else there was another kind that was chocolate. Grandma also sliced us off thick pieces of Leyden cheese, known as *komijnekaas* (cumin cheese), from a huge, red, wax-coated ball. For Christmas, the

Before leaving for the United States, the Damstra (then Dam) family posed for a final picture in the Netherlands. From left to right, they are Ted, Tys, Dick, Bert, Terri, Tina, and Al.

A twelve-year-old Tina poses with her doll carriage.

Tys and Tina Dam (Damstra) had this picture taken on their wedding day in the Netherlands.

grandchildren received brightly colored knitted socks with yarn shoelaces that went all the way up to your knees. She gave great hugs, squeezing so tightly you could hardly breathe.

Life during the War

In Germany-occupied Netherlands during World War II, my grandfather, Tys, made wooden shoes for sale. Work in his trade as a painter was scarce, so he carved shoes and traded them with others in the village for food and supplies. He said, "That went real good at the beginning of the war. There were hardly any shoes in the store anymore and everybody had to have wooden shoes. After the war there was not enough wood. Most of the trees were cut down in the war for heating." Toward the end of the war my grandfather did a painting of the view from his house. It shows tree stumps in a field; all the trees were cut down for firewood. Even today there aren't a lot of large trees there.

World War II left the country devastated. During the German occupation, my relatives were more fortunate than some because food was available in the countryside where they lived. However, the family lived in constant fear that Tys would be taken to work camps and that food and fuel would run out.

My uncle Ted was born in 1945. He remembers, "People would come over and tell their stories, about espionage and how they

Tys Damstra painted this watercolor picture of Harkema in the Netherlands in 1949 before he immigrated with his family to Michigan.

Pages of Tys Damstra's passport issued in the Netherlands in 1954.

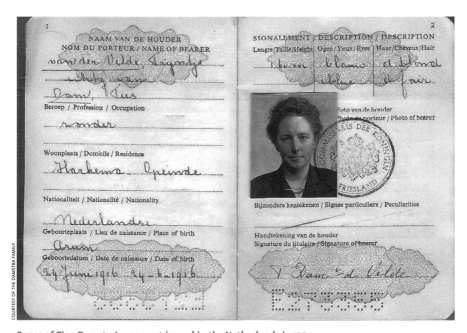

Pages of Tina Damstra's passport issued in the Netherlands in 1954.

sheltered some Jews and other people that the Germans were seeking. We had a corner closet, which had a hidden shelf on the bottom. We actually hid people in there, neighbors that Germans were looking for—anybody that would violate the rules of the Germans, those who wouldn't cooperate with the Germans or were suspected of hiding other people or butchered cows when they weren't supposed to." My grandmother once quietly told me about seeing a man get shot by the Germans as he ran away from them.

My dad, Dick, was born in 1941. He tells stories about skating on the frozen canals in winter to visit friends in other villages. He was very young during the war. I remember asking my dad about the planes. "There were always planes flying over Friesland. They were flying from England to bomb Germany. We were poor, but compared to most people we were well off. We never had to do without food. My mom did hide guys that were in their twenties that the German soldiers would come look for to work in their labor camps. Harkema was a small village; it wasn't really occupied as such."

Saying Goodbye

After the war my grandfather had a difficult time making enough money to support his growing family. My grandma had another reason to move; "Our house [in the Netherlands] was too small. We had five kids with a two-bedroom house. Ed & Wilma [their friends], they go in '49 to the United States and then we sent letters, and then she write back, 'Come over here, there is plenty work for Dad.' And then we have to wait three or four years. We go on a waiting list."

In March 1955, Tys and Tina and their five children boarded the *Groote Beer* headed for America and ultimately Grand Rapids, Michigan. Saying good-bye to their friends and family in the small town of Harkema was heartrending, but also tempered with the excitement and promise of a better future.

According to Ted there were some sad things about leaving.

The trip was in March, and the weather in Friesland at that time is cold and rainy. I don't think my dad and I really realized that

Ted and his two brothers, Dick and Bert, ride the *Groote Beer* (Great Bear), a converted army ship that brought them to the United States in 1955 from the Netherlands. They came with their parents and other brother and sister. Their whole family was seasick from the turbulent March seas during the six-day journey.

maybe we would never see Grandma again. That was really sad for my dad and for me too. And at that time the shock set in. People were crying and thinking that we would be gone forever or that they would never see us again. That's when I started understanding that we were going to go a long, long way away and maybe we would never come back.

My grandma had family members who emigrated to Canada earlier, so she was glad to go and be closer to them.

My own family was over here too for some time. [My parents] had ten kids; six kids get to Canada. And she [Grandma's sister] said, "Do it now, the kids are small, but later on the kids go away and you stay over there." That was one of the reasons we do it too. And Dad [her husband] want to go over here so the kids get a better education.

Tina remembers her trip on the *Groote Beer*. During the thirteen-day journey aboard the converted army ship, the entire family was seasick from the turbulent March seas.

Ted, who was nine at the time, recalls the voyage:

We had to go again through all kinds of screenings and we boarded the ship and waved good-bye. The weather wasn't very nice at all—rainy, windy, and cold. The voyage across was horrible because of the storms in March and it took us a lot longer to get across. We went on a boat called the *Groote Beer*, which means "The Large Bear." It was a converted army ship, so it was cigar-shaped, which really tossed and turned in the ocean.

Ted's arm was in a cast from an accident in Friesland, and he had another mishap on the boat.

When I was there on deck they served really hot chocolate and it was crowded and somebody spilled hot chocolate down my back. So I ended up a couple of days in the hospital on board ship. I had some burns on my neck and on my back. It was a rough voyage. Going across, most everybody was seasick and kind of kept to the bunks. We had fairly good accommodations on the second floor, so we weren't too far from the top to be able to throw up over the edge of the ship.

My father, Dick, who was fifteen at the time, had these memories of the voyage:

I remember the boat stopped at England, and I remember going by those cliffs, those white cliffs. Then I remember nothing but water, and there was a big storm, big waves, and a lot of flying fish that we could see all the time. They went alongside the boat. Everybody was seasick. It was a big boat and they had several rooms for kids to play in—a lot of games and stuff for kids to do. You were always occupied. Half the time you were too sick to enjoy it.

First we went to Halifax, Nova Scotia. A lot of people got off in Halifax and immigrated to Canada. We were allowed to get off the boat in Halifax, and I remember that we wanted to buy some oranges, some fruit, and that my mom wanted some, but nobody spoke English, except Terri and me were supposed to know a little bit of English that we'd been taught in school. I remember going into a grocery store. I really didn't want to, but then we went in there and bought some oranges to take back on the boat. From there we went to New York. We were docked in front of the harbor in New York for almost a day waiting for a spot to dock. We went on the train from New York to Kalamazoo and then up to Grand Rapids. I remember them bringing food around and none of us would eat it because we didn't like it, because we had never had that kind of food before.

After arriving, they lived with friends (their sponsors) for a few weeks and then moved into a small house near downtown Grand Rapids. Sponsors helped find work for Tys, who had experience with carpentry and painting.

The Damstra family is amazed at all the snow in Grand Rapids.

Life in Grand Rapids

There was a lot more snow in Grand Rapids than in Friesland, and many more cars. My Grandma had to learn how to drive. I think Grandma had the hardest time with the transition. "Language was the biggest problem. Dad [Grandpa] was better than me, but I was in the house all the time. I learned it a little bit from the kids. But I like it over here right away and Dad like it too. Free, freedom ... but I like it. And Dad like it too. And you have to work harder over here."

My family settled in quickly. After a couple of years, my grandfather started his own house-painting and finishing business with his sons, two of whom continue T. Damstra and Sons today. They worked long hours, sometimes thirteen hours a day and Saturdays.

Ted liked Grand Rapids:

It was all very new. People were really nice. It was an exciting time. The biggest thing that I remember is we lived on a hill and it was always so hilly. It's flat in Friesland so you immediately saw that the land was a whole lot different. I was overwhelmed simply trying to learn the language. I think we were kind of a curiosity then, too. People looked upon us as the new kids coming in, like you were in a zoo or something. We didn't have a TV but our neighbor would let us watch the *Mickey Mouse Club* on their black-and-white TV. We didn't have any TV [in Friesland]. We had some radio.

School was a big adjustment for the children. Dick remembers, "We couldn't speak English. There were other kids here that could speak Friesian. Those were all families that had immigrated here. Dick recalled:

I remember getting teased a lot in school at first. You couldn't speak English, so they would take advantage of you. They would trick you; they would get you to say swear words in English when we didn't know what the word meant. You learned real quick. In the schools in the Netherlands, when you're in the lower grades you get taught a lot more than you do here, like algebra and geometry. We would know a lot more than the kids in our class did, but we didn't know any English. After a while school was real easy.

After "retiring," Tys polished his carpentry, design, and painting skills, setting up a complete woodshop in his basement. He built elegant grandfather clocks for all of his children and toys and furniture for his grandchildren. When he experienced a fatal heart attack at the age of eighty-three, he had been working on oak rolltop desks for his kids and a rocking horse for his grandson. Tys advice for his children was "What you do, do the best that you can, and as good as you can."

Land of Opportunity

Life was still a struggle for my family, but there were more op-portunities to make money in Grand Rapids. Dick started working right away: "I worked after school. I worked at the bakery, cleaning up pots and pans. We did yard work after school. We pretty much wore all hand-me-downs. My mom did a lot of shopping at the Salvation Army."

Ted also worked hard: "I think that what I did here is I became more of an entrepreneur, Dick especially did too. I worked in the bakery from when I was very young, like eleven or twelve. There were a lot of chances to make money, paper routes. I did some of that and sold lightbulbs door-to-door for the Calvinist Cadets. That was like the Cub Scouts. You could win prizes. Dick won a prize for selling the most lightbulbs. I think things are much more competitive. If you work hard you can be more successful here. More freedom and opportunity here. In the Netherlands my life and my education levels may have been prescribed for me, in terms of what I could do and what I could study."

Growing up in Grand Rapids, I never really realized that my family was different because they had immigrated. There are a lot of Dutch Americans there and I thought we were like all the rest. In many ways my family was very typically American. I think things would have been fine if they had stayed, I have visited relatives in Friesland and they are doing well. Ted shared his views with me:

> At that time most of my life I spent trying to become American. And now that I'm older I treasure my heritage and culture a whole lot more. There's an element of freedom here, how hard you work. You can be successful. There's a stress associated with that, too. There's a stress of recognizing that if you were hurt or incapacitated somehow you could end up on the street and not have a safety net or health coverage. You make your own way.

We Didn't Know How Our Future Would Be

In the late nineteenth century, changes in Japan's economy and tax structure led to increased emigration, beginning about 1885. Many of the first to leave went to Hawaii, where large plantations needed workers to grow sugar cane. Especially after 1900, Japanese laborers sought better working conditions on the Pacific Coast of the United States.

Japanese immigrants, although few in number, faced obstacles that Europeans did not. Like most other Asians, they were not allowed to become citizens. They were the acknowledged targets of anti-alien land laws in western states that excluded noncitizens from owning land. Japanese immigration was severely curtailed by a 1907 informal agreement between the United States and Japan, and entirely cut off by the National Origins Act of 1924.

The United States entered World War II in December 1941, after Japanese forces bombed Pearl Harbor. Anti-Japanese hysteria reached its peak in the months after the attack.

There were fewer than 130,000 people of Japanese ancestry in the United States at that time. Two-thirds of them had been born here and thus were U.S. citizens. Although many Issei—first-generation Japanese immigrants—had lived in the United States for decades and the second-generation Nisei were American citizens, other Americans distrusted them. Anti-Japanese prejudice increased the fear that some Japanese Americans might be working for the enemy.

After the Japanese attack on Pearl Harbor, Japanese American lives changed drastically when they were forced to leave their homes and sent to internment camps. On February 19, 1942, President Franklin Roosevelt signed an executive order authorizing the relocation of Japanese Americans from designated areas on the West Coast, and also the construction of internment camps where they would be held against their will. Between 110,000 and 120,000 Japanese Americans were held in internment camps during World War II.

At the Colorado River War Relocation Center, or Poston Camp, the Bureau of Sociological Research recruited internee Iwao Ishino along with eighteen other college-aged people for an anthropological study of camp life and conditions, and to act as observers and interviewers. This participation gave him a different perspective on life in the camp and how people there coped, and led him to his career in anthropology and teaching.

Iwao Ishino and Mary Kobayashi met while at the camp. Though they were released in 1943, they were barred from returning to California. In 1944, the Office of War Information in Washington, D.C., hired Ishino as an analyst. The Ishinos moved there and were married.

In 1949, Ishino was sent to Occupied Japan with the Public Opinion and Sociological Research Division, and later earned his doctorate in anthropology at Harvard. When Michigan State University offered a teaching position in 1956, he and Mary settled in East Lansing.

Now retired, Iwao Ishino is Professor Emeritus of Anthropology at Michigan State University. He served on the faculty for thirty-five years, specializing in Japanese studies, Asian American ethnicity, and applied anthropology.

In May and June of 1999, Martha Aladjem (Climo) Bloomfield interviewed Professor Iwao Ishino and Mary Kobayashi Ishino in East Lansing, where they have lived for over fifty years.

Japanese Roots

When the Chinese came to the United States in the late nineteenth century, they worked on the railway going from the West Coast to the East Coast. When that was finished, the Japanese came in at the right time in terms of growing produce like celery, lettuce, and

COURTESY OF IWAO ISHINO

Iwao Ishino with his parents. His father, Tomota Ishino, emigrated from Japan to San Francisco, California, in 1906. His mother, Tei Yoshizuka, came later. Iwao was born in San Diego in 1921.

tomatoes that could be exported to the Midwest and East Coast. The invention of refrigerated rail cars—all that came in the early decades of the twentieth century—made such shipments possible.

My father came to the United States around 1906 following the great earthquake in San Francisco, and he eventually migrated to San Diego. He worked as a salesperson for a Japanese import company.

Most of my parents' generation went into farming or fishing, or some other activities like that, but my dad somehow went into sales. Eventually he got enough capital to start a fruit and vegetable stand. Then the Depression came along and he lost that business and went to work as a janitor for a place called the Barcelona Apartment Hotel.

My mother came here as a "picture bride."[1] I'm sure she must have had a lot of problems in adjusting.

She was working at this fruit and vegetable stand, eventually learning a kind of broken English while working there. After we lost the fruit stand, my father and mother rented a two-story building on Twelfth Street. We lived on the first floor. The second floor was used as a rooming house, and Mother became the manager of that rooming house. My father worked as a janitor at the hotel downtown, but Mother ran this little apartment. In the meantime, she raised five kids.

When we lived on Twelfth Street, it was a very convenient place. My mother had friends who lived in the farmland areas. On their way to the wholesale market they would drop off a few pieces of whatever vegetables they were bringing in. We also had friends in the fishing business. San Diego was noted for its tuna-fishing business. So she bartered fish and vegetables. It was one way to go through the Depression years minimizing the cost. So relatively speaking, we ate fairly well.

The Japanese American Community

One of the centers of the community life was the church—that's where the linkages were established.

When my father came to town, he joined a group that was set

up by the First Congregational Church of San Diego. They set up a Japanese mission church, and father was one of the early deacons. I was born in that church—not in the church but the meeting place.

There was also a Buddhist church in town, and these two became the center of community life. We lived in a fairly tight-knit community, a small community, and our social life centered on these kinds of institutions.

The church had to raise funds to sponsor its activities. There were two major ways of raising funds. One was showing Japanese movies. This is one of my early memories, before sound movies came in. There was a professional who traveled with these movies, and he spoke the parts.

Later on, when sound movies came in (during the 1930s, when Japan invaded China), we got some of the propaganda films from Japan. One of the movies I can remember is a story about three Japanese soldiers who tried to go through the barbed wire, and they were carrying a bomb which exploded, and that is how the barbed wire was cut. That was the kind of propaganda films that the Japanese put out, and we were seeing on the West Coast. So you can begin to see some of the anxiety and uncertainty that some FBI members might have felt—that we were being brainwashed.

The other way to raise funds was to put on Japanese plays. Now remember, this is all prewar. The average age of the second generation, the products of the picture brides, was around eighteen years old. So it was an immigrant audience. The first generation still controlled the community life, ran the businesses, and ran the churches. The reason why I tell you that is because the kinds of plays they put on to attract—not only for recreation but to raise money—were these Japanese plays, Kabuki theater. My old man, my father, was a ham.

Another way to raise funds was through having church-sponsored social affairs and picnics. The basic source of developing a sense of community for young people was to engage them in all kinds of sports—baseball, football. The Japanese Americans in one town would play another town. Baseball was popular in Japan too. That was when Babe Ruth and others popularized baseball in Japan. There's a book by Whiting about Japanese baseball. *You Gotta Have*

"My old man was a ham. He acted in our church plays."

Wa—which means harmony. He is arguing that even though the game of baseball and its rules went to Japan, a dimension called *wa* gave Japanese baseball a different feeling all together.

Discrimination and Prejudice

There were various ways in which a community got together both between and among different communities on the West Coast. So we were a fairly well-knit community. You can see how the outside community, the white community, began to become suspicious because we didn't really develop into the larger community in any intensive way.

Another way of dealing with prejudice and discrimination in San Diego was to join the Boy Scouts. Those who ventured out ran into problems, so most of us stayed within our community. A number of our parents thought we may not find jobs in the United States, so acquiring the Japanese language was important.

Our church and the Buddhist church also had Japanese-language schools after regular school.

The Japanese played a very important role in the fishing industry in California. That came about when the Catholics were not eating meat on Friday. The tuna industry developed, and some of my friends' parents came to San Diego and helped to develop a new fishing technique.

We were considered dangerous because we were involved in

COURTESY OF IWAO ISHINO

Iwao Ishino (*center*) believed that one way of avoiding prejudice and discrimination within the community was by joining the Boy Scouts.

fishing and agriculture. There are newspaper editorials saying that you have to be careful of the produce that you eat because the Japanese may poison you. That kind of activity and prejudice was being circulated in the newspapers.

Asians were not eligible to become naturalized citizens. Later on, certain economic interest groups like labor unions and farmer's associations became jealous of the advances that Japanese Americans were making. The California legislature passed a law saying that those ineligible for citizenship could not own land. There were bills in the California legislature trying to keep Japanese residents from fishing.

In terms of agricultural land, the Japanese Americans often bypassed that handicap by becoming sharecroppers. More commonly, the parents would put the property in the name of the American-born children so they were able to bypass the law.

There were several other discriminatory laws that were passed. For instance, if a Japanese American woman with citizenship married an Asian man, she would lose her U.S. citizenship.

My generation became aware of these kinds of prejudices and a lack of assimilation into the larger America society. So the older people and some of my generation organized what they called the Japanese American Citizens League (JACL). The primary goal of this organization was to demonstrate to the American public that we were loyal citizens and we had a vested interest in American society.

When the threat for the ethnic cleansing of the Japanese Americans came up, this was the largest formally organized Nisei group, and it went to the government and said, "We are loyal, we will participate in the evacuation process." That stirred up a lot of controversy in the postwar years within our group!

Relocation

I blocked out the details of this thing—exactly how I felt. I think I am suffering post-traumatic stress disorder. In fact, I wrote a paper about this and gave it at a conference some years ago, before that became a popular phrase. I gave that paper some time during the Vietnam period in the 1960s.

There were a lot of very interesting things going on before the war. The Japanese government, the militarists, were going into China and setting up the Manchukuo government.[2]

On the West Coast there was tremendous opposition expressed in the newspapers. Most of my friends were critical of the Japanese government. We also knew that we were U.S. citizens.

When Pearl Harbor happened, drastic action took place. The future was uncertain.

Immediately after Pearl Harbor, the FBI went to the leaders of the Japanese American communities. The FBI had access to the Japanese organizations, so when the war started they were ready to pounce on the leaders, like the ministers of the Buddhist church and leaders in the business community. They grabbed these guys up and put them in separate camps. Mary's father was taken. So there were some families without the head of the household moving with them.

Those who were taken in right after Pearl Harbor were treated under the international laws. They had a trial. And those who were found not guilty were released, and Mary's father was able to come back and join his family. The rest of us who were put in these camps didn't go through any kind of trial—there were too many of us. It is kind of ironic that one group would be going through a very careful trial and another would not.

Executive Order 9066 was the order that President Roosevelt signed to permit the army to remove U.S. citizens, people of Japanese descent on the West Coast. When rumors of that came out, I thought that we, as citizens, would not be evacuated because we had our rights. That turned out wrong, of course.

There was an attempt to make relocation of people voluntary. A few people in our town, some two hundred, attempted to find farms in the Midwest. That did not turn out to be the solution.

In March of 1942 another executive order was issued that established the War Relocation Authority. The importance of this is while the army moved us away from the area in assembly

COURTESY OF IWAO ISHINO. PHOTOGRAPH BY GARY BOYNTON.

Mary Kobayashi carried her belongings in this suitcase from California to the Colorado River War Relocation Center at Poston, Arizona. Japanese Americans were only allowed to take what they could carry in two suitcases.

centers, the War Relocation Authority set up permanent camps in the interior of the United States.

The army put out announcements. There were bulletins on telephone posts and so on. They used channels in the churches and other groups. There was a newspaper that the Japanese Americans put out with some information in it, in terms of what was coming down the pike.

On April 1, we were ordered to go to the San Diego train depot to register. Each family group was given a number and information was given as to what we could take with us when we go. Theoretically, some help was to be given in terms of what to do with your farm or your business.

We were told, "Bring only what you could carry in two suitcases." Mary still has her suitcase that her family used.

Life in the Camps

The San Diego group was a very small group. Maybe 2,000 at the most got on a train and went to what they called the assembly center. There were some fifteen of these assembly centers. We from San Diego went to the one in Santa Anita Racetrack. The reason why an assembly center was necessary was that the permanent camps were not available yet. So where were they going to put 120,000 people?

We had to stay in this assembly center at Santa Anita, a very famous racetrack in Southern California. We lived in one of the stalls. We stayed there from April to August while the permanent camps were still being established.

In August, we moved out by train—a real old train with gaslight lamps—to Poston, Arizona. It took us to an Indian reservation a few miles from Parker, Arizona. The official name of the camp was the Colorado River War Relocation Center.[3]

Only the Nisei (second-generation Japanese Americans) were allowed to serve on the camp's Community Council. This caused resentment amongst the Issei (first-generation Japanese Americans). This, combined with bad food, shortages, poor living conditions, and extreme temperatures led to increased tension between the detainees and camp authorities.

In November of 1942, two suspected informers were beaten, and camp officials arrested two suspects. A general strike ensued, with demonstrations, picketing, and work stoppages. The strike lasted several days before tensions eased.

At the camp, there was some sort of sign put up giving us directions, and then there was the reception center, and they assigned us to a particular block. Usually these barracks were divided into four parts. Theoretically, one part would be assigned to a family, but if you had a very large or small family, you made some variation to that theme.

There were thousands of barracks built. They were not very fancy. The camps that were in cold areas like Wyoming, they had some insulation, but not these in Arizona. When we arrived, we didn't have mattresses, so we had to have ticks—canvas bags that you put hay inside.

COURTESY OF IWAO ISHINO

A typical barrack at Poston Camp. The barracks were hot in the summer and cold in the winter. "There were hundreds of barracks built. They could put one of them up in seventy minutes. They were not very fancy," recalled Dr. Ishino.

In the center of each block were toilets for men and women, a laundry room, ironing room, and a mess hall—they called it a dining room. My camp had thirty-six blocks with fourteen barracks in each.

It was on an Indian reservation and there was nothing but desert and mesquite trees before the camps started. In the summer, the temperature would go up to 110, 120 degrees, very hot and dry. Dust storms came up and blew the dust up between the cracks in the floor and the walls.

They tried to put up a double roof in our camp so that between the first roof and the second roof hot air could blow out. That was an interesting innovation. Eventually, some of the richer people bought fans from Sears and Roebuck. Then they put in a water system that somehow blew the cool air into the rooms. It was such a dry place in the summer. It was a welcome event, the humidity part of it.

In the winter, it got cold. We didn't have any stoves like those in the northern relocation camps where they had coal or wood stoves. We just suffered from the cold weather.

The social life was great—especially among young people. Teenagers really had great fun because of all the boys and girls together. People who had musical backgrounds performed in bands. There were frequent dances, movies, sumo wrestling, and of course to get away from the heat, swimming in the makeshift swimming pools—irrigation ditches, really.

They were trying to set up reasonable living conditions, hospitals and so on. They set up stores in the camp, a co-op type of thing. Sears and Roebuck and Montgomery Ward catalogs were used. Also, Caucasian friends and neighbors brought in stuff so that the camp became a little bit more livable.

They tried to make a sense of community development. You have 10,000 people living in a place like that without regular jobs. One of these projects was a camouflage net. The war needed camouflage nets to put over artillery areas. A lot these people worked on this project, but some objected. "We are prisoners. Why should we do this kind of thing?" They had to recruit. The pay was a uniform worker's pay. I have forgotten what the rate was in the assembly center. I know what it was in the permanent camp. It was a modest amount, like nine dollars per month.

There were other kinds of things that they tried to set up, like schools. Young people were hired as teachers and nurses. Even the newspaper was put out in camp to keep the community informed as to what was going on.

Everybody learned something about how you adjust to camp life, like lining up to go to breakfast. We were given cards that were color-coded. They divided up the eating times. You had to stand in line to get your meals. One of the problems that parents had was that the kids would go eat on their own. You couldn't say, "You have been a bad boy Johnny, you go to bed without eating!"

There were a lot of stupid things going on—with the war going on. Some of the Caucasian workers are believed to have shunted off some of the food and goods for personal gain. There were issues with informers, people who were ratting on each other. In one camp a strike took place protesting that kind of activity, and the army had to come in to restore order.

The War Relocation Authority (WRA) was not run by the army, but was set up by a civilian administration. The first director was President Eisenhower's brother, Milton Eisenhower. My thinking on this is that, in general, the administration tried to do a decent job. I thought the handling of the camp situation was humane and sympathetic.

Pressed into Service

Since I had three years of college by that time, the Bureau of Sociological Research (BSR) recruited me for a project. Eventually eighteen of us college-age people were recruited to act as observers and interviewers. I had my first course in anthropology working on this project. I also had a three-month training in public opinion research methods at the University of Denver. So that kind of participation gave me a different prospective with respect to the camp and how things worked.

Poston Camp was on an Indian reservation. President Franklin Roosevelt appointed John Collier commissioner of Indian affairs in 1933. He was a very interesting idealist in terms of changing it. He had his sights set on this particular camp, and he contributed white Caucasian administrators from the Indian Service. Presumably, they had some experience dealing with the different cultural groups, but also behind this—I think this is partly rumor—John Collier had the idea that maybe the Japanese would come to this place, this desert, and develop a farm system like they did in California. Then the Indian reservation would be much more productive.

To some extent it came true. We had a fifty-year reunion and we went back to Poston and it was beautiful. They had put in an irrigation system.

My life was shaped by this project. It was kind of an escape for me. I was involved in this research project. I rationalized that my parents and my sisters and my brothers were in camp being taken care of by the system.

The project became a model. There were months of work,

pulling together data, organizing it, and each of us writing a biography of that period. The project became an important part in mediating and helping to give the WRA administration an understanding of what was going on in the camps.

One of the co-leaders of the Bureau of Sociological Research, Edward Spicer, was sent to Washington to head up a comparable unit at nine other camps, so that the administration would be informed—as well as the people—as to what was going on.

About 1943, BSR director Alexander Leighton took fifteen of us to a Navajo reservation at Window Rock. That research eventually became a book called *The Governing of Men.*[4]

Also in 1943, the War Relocation authorities began a policy to move out as many people from the camps as they could. One of the earliest attempts was to take people of college age and get them into colleges. The Quakers established what they called a relocation project.

There was a labor shortage. Work groups were organized for temporary assignments outside the camp. There were lots of detainees who went out and worked on the sugar beet farms. All of these things were going on—recruitment, volunteers for military service, and so on.

I had some very personal problems I was going through at this time. My mother was having problems raising her kids. Eventually she lost her marbles and she was put into a hospital. One of the interesting accidents, I suppose you could call it, was that Alexander Leighton was a psychiatrist, so he helped us get my mother into a mental hospital outside of the Poston Camp.

I have memories of visiting her while she was in the hospital in camp. It is hard to resolve. She had these nightmares and would start screaming. The hospital was having a hard time keeping her calm, so she was put in a hospital outside of Poston Center. There she went through electrical shock therapy. She eventually got well enough to come back to camp. Meanwhile, my father and sister took care of my infant brother.

One of the ironies about the camp was, if we were on the outside we would be worried about making a living and taking care of the house and so on. But these things were taken care of by the camp system. So there were no worries about where the next meal is coming from, or how to pay the rent, or who pays for the hospital bill for my mother—those kinds of things. My sister raised my youngest brother like he was her own. Eventually my mother came back to camp and things settled down pretty well.

Alexander Leighton worked up a very interesting deal. The Office of War Information (OWI) had a system set up for interviewing Japanese prisoners of war in the Pacific. Many of the interviewers were Japanese Americans sent there to become interviewers, translators, and interpreters. Five of us from camp were assigned to this job in the OWI at the Pentagon.

The OWI was responsible for putting out propaganda for both the European and the Pacific theater. Leighton, through his connections, was able to set up a special unit called the Foreign Morale Analysis Division (FMAD). The co-director of that unit was Clyde Kluckhohn, a professor from Harvard.5 There was Ruth Benedict and a number of other anthropologists and future social scientists involved.

The responsibility of this unit was to go through and systematically collect documents and prisoner of war interrogation reports. The idea was to trace the morale of the Japanese soldier during the war. We developed a technique of doing content analysis of these reports, and we noted references to poor leadership, inadequacy of supplies, faith in the system, etc. Three months before the atom bomb was dropped on Japan, this unit put out a report that went all the way up to General Marshall saying that Japan was ready to surrender.

Released from Camp

The War Relocation Authority began to close the camps. We didn't know what the future was going to be. We didn't know how we were going to be treated. We didn't know what the outcome of the war was going to be—all of those uncertainties.

We knew that California was not receptive to us. We didn't know what our future job or business was going to be, and we were being asked to move out before the war ended, so the question was, if we go to the Midwest or the East Coast, how would we be treated? What kind of job would we find? There was a war going on, there were shortages of all kinds. There was a whole series of things happening.

Three important court cases raised the constitutional issue. We know now that the Justice Department and the War Department withheld vital information that the Supreme Court did not know about, and they made a decision that avoided the constitutional issue and justified the relocation as a military necessity.

There was pressure on the part of the legal system to close the camps because they were illegal. The other part of it was, the WRA director and others knew that the war would be ending soon and there would be lots of displaced people, lots of chaos, and therefore, the camps ought to be closed soon.

Then came the question from Congress: How can we close the camps and let all these "disloyal" people out? How can we separate all the disloyals from the loyals? So they had a stupid questionnaire put out, and I don't know the exact phrasing but it had to with do your renouncing your loyalty to Japan. For the young Japanese Americans who were citizens, they would ask, "Are you willing to serve in the US military forces?" The people who said no were those who were going to be put into this disloyal camp that they had set up at Tule Lake, California. That became an issue in the camps. Fortunately my parents answered yes, so they got out, no problem.[6]

The other issue was parents and children answering separately. Who would go with the parents, and how was the decision made? You can see that psychologically it was a very trying situation.

The WRA set up resettlement offices in different cities, Detroit, Chicago, Cleveland. These relocation offices were supposed to help the people find a place to stay, and to find jobs, and so on. Not always successful, but that is what the administration figured out. I am not sure of the figure—something like fifty dollars was given to an individual for readjustment and train fare.

Part of the interest in closing camps early came from the fact that the Japanese American soldiers were doing very well in the European theatre and demonstrating their loyalty.

Japanese Americans first classified 1-A were recruited. After Pearl Harbor, some were kicked out of the army and we were reclassified 4-C, so we were no longer worried about the army recruitment. We were put in a category comparable to enemy agents. When the volunteer Japanese American troops started doing so well, the War Department decided to reclassify us. So I was reclassified 4-C to 1-A in late May or early June of 1944.

I was told to report in three weeks to the recruiting office. I said, "Heck, I got three weeks!" I proposed to Mary in the first week. We got married in the garden of this lovely house at 2410 Wyoming Street where she was working as a maid and going to secretarial school.

We didn't have much money. We went on a honeymoon in Virginia the third week. The travel agent made reservations for us because we were quote "a Philippine couple."

I came back and reported in time for the draft. I appeared at the address and the sergeant started reading off the names, but he didn't call my name. So I went up to him and said, "Sergeant, my name is Ishino. Am I not on this list? You never called me." He looked down at his paper and said, "Oh, you. It says here you should report to your office." So I went to my office and everybody there is smiling at me. They said, "You got a Presidential deferment!" I said, "Oh, heck, I didn't have to get married then!" I thought I was going to be a deadbeat for all those guys going overseas—a replacement!

World War II ended and I was drafted into the army in January 1946. I was assigned to the Military Intelligence Service Language School (MISLS) at Monterey, California. The school was training recruits to serve in postwar Japan as interpreters and translators.

By this time, the military draftees were required to serve only for eighteen months. For soldiers like me with limited Japanese language skills the school asked us to sign up for an additional eighteen months in order to complete the language training and to serve in Japan in the Occupation forces.

I decided not to extend my enlistment because I had a letter from Professor Clyde Kluckhohn who suggested that I apply for entering graduate school at Harvard. So in April 1947, I applied and was accepted.

In Occupied Japan

I finished my oral exams in the summer of 1949. I was ready to go someplace to write my dissertation. Fortunately, a Harvard professor who was working in the Public Opinion and Sociological Research Division was coming back. There was a position opening up, and because I had that public opinion research training, I got this job in Japan with the unit, the PO&SR Division. This unit did surveys to study the impact of the occupation reforms, the land reform program, the educational programs, and so on.

Coming to Michigan

When the job in Japan closed up, I was the only one left in my unit, because all the guys found a job doing something else. There was a job open for somebody to do a survey on Okinawa. The Pacific Science Board had a project out on behalf of the army to find out what were the sentiments of the people in Okinawa. They had three choices: (1) to become an independent state; (2) to become a trustee territory like the South Pacific Islands were; or (3), revert back to Japan. So I took three of these Japanese scholars with me—a statistician and two sociologists—to do the survey in Okinawa.

John Bennett was the project director of Public Opinion and Sociological Research and he was already back at Ohio State University. He said, "Well, you don't have a job, come to Ohio State University and we'll get a grant from the office of Naval Research to write up the materials on the Public Opinion and Sociological Research Division." And I was part of that team. So I said, "Sure, I'll go there." I was there five years and was appointed assistant professor.

At the end of the five years there was a job offer from Michigan State University. MSU under President John Hannah started the overseas projects, and Okinawa was one of the early ones. I knew that they had this project and I knew that that would be a possibility for future research, so I opted to leave Ohio State and come here. I didn't get to Okinawa until 1963, however. I took my family with me and stayed there for two years.

Conclusions

There are some rather interesting things happening in the United States, like what is happening with ethnic relations. We are beginning to define what assimilation means. It used to be assimilation to a European background, but it is now becoming a much more diverse kind of thing. It is a very interesting issue going on right now, with immigration and all of these other kinds of things. The question of the new image of American society is developing as a result of these kinds of changes taking place.

For example, I just showed you the picture of my grandson getting married. Among Japanese Americans in my children's generation, over half are married outside of the Japanese community. What is going on is a definition of a new kind of society, with different kinds of lineages coming in.

We are in a process of formulating a new concept of what American society is. All kinds of interesting things are coming out of this chaos. Somebody called the whole process *chaordic—cha* from *chaos, ord* from *order.*

NOTES

1. Picture brides or mail order brides were Asian immigrants who came to the United States in the early decades of the twentieth century. Matchmakers arranged the marriages using photographs and biographical information from the immigrants.
2. Manchukuo, meaning "State of Manchuria," was a puppet state in China founded and administered by the Japanese government in 1932.
3. The Colorado River War Relocation Center, or Poston Camp, operated from May 8, 1942, until November 28, 1945. Consisting of three separate camps located several miles apart, it was the largest detention center in the United States. At its peak the camp housed 17,814 detainees. Poston was situated on 71,000 acres of Colorado River Indian Tribes reservation land, against the wishes of the tribal council. Poston was the only camp administered by the Bureau of Indian Affairs, rather than the War Relocation Authority.
4. Psychiatrist Dr. Alexander Hamilton Leighton was commissioned as commander in the U.S. Navy Medical Corps after the United States entered

World War II in 1941. He was assigned to conduct a study on the treatment and conditions of Japanese Americans at the Poston War Relocation Camp. He later became chief of the Foreign Morale Analysis Division of the Office of War Information.

5. Clyde Kluckhohn was a cultural anthropologist and psychologist who studied the Navajo culture. Kluckhohn was a curator of ethnology at the Peabody Museum until his death in 1960. A couple of books eventually came out from this research. One was called *Human Relations in the Changing World*, which gave all of the technical details. Ruth Benedict also got the basic data for *The Chrysanthemum and the Sword* book, which is a classic Japanese anthropological study.

6. According to the National Japanese American Historical Society, *The Bill of Rights and the Japanese American World War II Experience*, pp. 6–7, 1992:

> Questions of Loyalty: On February 8, 1943, the WRA and the Army distributed applications for leave clearance titled "Statement of U.S. citizenship of Japanese American Ancestry." All inmates seventeen years old and older were required to complete the questionnaire, one which was to provoke the greatest upheaval within the camps.

Two questions, intended to separate the "loyal" from the "disloyal," most disturbed the internees:

> Question #27 asked: "Are you willing to serve in the armed forces of the United States on combat duty wherever ordered?"
> Question #28 asked, "Will you swear un-qualified allegiance to the United States of America and faithfully defend the United States from any or all attack by foreign or domestic forces, and forswear any form of allegiance or obedience to the Japanese emperor, or any other foreign government, power or organization?"

WRA director Dillon S. Myer later admitted: "A bad mistake was made in the loyalty question." For one thing, question 27 put to the *Issei* whose average age was 54 was not conceivable, while question 28 forced them into an untenable position: they had not been allowed U.S. citizenship, and now they were being asked to renounce allegiance to the only country of which they were citizens.

The Nisei were understandably outraged. Among other citizens loyalty was never questioned, yet the Nisei were once again asked to prove theirs.

Also, they knew that, should their parents answer no to both questions, a yes on their part would mean certain physical and emotional separation from them. These questions most disturbing to the internees were intended to separate the "loyal" from the "disloyal." Most internees felt they were again put on trial to prove their loyalty. The requirement to fill out the poorly worded questionnaire resulted in dissension among camp inmates as people were classified based on their answers.

We Have to Make the Best of the Situation

Mary Kobayashi's grandfather grew peaches and oranges on the Japanese island of Shikoku in the late 1880s. He owned a towboat and barges for hauling coal and fruit to other parts of Japan. When a typhoon hit the island and destroyed boats, the business was ruined.

Japanese tradition dictates that if a family loses its money, the oldest son of the family must pay back any debts incurred. In 1912, when Mary's father, Sahichiro Kobayashi, was sixteen years old, he immigrated to Arizona to seek his fortune. He went to high school there.

After several years he returned to Japan to marry Misao Kitaya, a seamstress from Gogoshima. They went to San Francisco in 1915. Sahichiro and Misao had five sons before Mary was born in 1923. Sahichiro eventually owned and operated a prosperous chicken farm in Santa Ana, California.

When the United States government issued Executive Order 9066 in 1942 after the attack on Pearl Harbor, all Japanese Americans and Japanese living in California were ordered to move to relocation camps.

Mary's father was falsely accused of anti-American activities,

Mary dressed in traditional Japanese clothing including a kimono and parasol for this picture in Bolsa, California. The kimono is the traditional dress of a young Japanese person.

arrested, and sent to jail in Missoula, Montana, where he was held for several months.

In May 1942, Mary—along with her five older brothers and their mother—were sent to a relocation camp in Poston, Arizona. Mary worked as a secretary and a gym teacher. After months in jail, her father was tried and acquitted, but was still not free. He joined his family at Poston.

At Poston Mary met Iwao Ishino, whose parents were also Japanese immigrants. When they were finally allowed to leave the camp, the United States government would not let them return home to California, so they moved to Washington, D.C., where they were married. Eventually, they moved to East Lansing, Michigan, where Iwao Ishino became a professor of anthropology. Mary taught Japanese flower arranging and made ceramic pots. Mary and Iwao Ishino raised four daughters, Marilyn, Catherine, Ellen Susan, and Tomi. The Ishinos have seven grandchildren and two great-grandchildren.

In May and June of 1999, Martha Aladjem (Climo) Bloomfield interviewed Professor Iwao Ishino and Mary Kobayashi Ishino in East Lansing, where they have lived for over fifty years.

———————————

Japanese Roots

My mother and father came to the United States in 1915. I was born in Stanton, California.

My grandparents lived in Shikoku, Japan. They used to grow oranges and ship them up north. My grandfather had barges that he would load up with oranges and coal and take up to the northern islands.

One year there was a typhoon and my grandfather lost all of his barges. My father was the oldest son, so he was told to go to America and earn money to pay off the family debt. He came to the United States, to Arizona.

After he finished high school, he decided to go back to Japan and marry my mother. She is from the same island, called Gogoshima. He knew her from before, and he must have been a fast talker

Mary Kobayashi's parents, Misao Kitaya and Sahichiro Kobayashi, came to San Francisco from Japan in 1915.

COURTESY OF MARY ISHINO

because her house in Japan was beautiful. We saw it when we traveled to Japan in 1993. They had a receiving room with chairs and everything. In back was a Japanese room as big as our living room. They had other rooms, kitchen, and more. I don't know why she came to the United States because she was living real well.

While on our trip, we were in a tobacco store. An older man had said, "You should go to the village office and look up your relatives."

So we went to the village office. I told the clerk there that my father's name was Kobayashi—that's like Smith here. He went through records and records and finally he said my brother's Japanese name. I said, "That is my brother's Japanese name! Is my name, Tomiko, down there?" My name was crossed off because I was an American citizen. We told them my mother's name and he said, "Your uncle was my elementary school teacher and your aunt is still alive!"

The second clerk says, "I will take you there, because they live only a block away from me!" So we went over there, and my cousin was a little bit leery—three people showing up at the door and claiming that they are relatives. The clerk told them who I was, and my aunt said, "Oh yes, by all means, come in." She was ninety-nine years old! She was my mother's sister-in-law—my mother's brother's wife. We talked to her, and my daughter, Cathe, interviewed her.

Farming in California

My father heard of this property being sold in Bolsa—now called Westminster, out in Orange County. At that time, Japanese people were not allowed to own property. Since my father studied English and knew about these laws, he put it in my two older brothers' names. We had five acres. We grew alfalfa for the chickens. We had about 5,000 birds.

They used to have these nest boxes where the chickens laid their eggs and we cleaned them. Also, my mother weighed the eggs when she didn't know which was medium or large.

Next door to us was another poultry farmer. On the corner was a strawberry farmer. There were celery farmers who were Nisei (second generation Japanese Americans).

We were the first people to provide Knott's Berry Farm with chickens.[1]

Assimilation

My father always said, "You are living in America, so you better learn how to live that way. Not the Japanese cultural way, but the American way." Some children went to Japanese school after school. My father told us to go out for after-school sports and club activities.

My mother didn't speak English completely. She mixed English words with Japanese words. She said words in Japanese that were difficult for her to put into the English language.

COURTESY OF MARY ISHINO

Misao Kobayashi is holding Mary in her arms, with her five brothers.

COURTESY OF MARY ISHINO

Before he was relocated to Poston, Sahichiro Kobayashi owned this Rickenbacker car.

After Pearl Harbor

The day after Pearl Harbor, my brother wanted to go into the Army Air Force. They turned him down because of his Japanese ancestry. I thought that was strange. I was in my first year of college at Santa Ana. The FBI came to our house and searched our house for shortwave radios, cameras, and any other things, like guns. We didn't have any, but they took my brother's Boy Scout knife. That scared the daylights out of me!

They questioned my father and he spoke English, so they wanted him to come and work as an interrogator, but he said no. He had too many friends and didn't want to become an interrogator.

My father was incarcerated in jail. Eventually, he was held in a prisoner of war camp in Missoula, Montana, for about eight months.

My father said he was the one who knew English the best, so he bribed the guards to bring in the newspaper and knew what was going on in the world. He would tear it up and flush it down the toilet after he read it and told all of the other people the news. He wrote letters to my mother and she kept them. I still have them.

After he was cleared, he came to Poston, Arizona. From a cold place to a hot place—120 degrees in the shade in the summer at Poston!

We said, "Oh my God, we are back as a family!" It was good to see him back. My mother was going through menopause at the time. It was hard on her. When he came back, it was a big relief.

Relocation

We got a notice. I think the executive order came out in February and we left May 9. We went directly to Poston, Arizona. I thought we went by train, but my brother says we rode on busses. It seems as if I am mentally blocking that time out. I didn't want to go through it. He also said we were able to rent out our place before we left.

We had a Nisei group that met at the First Baptist Church in Garden Grove. The advisor to this group had a barn. They took in all of our extra furniture that we couldn't take with us. We took our valuable dishes. They kept our car for us. Eventually they drove over to Arizona, and we were able to use the car to go out East when we left camp.

Life at Poston Camp

When we first got there, we had to fill the mattress ticking with straw and make up our metal cots. I remember doing that. I said, "We are here, we have to make the best of the situation. There isn't anything that we can do."

There were four units in a barrack. As a block manager, my brother was able to get us an end unit for our family. My brother, who was married, was in the next unit, which was smaller. Then there were my mother, my two older brothers, and myself. Four of us were in the one end unit.

My married brother and two younger brothers were able to get into the other unit for four, because eventually my father was going to come. So there would be five of us in the end unit.

Since my three brothers had graduated from Cal-Poly in San Luis Obispo, they managed the poultry farm at camp where they

Mary Kobayashi's older brother lived in this small but neat corner of a barrack.

"Over time, people improved the landscape around our homes [at the camp]. . . . They planted trees, built gardens and small bridges. We had to be strong. We told ourselves, 'We have to make the best of the situation, there isn't anything that we can do,'" said Mary Ishino. Detainees created this Japanese garden in the desert at Poston.

raised birds. I remember that it was dusty and hot. My brothers had this motor from an incubator, and they set up a fan. They somehow had water going through the excelsior, and the fan blowing it into our room. Wasn't that clever?

The detainees built Japanese gardens with trees and a footbridge. There was a swimming pool. They brought the Colorado River in through a ditch.

At first, I worked in the block manager's office as a secretary. I didn't know how to take shorthand, but I knew how to type. Then they wanted someone for an assistant physical education teacher for middle school and junior high kids. I had almost completed my first year of college, so I became a teacher.

One day I had to take the children over to the hospital for physicals so they could participate in sports. I had to go through the administration building, and Iwao was sitting in one of the offices.

Iwao Ishino wrote in his diary on August 10, 1943: "With the continuous days of hot weather, many residents have been going to the river to fish and swim."

I thought, "Boy, he is good looking!" I found out that he lived in the same quad in the bachelor's quarter that I did. My friend who was the head physical education teacher knew him because they were from the same area in San Diego, and so we all started to get together. We would play volleyball and badminton. We would go to the church or a movie.

This is what I say when I give talks with Iwao. I give the lighter side. I say, "How many of you are eighteen or nineteen years old? How would you like to be put into a camp, where before you maybe knew twenty people in your hometown, now you have hundreds of people with different occupations and come from different backgrounds? Where else could an eighteen or nineteen year old have more good-looking guys to date? They laugh and giggle. Then I say, 'But you can't go anywhere alone, so you all have to go in a group.'"

I know of a case where one young man wanted to marry into an outcast group. In Japan, the Eta are the ones who killed the cattle and the animals. He wanted to marry this girl, and the parents objected to it, so the couple went over to the administration building and got permission to get married. The parents couldn't do anything to stop them, so they got married.

We had these outdoor showers with a cement floor and a grate. You stood on it so the water would drain through the open slats. My mother was taking a shower and got stung by a scorpion, so I took her to the hospital and they treated her.

We had to eat mutton and rice. Oh, did it smell! I still remember it, and I still hate it to this day.

Another bad thing was the toilets. They were open johns—just the back and the sides were closed. You didn't have a front door.

They had sinks, big tubs that you could wash your clothing in. Somebody wanted to go do some laundry, and it was dark in there so they switched on the light, and there were people in the tubs washing themselves!

The odd part is, they have those community baths in Japan, but they didn't like the showers. I think it was more the Nisei who didn't like the showers. I think the main thing was privacy in the shower and toilet.

My daughter said, "How come you didn't strike or raise a protest or anything?" I think it was a cultural thing. I think, what the authorities told us to do, we did. I think all of us said, "We're here, make the best of the situation." We were there from May 1942 until August of the following year.

Leaving Camp

I don't know how many people were left by the time they closed it. They said eight thousand in our camp, number one. They gave you $50 and that was it. Good luck! Just imagine when they closed camp, how many homeless people that they had.

I was going up to Washington, D.C., because I had two brothers out in Maryland. Secretary Ickes' wife had a poultry farm.[2] She wanted a manager for the farm, so my two brothers and their wives went out to Maryland.

My oldest brother and myself were the only ones from our family left in camp with our folks. My other two brothers had gone to Secretary Ickes' wife's poultry farm. My other brother Jim went to Chicago. My oldest brother was going out to Maryland, and I decided to go, and my folks said okay. So I went to Strayer Business College and worked as a housemaid in Washington, D.C.

Reunited

IWAO ISHINO: This is a story Mary should tell you, but I want to tell you. Harold L. Ickes was Secretary of the Interior, which included the War Relocation Authority and the Public Works Administration. Ickes was in favor of closing the camps and trying to encourage the American public to provide jobs for Japanese Americans.

Mrs. Ickes had a poultry farm in Maryland, near Washington, D.C. Mary's brothers were given a job out at the Ickes farm, because Mary's father had had this chicken farm in Santa Ana.

Knott's Berry Farm had a place like Zehnder's over here, where on Sunday's they had these fabulous chicken dinners. Mary's father provided the chickens for the place. He had the foresight of sending three of his sons to Cal-Poly to learn poultry husbandry. He had visions of having his poultry farm expanding.

So Mary went to Washington, D.C., with her brother, and I came out to work for the government. The reason that I tell you this, this is how I met and married Mary.

MARY KOBAYASHI ISHINO: There was a Japanese American Citizens' league that used to be in Washington, D.C. They started a USO program and had dances on the weekend. These men would come in that were going overseas to Europe. Before they went overseas we would have these dances for them.

At one of those dances, Iwao came. We talked and he said, "Would you like to go to church on Sunday?" I said, "Yes. However, I have been going with my girlfriend." He said, "That's all right." So we went, and then we started dating from then on.

We got married in June of 1944 because he was going into the

The Kobayashi family raised chickens before being relocated, and later at Poston Camp.

service. We went on our honeymoon and we came back and he reported to his board.

In Occupied Japan

When the U.S. occupied Japan, we went there because Iwao went to work for the Public Opinion and Sociological Research Division from 1949 to 1951. I didn't have the foggiest notion of what I would encounter or experience over there.

My brothers Fred and Jim were already there with the occupational forces. One worked for the CIC (Counter Intelligence Corps) and the other one worked for the education department.

I got along with the Japanese people because my husband was in the same office with several professors that were there. I would meet this Japanese lady who was the wife of one of the professors. I would give her coffee and sugar and she would give me rice. The rice was rationed in Japan. If she went to a restaurant, she had to take her rice with her for them to exchange.

We lived in a housing project that was at the U.S. Army base.

Iwao had a rank of GS12 or 13—I don't remember. We were in a housing area equivalent to majors and lieutenant colonels. All we met were Caucasians. My brothers lived in another housing unit and we would see them there.

Coming to Michigan

We couldn't go back to the West Coast for a while. It was the law at that time, because we were still at war with Japan. They were afraid there might be some sabotage. I didn't want to go back anyway.

I think it was very good that they scattered us throughout the United States. Not congregating us in California or in New York or Washington, D.C., or Chicago. I think the reason why they scattered us through all over, they considered us as individuals rather than a racial group. They didn't want us congregating in one area.

My folks wanted to go back to their poultry farm and my brothers did too. I was married and I was happy with where we were. Wherever Iwao went, we just made the best of the situation.

Life in Michigan

After all we've been through, we were still able to participate in various activities—yes, football games—and enjoy life in Michigan. While making a life in Michigan, I furthered my studies in Japanese flower arrangements. Originally, I had started lessons in 1950 and had received teacher certificates from the Ikenobo School and Sogetsu School in Japan. I am also the ikebana arranger at Michigan State University's University Club and was the president of the Ikebana International Lansing Chapter from 2007 to 2009. I have taught ikebana at Michigan State University's Evening College and at the University Club of Michigan State University.

I also joined various clubs including the Michigan State University Faculty Folk Club for faculty wives. I was president of the club in 1992–93 and Woman of the Year in 2007–2008. I was also co-president of the East Lansing Women's Club in 2003. Iwao and I are members of the Japanese American Citizens League and the

Mid-Michigan Asian Pacific American Association. I am also a member of the Asian Pacific American Women Association.

I also love to play golf.

NOTES

1. In 1920, Walter and Cordelier Knott began selling berries, jams, jellies, and pies from a roadside stand near Buena Park, California. In the 1930s they started serving fried chicken dinners along with their famous boysenberry pie. To entertain the customers who waited in line, sometimes for hours, Walter Knott built a ghost town, and later added attractions like a narrow-gauge train ride and panning for gold. By the time Disneyland opened nearby in 1955, Knott's Berry Farm was a full-fledged amusement park with roller coasters and theme parks.

2. Harold L. Ickes was Secretary of the Interior under Franklin D. Roosevelt, and was an outspoken critic of the Japanese American internment policy.

From Korea with Love

Prior to World War II, only about 2,000 Koreans had immigrated to the United States. After the war, some Koreans began arriving here, some as spouses of military servicemen. The liberalization of American immigration laws in 1965 coincided with rapid industrialization and urbanization in South Korea, spurring a new wave of more than half a million immigrants in the 1970s and 1980s.

One aspect of this immigration was the effort to place Korean children in American families. The Korean War had left many children orphaned. Unmarried mothers faced the stigma of single motherhood and knew their Amerasian children would be ostracized. Since adoption in Korea traditionally occurred only within extended families, the South Korean government welcomed the interest of Americans and other Westerners in adopting these children. About 100,000 children have found new homes since 1954.

Oh Ae Kyung was two years old when abandoned on the streets of Seoul. She lived in a Korean orphanage for five years. In 1972, when she was seven years old, Shirley and Richard Hanna of East Lansing, Michigan adopted her. She flew to America with about thirty other adopted children. Her parents renamed her Jennifer Hanna.

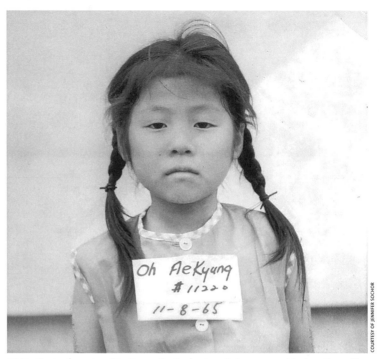

COURTESY OF JENNIFER SOCHOR

Oh Ae Kyung (now Jennifer Hanna Sochor) was only two years old when the police found her walking the streets of Seoul, Korea. They took her to an orphanage where she stayed until age seven. The orphanage sent this picture of Jennifer to prospective adoptive parents in America. It shows her Korean name, her birth date, and her identification number.

She grew up and went to school in East Lansing. Today, Jennifer lives with her husband and their four children in St. Johns, Michigan. She has worked for the Michigan Historical Museum for more than twenty years.

Martha Aladjem (Climo) Bloomfield interviewed Jennifer on April 28, 1999.

Life in a Korean Orphanage

Someone found me walking on the streets in Korea and took me to the police station. No one claimed me, so the police put me in an orphanage. Supposedly I was two years old.

I forgot the name of the orphanage, but it is an hour north of Seoul, Korea. I lived there for five years until I came to the United States on Christmas Eve in 1972.

It was a ten-story building and it had brick walls around it so you couldn't get out. They had Doberman dogs to watch us so we couldn't escape. One time—and I don't remember how old I was—I tried to climb out. I got scratches on my face from the dogs. After that, I realized I would be there for a while until I got adopted.

There were a bunch of different rooms on the floors—I think about ten. In one room, they had a big huge blanket on the floor. You slept underneath it. They put children who still wet their pants in a separate area in the same room. I asked if I could help take care of the infants and babies. I guess I was good with babies and kids. I did that right up until I left for the United States.

Each room had a different foster parent. We had to ask permission to go to play outside. I was the go-getter. I would say, "Let's go!" I told the other kids that our foster mother was away and she will never know. So everybody listened to me and we went outside and we played. Then we said, "Here she comes." We all ran back inside and pretended that we were all sweeping and cleaning and nothing had ever happened, but she knew what was going on. She made us take our pants off and spanked our hands and butts with a two-inch-thick piece of wood. I thought this was all my fault. I felt bad. Nobody blamed me because everybody was really nice. We never did that again! After that, we always asked permission to go outside to play. I don't think they ever allowed us to leave the building even to go somewhere else—to be adventurous.

When I was in the orphanage, I met a grandmother. She was probably eighty years old. She was really nice to me. She really liked me because I was always happy and I liked to have people around. I visited with the grandmother as much as I could, maybe one or two days out of the week.

We went to mass every Sunday. I remember going there and singing and learning English. They wouldn't let us learn too much—just simple things. I believe I just learned how to sing Korean songs.

We always had to eat our food or something bad would happen.

One day this new boy came along and he didn't like spinach. I told him he had better eat all of his spinach or else something really bad would happen to him. So he said, "Oh nothing bad will happen to me." He didn't eat the spinach. He had to go underneath the stairs and stay there for a couple of days without any food. They gave him water, but I sneaked food to him so he wouldn't starve. If I got caught I would have really been in trouble! After that, he ate his spinach. Everybody ate their food, but sometimes if they couldn't eat it, I tried to eat it.

Once a month we celebrated everybody's birthday and we had cake. Otherwise, we never had sweets. We weren't actually allowed to eat sweets or anything like that, so that is why they gave us cake once a month. We never had candy or gum.

I kept a positive attitude, hoping that one day I would be adopted. One of my friends had already been adopted before I was. She told me that I would be next. She told me to have a positive attitude. As long as you are always happy and helpful, God will give you the opportunity to go somewhere. I just kept thinking that.

She left a year before I did. I haven't heard from her since then. I sometimes wish we could meet so I could see what her life was about. She might have moved to California, or to who knows where.

Flying to a New Home

I was really happy when I found out that I was going to be adopted. I was glad that I wasn't going to be in the orphanage for the rest of my life. I knew that if I had stayed there I would probably be dead or sickly. I think most kids who lived there didn't survive very long, because of the way it was. I probably would have survived the longest because I always had a positive attitude. I always helped out. Most people were sad and gloomy. I always told them if they were happy there is a way to get out or somehow, in the future someone would adopt them.

My adoptive parents, Shirley and Richard Hanna, sent me some pictures of them three or four months before I came to the United States so I would know what they looked like when I got to Michigan. I had a picture of my mom in the kitchen, my three

Jennifer's mother, Shirley Hanna, cooks in her kitchen in East Lansing. Shirley sent these pictures to Jennifer in Korea so she would recognize her new family when she arrived in the United States.

Jennifer's new adoptive sisters, Catherine, Mary, and Ellen (*from left to right, oldest to youngest*), outside their home in East Lansing.

COURTESY OF JENNIFER SOCHOR

Jennifer left an orphanage in South Korea when she was adopted by a family in America. This is Jennifer's new home in East Lansing.

sisters—Catherine, Mary, and Ellen—outside and my dad on his motorcycle. I sent them pictures of me so they would know what I looked like when I got off the plane.

I remember going to the airport in Seoul, then flying and sleeping a lot. When I was awake on the plane, all I thought about was going to America. When I wasn't sleeping, I walked around and helped the other kids who were being adopted—to keep my mind off the ride.

I had motion sickness. I had to go to the bathroom because I was so sick. One meal they gave me was an American style meal. They gave me Coke and some type of sandwich and the airline peanuts. After I drank that Coke, all that sugar made me sick for five hours. I was so sick I didn't even think about coming here. I just wanted to go to bed. The flight was too long for me. All I wanted to do was sleep.

I guess I was special or something because I was the only one who wore a hanbok—a Korean traditional dress. It's made of silk. I still have it. I'm hoping that when my girls grow up they can fit into it and see what they look like. My mom couldn't figure out why I was the only one dressed up. Most of the kids were just wearing pants and a shirt. Even my friend Rachel, who was adopted and

Jennifer wore this colorful, traditional Korean dress, a hanbok, when she came to America in 1972. At age seven, she was the oldest child on the plane and the only one who wore a hanbok among the thirty children who were coming to be adopted in the United States. Her Michigan family drove to Chicago to pick her up at the airport on Christmas Eve.

Jennifer Sochor wore these traditional, colorful shoes on the airplane when she came from Korea to Chicago in 1972.

Jennifer in the arms of her new father, Richard Hanna, at the Chicago airport. Her family brought her the balloons to greet her.

went to the United States before me, she didn't have a hanbok. She just wore normal clothes, like shorts and a T-shirt, because she came in the summer.

When I got off the plane, I was trying to find my parents. I was the last one to get off the plane, but my mom knew it was me. She was amazed that I was wearing that dress. She knew that I must have been special because I wore that dress and nobody else did. The interpreter was saying that very rarely do you find someone wearing a hanbok because it's so expensive. I have no idea who gave it to me. My parents have no idea. Maybe it was the grandmother. I guess we'll never know.

I remember my dad hugging and squeezing me so tightly I couldn't breathe, but I didn't say anything. He was so big and I was so small—he is six feet five. My mom is only five foot two. I remember being on my dad's shoulder and looking down and thinking, "Oh my goodness" because he was so tall.

My dad gave me five balloons. There was a girl who saw my balloons. My mom was surprised that I gave two of the balloons to the little girl. She thought that was cute and special. Then she knew I was a kind person, always thoughtful. She didn't have to worry about her teaching me any manners. I felt bad for the little girl because she didn't get a balloon when she got there, so I gave

Jennifer celebrates Christmas with a tree in her new home in East Lansing. She arrived in America on Christmas Eve. She could not celebrate Christmas until a couple of days after the actual holiday because she had been sick from the plane trip and slept a lot when she arrived at her new home.

two of them to her. I tried to bite the string but my dad used a jackknife he had.

The orphanage sent documents to my adoptive parents that said I liked to talk, sleep and eat a lot. That still holds true today. My husband just laughs about that. When he read that piece of paper, he just about died! I just love to eat. I've always been like that. People always ask me how I stay so small and thin. I can eat so much. My colleagues at the museum say they don't know where I put it. My mother-in-law says that, too. I must just have a high metabolism.

My mom told me that I've always had a positive attitude. I don't know how I got it. She said I was very independent and outgoing. I was never shy. I talked to people—strangers, whoever. It didn't matter who it was. I just did that. My mom would say sometimes that you have to be really careful when you are little and are not supposed to talk to or take something from strangers. I knew that. I just liked to talk to people.

They said that I never complained or cried. They were always curious because I didn't really smile. I always had a gloomy face. In their mind I guess I did, but to me, I was always happy.

Starting School

Going to school was totally different from what I expected. My mother went to Pinecrest Elementary School to set everything up. At first, I was afraid of going to school because I thought I was going back to the orphanage. My mom explained to me that my kindergarten teacher knew all about me ahead of time. She said that my teacher, Mrs. Olmstead, would help me get around and I shouldn't be afraid. If the kids teased me, I should let my teacher know. My teacher had already told the class about me. I remember that I stared at everybody. I didn't say anything; I just looked around.

A couple of days after school started, I realized that this wasn't an orphanage. My mom couldn't believe that I wanted to go back to school. I told my mom all about my friends at school. What I liked about it was playing and taking naps. I was learning a lot of new words from everyone.

In the beginning, I was listening to what people were saying.

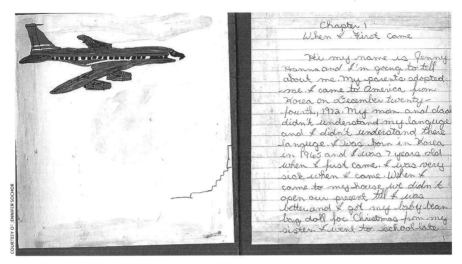

Jennifer Sochor, originally from Korea, wrote this diary as part of a school project in 1976, the same year she became a U.S. citizen, at Whitehills Elementary School in East Lansing. She began her retrospective journal with her airplane trip from Seoul to Chicago.

I wanted to be able to talk properly. Even though they thought I couldn't talk, I really could. I just didn't want to say anything because I wanted to make sure everything was okay. I do remember singing "Mary Had a Little Lamb" and "Twinkle Twinkle Little Star." They tape-recorded that. That was all the English I could speak at the time. I listened to what everybody was saying. That's the reason I repeated those words. So that I could hear the sound and I wouldn't make a mistake.

My mom remembered that when we were crossing the street I would squat down. I used to do that because the traffic lights took so long. My mom said I would squat and talk to people. It was funny; people wondered what in the world I was doing. My mom said that it was just my way. They laughed and they thought it was kind of cute. Sometimes I would do it at school and they couldn't believe that someone that little would do that.

Someday I should go visit Mrs. Olmstead. She would remember me because she remembers everyone's names and faces—even though it has been a long time.

I loved playing in the snow. I had only seen a little bit of snow in

Korea. I loved going outside and making snow angels, making forts, and throwing snowballs. My dad would always take me sledding at Angel Hill in Lansing over by Marshall Park. Someone ran into me and I was knocked out. The ambulance came and my mom and dad were afraid something serious had happened. I was fine, though.

I decided to try tennis. I wanted to make the East Lansing High School team and I worked my butt off. Most of these students had been playing since they were three or four years old. I did pretty well for a late bloomer. I didn't make varsity my freshman year because there were too many people who were trying out. I made it the second year through my senior year. My sophomore year I was second in doubles and fourth in singles. I really worked that summer. I had played tennis all year round.

Return to Korea

My parents gave me a high school graduation gift, a trip to Korea. They wanted me to go there and experience the culture I was born into, so I'd have an idea of what was going on.

I went there for two weeks. We got to meet the mayor of Seoul and the president of the International Children's Service. We met the daughter of the person who started the adoption program. Harry Holt was the one who started it. He passed away, so his kids are the ones who are running it now.

I knew I wouldn't be able to find my real parents or any brothers or sisters. Thirty of us went on the trip and five of us could not find our siblings. My orphanage was too far away for them to take me there because it was an hour north of Seoul. The other students had lived in an orphanage right in Seoul, so they got to visit the orphanage and meet their siblings or parents. I wanted to at least try. We went to the courthouse where all the records are kept and I got to see my card. There was no information there because I was abandoned in the streets. Then I thought, "It's not worth it to struggle with this and have it on my mind." My adoptive parents are like my real parents. That's what I consider them.

They did a TV interview with all of us. When we did the interview, a lot of people cried. The reason they decided to have the interview was to find out why their parents put them up for adoption. Most of their parents said they couldn't afford to raise them back then because of the war. The other reason was they weren't allowed to have girls and they were only supposed to have one kid and it had to be a boy and if it were a girl they would actually kill them. Most of the girls were put in the orphanage. It is kind of like in China. They always want a first-born male child and they are only supposed to have one or two children. That's why you don't see too many that have more than one child. That made me sad and disappointed. Why would people do that?

We traveled to different places to sightsee and get an idea about what Korea was like. In addition to Seoul, we went to several different cities. Pusan was a dumpy place. All the buildings were close together and there were clotheslines all over the place and it was mostly run-down. I felt sorry for those people because they didn't have any money. Then we went to Daegook. We went to the university there to see what the schools were like in Korea.

We went to this place called Itaewon in Seoul. All the Americans go there for shopping. It is supposed to have Gucci and other name brands. They had KFC, Burger King, McDonalds, and Wendy's, but it wasn't the same. The hamburgers were a little different.

I remember trying different foods that I hadn't had before. They ate their meat raw. I didn't like that. I like mine cooked. When I found out they ate dogs and horses, I said, "I don't think I am going to eat this!"

There are dangerous drivers there. They drive too fast. I had a screaming fit one time. I thought the bus was going to hit this car. Everyone looked at me. They are maniac drivers. That is the way they have to be because it is such a small area. They said they have few accidents. We saw one, but it is very rare.

I didn't know what to expect there. I didn't know if people would put me down because I was adopted. I thought people would disgrace me or wouldn't like me. Everybody in Korea was really friendly. I was really surprised. I was glad I saw some people who were shorter than I was. All of these older people—their backs are crooked because they worked in the rice fields. I was amazed how they survived from that. I saw people working in the rice fields and it was kind of neat to see what it was like—to put the seeds in the water, plant the rice. Everywhere you go you see rice paddies.

Friends and Family

It was nice to have three sisters who helped me even though they weren't my real sisters. To me, they were. It didn't matter to me because I didn't think of it that way. They were like second mothers. They watched out for me all the time and they still do.

I remember that they took me to a bar when I was in middle school. I don't think my mom ever knew about that! They just wanted me to see what it was like. They would take me to the R-rated movies. My mom would have died!

I had two friends here who had been adopted from Korea. My best friend was Rachel, who was adopted here before I was. She used to live in Mason. We always went to the Ingham County Fair together. We got along because we acted like we were sisters. We were both alike and everybody thought we looked like sisters.

Rachel and I used to talk about when we were kids. We always wanted to find our real mothers. Sometimes it makes me sad because I wish I had. Then sometimes I think, "No." People would ask me all the time about my real parents. I told them that my adopted parents are my real parents. I do wish I could find my biological parents, but I don't think I will be able to. I want to ask my biological mother why they gave me up.

I have another friend who is also adopted from Korea. She has a totally different attitude. She hates having been adopted. She doesn't like to talk about it at all. Her adopted dad wasn't nice; he was pessimistic. Every time I was around her, people would come up and they would be curious about what nationality I was. I have always been outgoing and not shy. I would tell them that I am adopted. She would say, "Why do you say those kinds of things?" I would tell her, "Because that's who I am. I like to talk to people and I want people to know who I am."

My parents always showed love and affection and made sure I was brought up right. That's how I'm bringing my kids up.

Every year on Christmas Eve, my parents always did something special whether it was going out to dinner or they would remind me, "Do you know what today is?" December 2002, my kids and husband and I went to Cocoa Beach, Florida, on a winter vacation. I got a $30 check from my parents to remind me on Christmas Eve what day it was. I had been in Michigan for thirty years!

Sharkey S. Haddad, a Chaldean from Iraq

Call Your Brother in Michigan

W hen Sharkey Haddad turned seven years old in 1968, the Baath Party, took control of the Iraqi government for the second time since his birth. Party leaders knew that many Iraqis objected to Baath rule. Between 1968 and 1973, Baath dictator Saddam Hussein ruthlessly eliminated any group or person suspected of challenging Baath rule through a series of sham trials, executions, and assassinations.

While Saddam Hussein and his Baath Party ruled Iraq, Sharkey's father was arrested. Saddam Hussein supported Islam. For people such as Sharkey's family, who are not Muslim, Iraq was a dangerous place to be. Sharkey Haddad left Iraq in 1977, and since then, much has changed.

On December 13, 2003, United States forces captured Saddam Hussein, and he was brought to trial by the Iraqi government. He was convicted of crimes against humanity, sentenced to death by hanging, and executed on December 30, 2006.

Martha Aladjem (Climo) Bloomfield interviewed Sharkey S. Haddad in 2000 at the West Bloomfield High School. At the time he was the Community Liaison Specialist for the West Bloomfield School District. He then went to work as a Linguist Specialist for Global Linguist Solutions of Southfield, Michigan, where he

Sharkey S. Haddad (*second from right*) and his friends spend a night out.

recruited, screened, and tested Arabic translators to support the U.S. Military's mission in Iraq.

Chaldean History

Chaldeans trace their ancestry and history to the Babylonian Empire, which was about six or seven hundred years before the birth of Christ. Up until today Chaldeans still read, write, and speak the ancient Aramaic that was spoken by the Chaldean people and the Chaldean Empire of Babylon. Chaldeans still have names, last names mostly, that you'd find if you read the ancient history of Babylon.

The reason we were able to survive—despite all the dynasties that conquered what is now called Iraq and used to be called Mesopotamia, despite the invasion or takeover by the Persian Empire under Cyrus the Great, by the Greek Macedonians under Alexander the Great, by the Roman Empire, by the Arabs who followed Mohammed and his prophecy, by the Ottoman Empire around the 1800s, which ruled most of that region until World War II, when the Ottomans were defeated and the Ottoman Empire was broken up, despite the toll of these invasions on the Chaldean population of 600,000 (at one time millions) in that region as a religious and ethnic speaking group—is that we migrated to the northern part of Iraq and lived in villages in the mountains.

We felt that living away from the big cities, the big armies, and the government of whatever empire was governing Iraq at the time, not being involved in political situations in that region, and following the policy of the Chaldean priests for the past five or six hundred years, would relieve us from persecution. And sure enough, it did! That's why we still have churches that were built five hundred years ago, even eight hundred years ago, still untouched in the Christian villages of the northern part of Iraq.

[Eventually] more and more Chaldeans sought higher education. Our churches only had education until sixth grade, so the Chaldeans had to migrate from those Christian villages to bigger cities where they had high schools and universities. Employment then became an option instead of going back to the villages. Around 1850 Chaldeans were migrating from the Chaldean villages in the northern part of Iraq and going to big cities like Baghdad and Basrah in pursuit of higher education. Chaldeans ended up staying in those big cities after receiving their education and working in different professions.

Since 1850, until around the turn of the century, Chaldeans were building their own churches in those big cities. Those churches are not as ancient as those in the villages. There was a period of time where the churches and the synagogues—because there were a great number of Jewish synagogues and Jewish people in what is now called Iraq—were all destroyed. That was because of the way Islam looked at other religions. There were at least 200 or 300 temples and churches in what is now called Iraq, most of them were in big cities like Basrah, but yet there is no trace of them now.

Family Ties

The first thought that goes through my mind about my childhood is the playground area. Boy, we had a lot of fun, us kids. I guess that goes back to when I was three or four years old, playing with the children of the neighborhood. We lived in an area in the neighborhood that probably was considered a lower-income community. The neighbors all knew each other—the children played together.

It started on the playground, a lot of fun, a lot of loving and support. And we didn't have a lot, we certainly weren't wealthy. I didn't know it at the time. But now, when I look back, we lived in a lower-income community or neighborhood. But life was still fun and fulfilling. The entire country was not well off because the impact of oil production had not hit everybody at the time yet.

I remember being surrounded by aunts and uncles and my grandfather and grandmother living in the same household. It's always fun for children to be surrounded by adults. I remember receiving a lot of TLC. When my mother or father disciplined me, there was always somebody else I could go to and feel loved and wanted.

We lived with Grandma, Grandpa—my dad's parents—and my dad's seven brothers and sisters. In the Middle East, it is expected of the oldest member of the male children to continue to live in the same household as his parents because it's looked upon him to replace the father if the father passes away, to take charge of looking after the welfare of the family. Most of, if not all of, the older sons get married and continue to live in the house. They have a section of the house for themselves and their newborns. That was the case with my father because he was the oldest among his four brothers and three sisters.

That's really powerful and important, I think, because one of the biggest challenges facing the Chaldean family in today's society living in Michigan is that they don't enjoy that close-knit family as much any more. Our children tend to grow up with a great deal of dependency on Mom and Dad for guidance, supervision, and emotional and social support. Unfortunately, you find the fathers in the Chaldean community working long hours to make ends meet. The mothers are so overwhelmed by the household chores and taking care of the children, that they don't provide enough parental support. When they turn around, the aunts and the uncles are also overwhelmed and they don't live in the same household. The Chaldean family links are missing. It has been hurting the Chaldean youngsters in this generation.

Growing up, I lived in the port of Basrah, the third largest city in Iraq, located on the Persian Gulf in the southern part of Iraq bordering Kuwait. This is where the conflict took place in 1990 and 1991 and where the majority are Muslims, an Arabic-speaking population. There were very few Chaldean families in that region. We had about two or three Chaldean churches in the area that addressed the spiritual needs of the Chaldean people.

My grandparents on both sides were born in the villages in the north. My parents were born in the cities. That's how I trace my childhood. My parents would trace their childhood to Baghdad as well, but remember visiting the villages because their parents were born in the Christian villages—the Chaldean villages.

I was born in Basrah because my father sought employment there with the oil industry. His father made the decision to go down to Basrah to seek employment but not necessarily education. That was the case with his father and he decided to bring his entire family with him to Basrah and to Baghdad. First, he located in Baghdad. Some of his sons and daughters were born in Baghdad, and then he decided to make a move to Basrah to find employment as well. That's when my dad became employed, and we also stayed there.

I remember that my father decided to move out of his parents' house and get a section of a house. This is common in Iraqi neighborhoods. If you have a large house, you will have an attachment, an area where you have two bedrooms, kitchen, and a bathroom and a family room and a door that can be locked. That section could be leased to people as extra income for the family or sometimes they have an attachment so the son can live next door instead of moving away. I remember that my father and my mother decided to move out of the house but not too far because they wanted to be close to the relatives.

This is still common in Chaldean culture. The majority of Chaldeans buy homes in the same neighborhood where other Chaldeans live, and it is not unusual for the Chaldean wife to look at an area for a house that is close to her mother. In American society, the mother would consider herself lucky if her daughter or son decide to live in the same state. In the Chaldean community or culture, the Chaldean wife will generally convince her husband to buy a home close to her parents for the support that grandparents provide.

For example, many grandparents take care of their grand-children, especially if the mother works. In my family, my wife's mother watches our children three days a week and my mother watches them the other two. They both live within two miles of our home. We chose the location of our home not simply because we wanted them to watch our kids but because we knew the proximity would make our families closer.

I think that my father lived his own life and my mother lived her own life. The Middle Eastern society at that time did not allow women to participate in employment, in supporting causes or events that impacted society. Women played a traditional role. The expectation of women was to raise their children and look after the house chores, and for some women to take care of their mothers and fathers. So I watched my parents live separate lives.

Moving to Saudi Arabia

I witnessed my father working hard, trying to accomplish things his own father could not. The fact that he accepted a position with Chrysler in Saudi Arabia in Jeddah, which is a port on the Red Sea and one of the largest cities after Riyadh, the capital, is proof that my father wanted to do better for us, for the family, for himself. In 1967, my father connected with a friend who also was Chaldean who was working with Chrysler in Saudi Arabia. "If you come to Saudi Arabia, I'll provide you with the following salary"—which is something my father could not have dreamed of making in Basrah. So it was a big move for us.

I was about five years old when we moved, but we didn't move immediately. I remember living without our dad at the age of five. I don't know if I remember missing my dad, but I do remember looking forward to meeting him because he went to Saudi Arabia ahead of us, about six months ahead of us, just to make sure that life in Saudi Arabia was good enough to raise a family, that the income was stable, and that the job was comfortable.

I remember traveling to Saudi Arabia. I still remember the fear and the hardship of that journey, that migration from Basrah, Iraq, to Jeddah, Saudi Arabia. I remember our being in a different culture, among a different people who did not speak the language. My mother was very powerless. She didn't know what to do, where to go.

Then I remember being in Kuwait and again my mother struggling as far as trying to find out how to get on a bus or what transportation to take. That's an example of how women in that region didn't make decisions and could not survive on their own without a male, or a husband.

My father was not on that trip and we were scared. We didn't know whom to trust. We didn't know what to do. I had similar feelings, not as bad, when we came to the United States. We didn't know the language. We didn't know how to communicate with people. We worried about that. We didn't know how we were going to like it. And we didn't know if we were going to survive. And when I say survive, I don't necessarily mean life or death, but I mean as far as living the same lifestyle that we were used to. We worried about losing that and living a lifestyle that we were not accustomed to.

But we made the migration to Saudi Arabia. We experienced hardships. The main reason was that my mother felt helpless, but we ended up meeting our father. I remember it was the summer of '67. It was very hot. I looked forward to meeting and seeing him again. My youngest brother could not remember him and was afraid to hug him because he had forgotten him. He did not want to go to him until after about five or six hours of being in his company. My father had left when I was five; my brother was about two years old. There are four boys in my family—no sisters unfortunately—and we are all one year apart. We lived in Saudi Arabia. My father had a good job. My mother did not work. She stayed at home raising us.

We went to private schools in Saudi Arabia, at first where foreigners mainly go. They're Arabic-speaking foreigners—Egyptians, Palestinians, Lebanese, Iraqis, any family who came from the Middle East, who were not Saudis. Their families come for employment. In Saudi Arabia, around that time in the sixties and

A group photo of Sharkey (*third from right*) and his friends camping in Saudi Arabia, the summer of 1971. Sharkey said, "Family recreation in Saudi Arabia was as simple as driving to the desert outside of the city and camp[ing] with other families and friends."

the seventies and even the fifties, their labor was almost zero. Their labor force did not exist. Oil came in a very short period of time and because of oil, things were happening very fast. Hospitals and schools were built.

All of sudden Saudi Arabia discovered they had a lot of oil and things were being built left and right but there was no labor for it. They didn't have any teachers. They didn't have any doctors. They didn't have any engineers. They didn't have any employees who could fill in the labor force. As a result, they had to depend on Arabic-speaking individuals from the surrounding, neighboring countries, Egypt, Lebanon, Palestine, Iraq. That's how my father got his job.

My father spoke Arabic and Chaldean, which are two very different languages. In Saudi Arabia, they speak Arabic as well. They speak with a different dialect than that from Iraq but it's still Arabic. I only spoke Arabic at the time because we lived in Arabic neighborhoods in Basrah and we used to listen to our parents speak Chaldean when they didn't want us to understand anything, which is a common practice with most families.

We lived in Jeddah, Saudi Arabia, for about four years. My dad got a promotion to Riyadh, the capital of Saudi Arabia, and so we moved again. This time we switched from the private schools that we were used to, with very few Saudi students and teachers who were also from outside Saudi Arabia, to schools where we were the minority.

We noticed the difference right away. Unlike in private schools where everyone is a foreigner, we were the minority. One in 500 was not Saudi, who spoke with an accent, not a Saudi accent. That's when discrimination started. We realized that there were people in Saudi Arabia who didn't like us. And of course, that was even before they found out that we were Christians. When they found out we were Christians, even more discrimination took place against us.

That's when my dad started telling us to hide our religion, our identity. That was his way of helping us to escape discrimination and kids picking on us. I still remember them calling us "the infidels" because we were not Muslim. Anyone who was not Muslim was an infidel in their opinion. I used to walk with a buddy of mine, a friend of mine in the neighborhood, and another group of kids would be walking across the street and they'd say, "Hey, there's the infidel, the Christian boy." And of course that didn't feel good. But, you know, it created the scars that I still carry with me today and sometimes I wonder whether it's because of these scars I'm so committed to building and improving race relations in the Detroit metropolitan area.

I remember a story. I used to enjoy playing soccer and I was very good at it. I remember it as if it just happened yesterday that we were in the neighborhood one day and the two captains were picking players. One of the captains picked me at the beginning stages because of what they saw, of the way they saw me play. I remember the other kids behind the boy said, "No, don't pick this boy. He's Christian." And sure enough I was not picked because of that. I remember the experiences of exclusion and discrimination, of not feeling welcome, from a long time ago.

Back to Iraq

In 1974, my dad decided that enough was enough. For us to celebrate Christmas, we had to sneak into the American compounds. There were American families who worked in Saudi Arabia because of the oil industry. They used to live in homes that were modern, like the ones that you build out of trailers, but they used to be surrounding those neighborhoods with a big yard to separate them from the natives, the Saudis.

You can imagine how big that wall was. It was like a mini-neighborhood where they had their own youth center, their own swimming pool, you know, things that the kids of those families had to do, so I remember sneaking there. It was during Christmastime, and sitting in a mass at Christmastime, secretly, because we didn't want the Saudis to know that there was a building, a hall that was being used as a church. The Americans used to be very cautious about inviting Arabic Christians or Chaldeans, because they didn't want the word to spread and the law enforcement agents to say, "Hey, what are you practicing Christianity in Saudi Arabia?" I remember that very well.

My father decided to move back to Iraq because he felt that working in Saudi Arabia for eight or nine years, he had made enough money to go home. He sent the family first to get established and left that responsibility to my mother, again. I stayed with my father because I did not do so well in the eighth grade. In the Middle East, you have seven classes during the year in the school system. If you fail one of these classes, you get one more chance to take the test again in the summer. If you fail that test, you end up repeating the entire school year, not just the one class. Even if you got an A in math, you still have to take math again. Even if you got an A in social studies, you still have to take it again. So you repeat the whole school year. I had failed math and had to stay behind to take the test again in the summertime because I didn't want to fail that class and have to start a year behind back in Iraq. I ended up staying, studying hard and passing. I ended up joining my family in Bagdad about three months later.

My father put me on an airplane by myself and I traveled to

Sharkey S. Haddad (*back row, fourth from left*) was a member of the Zawra Soccer Club in Baghdad in the summer of 1975. Sharkey remembers, "Soccer was the number one sport in Iraq, and like many other youth, my dream was to play pro."

Iraq. I was about fourteen. At the age of fourteen, neither my three brothers nor I enjoyed a close relationship with our father or mother. We did have a better relationship with my mother because we spent more time with her.

This is a very common situation among Chaldean youth today. Unfortunately, when they don't see enough of Dad, there is very little room to create any closeness, that father-son, father-daughter relationship. As a result, during the teenage years, there are more situations of Chaldean youth rebelling, more so among males than females, because the females tend to spend more time with their mothers because the mothers are around. They tend to have heart-to-heart talks particularly about female issues. As a result of that, a relationship between the two develops. However, in most cases, the males don't enjoy that. They can't talk about their issues with their mothers. The father isn't around for them to establish a relationship, so they end up relying on their peers or their older brothers sometimes. If their older brother is mature with a good head on his shoulders, then he's a good role model. If the older brother is someone who needs help himself, you can see what kind of impact he's going to have on his younger brothers. In the old country, the rebellion of teenagers was not as frequent because there were other role models surrounding the youth, uncles, aunts, cousins who were older and responsible. They would always take the teens under their wings and give them support.

Anyway, my father returned to Iraq about six months later during the winter of 1975. The day that my father came back to Iraq, he was hurt because I decided that I needed to play soccer with my friends in the neighborhood instead of waiting at home for him to arrive. I don't know why I did that, but I was a child, and most fourteen-year-olds are pushed to do things based on their feelings. And maybe the fact that there was a lack of closeness was a reason that I could say, "I can always see my dad as soon as I finish up my soccer game so."

It was that winter, sometime after my dad returned to Iraq from Saudi Arabia, that the incident took place that changed our lives forever. One day, I remember vividly, my dad didn't come home. We were very concerned. The following day came and he was still not home. We saw my mom cry and, of course, when she cried, we all became scared. My mother started making phone calls to her brothers and sisters asking for help, saying he had not come home. Something happened.

I remember being scared—too scared to even go to the police department. If they thought that my dad had done something wrong and that they did something to him like kill him or throw him in jail or whatever, we felt that anyone who went to ask them would get the same treatment. The reason we were fearful was because of previous experiences our parents and relatives told us about. The police mistreated mainly the Christians and Jews and other minorities because we didn't have any backbone. We didn't have any people in high positions to stand up for us and say, "Hey, wait a minute. What are you doing this for? This is not right." Of course, no civil rights existed in most countries. They still don't in most Middle East countries. So we were afraid to ask about our own father.

"I Want You to Call Your Brother in Michigan"

Three days later, he showed up—very, very tired, not bathed, with a beard, almost a full beard. And the first words that came out of his mouth were, "Listen to me and listen to me very carefully." He was addressing my mother. We were all so overwhelmed and happy, yet crying because we couldn't believe he was actually back. Then he said, "I want you to sell everything we have! We're getting out of this country. I want you to call your brother in Michigan." The uncle that my father was referring to was my mom's brother, who had gone to study in Montana and then went to Michigan to work as an engineer for a company in the fifties.

At the time, he just never had any interest in coming back home. I take that back. He did decide to come back home. He did work for a company. He just couldn't tolerate it. He was comparing the workforce and society and the environment in Iraq to Michigan and he decided that it was better to work in Michigan. Now, keep in mind that this is all in the seventies, and in the seventies we had a small Chaldean population in Michigan. There were probably about 10,000 to 15,000 Chaldeans. So my uncle wasn't alone there and we wouldn't be either. They had their Chaldean get-togethers, Chaldean weddings where they saw everyone. They had their Chaldean coffee shops where they got together. There was enough reason for him to say, "Forget it. I don't enjoy working in Baghdad, Iraq. I'm not going to go back."

Getting back to the story, my father said to my mother, "Sell everything. I'm leaving first to make sure they don't catch me again. And then you need to catch up with me." Yet again, my mother was put in a situation where she was given a big responsibility but very little experience in which to deal with it.

My father shared with us what happened that day that he didn't come home. It turned out that this was all because he was driving an American car. In the sixties and seventies, it was very uncommon to drive an American car because after 1967 Iraq cut relationships with America because of America taking sides with Israel and their war in 1967 with Iraq with the Arabs. Because of that, some Arabic countries cut diplomatic relations with the U.S., boycotted the

U.S.—for example, Egypt, Iraq, Syria, Yemen. And because of that, they figured, "What's an American car doing in Iraq?" My father had bought an American car because he worked for Chrysler. He was allowed to bring one vehicle without paying taxes on it. He figured, "What the heck? I worked for Chrysler. I have money. Let us enjoy driving a nice car." So he brought an American car with him.

He was stopped by the secret police. Of course, they didn't need a reason to stop anyone over there. They stopped him for questions. He showed them his passport and they saw he had been living in Saudi Arabia for eight or nine years. That's when they were alarmed and decided they needed to take and keep him for three days of questioning and interrogation. My father told us that he didn't know if he was going to come out alive.

They didn't torture him, but they treated him as if he were an animal. They didn't allow him to take a bath. They didn't provide him adequate food. They didn't do the things that any humanitarian agency would do. Anyway, to him that was enough. Enough was finally enough.

He took off to Saudi Arabia. As soon as he got to Riyadh, where he still had ties, he contacted the American Embassy, and the American Embassy got an application from my uncle in Michigan.

We decided to go to Saudi Arabia in our effort to go to America. Before we got to Saudi Arabia, we were very, very scared that someone would find out, because at the time, the Iraqi government did not allow any family or any person to leave the country. It's not like in America where you say, "I want to move out. I want to go somewhere." People did not enjoy freedom, so we had to lie to people. People were asking us, "Where are you going?" We had to lie and tell people, "We're going back to Saudi Arabia, because my dad got a new contract." Of course, our relatives knew. But, it's unbelievable how concerned we were and scared, because if they would have found out, they could have kept us as hostages until my dad came back, and then they would have applied consequences to him for trying to escape the country.

They didn't have a problem if we were going to Saudi Arabia for employment. But the restriction placed on Iraqis going to America was a problem. On our passports, it said we were allowed to go anywhere except Israel and America. Because of this restriction, we couldn't get a visa from Iraq. It was very secretive. And we were very much afraid that at the last minute someone was going to catch us. Another thing that we were worried about was that you couldn't get your money out of the country. You couldn't get your own money that you worked so hard to earn, out of the country. After selling our home—selling everything, my mother risked taking a large sum of money, stashing it in the luggage to take it out, because we couldn't do it through the banks. It was illegal to take money out and of course, we couldn't leave it behind or how else were we going to immigrate to America when we had a substantial amount of money and couldn't use it. That was a big risk and that made my mother very fearful. Luckily, she went through with it. And again, I commend her for being such a strong and brave woman.

We traveled by plane. This time my father was waiting for us. He had already rented a house so we had somewhere to stay. He told us we were only going to be in Riyadh for six months according to the American Embassy, that it wouldn't take more than six months for the immigration papers to be completed at that time. And of course, we're talking about the seventies at that time. In 1977 the immigration quotas were very relaxed for an applicant. It could take one to six months, whereas now it can take up to four to five years for any relative to join you, sometimes ten years. It's a lot stricter today. I remember that within six months, our papers were ready and we went to the American Embassy in Riyadh.

I remember visiting with the American consul, American ambassador. He asked, why do we want to come to Michigan? And I remember going through the medical exam and that we were very excited, very happy that we are going to Michigan and that we had relatives in Michigan. By the way, by then, I would say, about one-third of my first cousins, not their parents, from my mother's side, had already escaped from Iraq and had gone to Michigan. So, it was very exciting to join our cousins in Michigan.

I remember the counselor. He was so kind. Sometimes I think about him. Sometimes I think about researching who he was at that particular time to see if I can send him a letter and find where he is and say, "I remember meeting you. And I remember that you made our transition very comfortable." He was a good man. He was a younger man. He was probably in his forties. And he really enjoyed meeting us. He was bragging—no not bragging—showing off how many Arabic words he knew. Stuff like that. So anyway, it was a nice touch.

Anyway, six months later, in August, we got on a plane. The plane stopped in Turkey. It was on that plane—a situation that still amazes me—as we were sitting on that plane, more passengers came. Another Chaldean family got on that plane and we recognized them as our neighbors in Basrah. Talk about a coincidence! The father, the mother, and their five children got on the plane. And they were very happy to hear from us. They had not heard from us in a while. And, of course, we started sharing our stories, and then they told us they themselves escaped from Iraq and they were going to Michigan as well. So we arrived in Michigan, on the same plane, at the same time. And I thought that was a unique story.

Before Michigan, we arrived in New York and we were amazed at how huge the airport was. I stood and I still remember waiting to get on the bus to go from one terminal to another. Back home in Iraq, there was only one terminal, only one door to the whole terminal, one door where people existed, and there were probably only five or six planes on the runway.

We got on another plane and then we finally arrived in Michigan. I remember it was late at night and there wasn't a lot of traffic, but I was amazed at how huge, how big, the airport was. We went to another terminal—I think it was twelve o'clock at night—and were greeted by our uncle and his wife. They came to pick us up at Detroit Metro airport. We were very excited, very happy!

I remember fighting with my brothers to get a window seat in the car because I figured even though it was dark; I wanted to see out there. I wanted to see what America looked like from the window of the car, and I was amazed looking at the freeway. It was huge. We didn't have any freeways in the old country. Back then, my uncle lived in Southfield, Twelve Mile and Greenfield, to be exact. You're talking the seventies—very small homes. So we stayed there with them.

We were still full of energy. We weren't tired. They turned on the TV for us. Boy, what an eye-opener that was. In Saudi Arabia, there was only one station of TV, and the programs were either religious, political, or they would show one hour of cartoons, and then at night after nine o'clock, they would show what they considered entertainment. And their idea of entertainment was not movies, it was singing, Middle Eastern singers to be exact, and they'd show about an hour or two.

When we came here, we had the opportunity to experience the remote control for the first time. The remote control was something we were fascinated with. We were going crazy. We were wondering, "How many channels do you guys have?" you know, and so we did this all night long. We enjoyed all the stations. I can't remember if I slept that night, but the following day I was so excited to go out and about and explore my new home.

We arrived here on August 12. I turned sixteen on August 23, eleven days later. It was a tough age for me. I had almost mastered the Arabic language and knew no English, and at the time it was difficult for me to learn another language. It was a little bit tougher, because the older you get, the more difficult it becomes for you to learn a language.

I remember the following day. I looked for soccer on the numerous TV channels, because in the Middle East, like all over the world, soccer is the most popular sport. If you don't love soccer, something's wrong with you! And I turned the TV channel and there was no soccer. Instead I saw a football game. And I was thinking, "Why are those people hitting each other?"

I said to my uncle, "What's wrong with these people? Why are they hitting each other? Why are they hurting each other?"

My uncle said, "Dear, this is a sport called football."

I was confused! I knew football and this wasn't it, so I said, "No, this isn't football. Football is football. A sport you play with your feet. Those are holding a ball and hitting each other."

He said, "No, that's American football."

I said, "These guys are crazy. That's stupid. I'm not watching this game again." I was disappointed.

New Kid in School

We stayed with my uncles in his small house for one month. A month later, we moved to our new house. What had happened was that my father had wired my uncle money in order to purchase us a home ahead of time. Chaldean families stay with their immediate relatives for six months, sometimes one year. I remember in the seventies one family stayed with their immediate relatives for two years. That's an extreme, of course. But it's anywhere from six months to two years, until they get established, until their relatives get them a job and get them a place to stay and rent.

But we did it differently. My dad's financial situation was good compared to other immigrants who came here only with the shirt on their backs. So my uncle ended up buying us a home in a good school district at Evergreen and Thirteen Mile Road, Southfield City, but Birmingham School District. The homes were not very expensive. They were more expensive than the rest of Southfield, but they were less expensive than Birmingham. The advantage was that we got to go to Birmingham schools.

One month later [we moved to our new house], and of course, one excitement after the other, no setbacks, no tragedies, thank God! We were lucky, unlike many other immigrants that we had heard stories about, where they had to sleep one night out on the street or whatever difficulties they had to go through. We went to our house. We met our neighbors. Our neighbors were excited. They couldn't believe that there was a family from another part of the world who didn't speak English. We tried to communicate with them as we played with them. They were kind. Luckily there were enough kids on our street that we managed to have a good time. Soon enough, school started.

I went to Birmingham Groves, which was located a mile away from my home. I ended up walking because transportation was not provided for homes that were up to one mile away from this school. My three brothers went to Berkshire Middle School in Birmingham. It was a very tough first year, very tough.

The hardest thing was to sit in the classroom, look at the teacher who was explaining the subject matter, and to not understand

Sharkey S. Haddad (*front row, left*) and his Groves High School soccer team paused for a picture before a game at the Pontiac Silverdome in the fall of 1978.

one word that he was saying. I got angry and became frustrated. I even hated my parents for doing this to me because it was so tough. Luckily, and this demonstrates the wisdom of Birmingham as a school district, in 1977 Groves High School hired a part-time bilingual tutor. I mean, in 1977, you say bilingual education and people laugh at you. They'd say, "You don't need that. You come to this country, you speak English whether you like it or not, no matter what. You learn."

Birmingham schools, because of their wisdom, were probably one of the first to hire a bilingual tutor, and that bilingual tutor happened to be Chaldean. Her name was Josephine Sarafina. I mention her name every time I do a presentation about Chaldean history and culture because of the impact she had on my education and in turn, my life.

She's married to the late Sarafa, the Sarafa family. They're very well known in the Chaldean community. They were very big on education. As a matter of fact, the first minister of education in

Iraq was Mr. Nahim Sarafa, who in the 1960s had managed to get a Ph.D. from Wayne State University in education. Because of his degree, the Iraqi government appointed him as the minister of education in Iraq. Of course, education was very high and deep in the Sarafa family and that was one of the reasons why she became a bilingual tutor.

If it wasn't for her, I would have done what most of my cousins have done, which is drop out of high school. They said, "We don't need this. Why do we go to a place that we feel uncomfortable, frustrated, and angry? And, on top of that, other kids make fun of us because of the way we look, because of the way we talk or don't talk, because we don't know the language."

Teachers were very understanding of the fact that I couldn't speak English, and they were just trying to help me the best they could. At first, there were no programs for English as a second language for students. There were very few students who came to that district, who could afford to live in Birmingham. Most immigrants, most Chaldean immigrants, when they come to Michigan, they end up first locating on Seven Mile and Woodward area, and that's the only pocket in Detroit where we had a Chaldean church and Chaldean neighborhood. The reason they ended up locating there first is because they didn't have a lot of money, and lower housing was more available for them in that neighborhood than in somewhere like Southfield or Bloomfield.

Michigan was the state that some Chaldeans originally came to at the turn of the century when Henry Ford was offering five dollars a day. Most immigrants came here to work. Not all of them had the privilege of getting a job. Unless you knew how to speak a little English, you couldn't work. There were several cases of Chaldean pioneers, pioneers who came here and could not get a job with the Henry Ford factory. As result of that, they ended up working with Lebanese grocers, where at the time you had a Lebanese community, a Christian-Lebanese community, because very few Muslim Arabs had a reason to come to immigrate to the United States.

What happened later, because the Chaldean people were such hardworking people who worked for the Lebanese stores, they ended up buying those businesses, buying another business, or starting their own businesses. And then, of course, the idea was not to stay, unlike the Lebanese. Maybe the Lebanese had the same idea, to come make money and then go back to the old country and buy a farm in the Chaldean villages. We're talking about 1910, 1920. So after they established wealth and got adjusted to the American way of life, when they went back to the old country, instead of settling there, they ended up going back, getting married, and bringing their wives here.

That's how the Chaldean community started here. Then they started bringing their relatives here cause of the close-knit Chaldean family. After that, they started bringing their brothers and sisters and their families, their children. So, by 1950, we had about ten to fifteen thousand Chaldeans, which was still small if you think about it.[1]

Challenges and Sacrifices

In high school I started to struggle with the fact that I was in a coed school. In the Middle East, boys go to schools separate from girls. In America, I had to adjust to the fact that I was sitting, interacting with females at the age of sixteen when I never had that opportunity in the old days. That was a very difficult adjustment for me, how to conduct myself among girls when I had that opportunity, what to do and what not to do.

The second challenge was the language acquisition. It was very difficult for me to gain enough social English for me to get by. We're not even talking academic at this point, just social.

The third difficulty was the cultural differences. I had to guess what to say and do what would be appropriate in the eyes of my peers at the high school. Think about it. A lot of us take things for granted. These are the things you do and there are things you don't do in America, and I didn't know what was appropriate. Imagine going to another country and not knowing their culture. A lot of the countries that we travel to are more forgiving when tourists do things that are not appropriate: "Well, they're tourists. They don't know our way of life." But I wasn't a tourist, I wasn't a visitor. I was going to school and people did understand that I was here to stay. So a lot of the kids expected me to behave just the way they were behaving, and that was very difficult for me to adjust to because I didn't know how to.

The fourth difficulty was that I did not know how to introduce myself, and I had even more difficulties when I said, "I'm from Iraq." And the kids would say, "Where the heck, where the hell is Iraq at?" Very few kids knew about countries in the Middle East. So it was a constant struggle being part of the school environment, student body. Add to that, I was very pessimistic at my chances to graduate from high school considering my limitations.

The fifth issue was that parents did not know what their role was as parents in their children's education. In the old country, parents had a very limited role. They didn't do anything. They just put the kids on the bus and sent them to school. The teacher did everything. That is what I would tell teachers in America. They didn't understand and said, "Wow! And that worked?" And I'd say, "Yeah. There was a 90 percent turnaround success." As a matter of fact, parents used to threaten their children when they did something wrong in the house that they're going to tell their teacher the following day. Parents didn't have a reason to go to the school unless their kid was being suspended for being a problem child. But that very seldom happens. And that is the authoritarian model of schools we had.

The teacher was in charge. You didn't ask a teacher anything. You never raised your face, your eyes, to a teacher. When you spoke to a teacher, you looked down. If the teacher hit you, that's okay. If you did something wrong and you got smacked by the teacher, you wouldn't dare ask why. You just bit your tongue and hoped that he didn't smack you again. I was smacked by teachers. I was smacked on the palm inside of my hands because I did something wrong. And now I look back, and I say I deserved it. I misbehaved.

When the Chaldean parents came here, if they had gone to school in the old country, they were going to assume schools are similar all over the world. The teacher is in charge. The parents don't need to be as involved. Now, add to that, they don't know any better. They couldn't speak English that well, so even if they wanted to be part of their children's education, they couldn't communicate. So I was left on my own. I had to make all the decisions in my school, my high school—when to drop a class, when to take a class, which class I needed to study for, which class I skipped. With American society, it's very easy to be distracted from education and find other priorities. I had to learn how to have fun and balance school in this very different school atmosphere.

I think the only reason I decided to continue my education was a combination of two things. One, I was surrounded by kids who played soccer with me on the team. Soccer was a major, major factor. All the kids who played soccer with me went to college. And they kept encouraging me to go to college. And I still remember the words of a friend of mine. His name was Charlie Sanders. He was the only one in my experience who said to me, "Sharkey, I think you can go to Michigan State and do a great job." He believed in me and he told me that he was going to Michigan State and that he didn't think he was better than me. He told me that I could go to Michigan State and do as good as he was doing and play soccer for Michigan State as well. So he was a motivator to go to college. His words meant a lot to me, and I started thinking about college and that that was something I wanted to do.

My father wanted me to go to college, and most Chaldean parents were pro-education. In Iraq for a Chaldean to graduate from a college—only in the cities in Iraq—it's no big deal. To get a master's and Ph.D., that's when you need to brag. So education runs very deep among Chaldeans in the big cities in Iraq. All of the parents used to compete about how their sons and daughters graduated from this college or that college in Iraq.

When they come here to America, education does not become a priority. Survival becomes a priority, but for some reason my dad did not make that an issue—the survival. He kept saying to me, "Go to college." The problem with his encouragement was that my father didn't know how to encourage. He did it in the way that Middle Eastern fathers know best—with negative criticism instead of positive example. He's say "Oh, you're no good, you're not going to make any good of your future because you don't want to go to college or because you don't think about college." To be honest, I

Sharkey S. Haddad with his family celebrating his son Blake's First Communion. *Back, from left:* Tess, Hilda, Sharkey, and Sindel. *Front:* Blake.

don't know why it worked with me, Maybe it worked because of the lack of relationship between me and my father and how I always struggled as the oldest son to prove to my father that I am capable of whatever I want, despite his negative criticism of me. I think that the combination of that and the support I got from my peers on the soccer team contributed to my decision. Also, the strains on my relationship with my father, where he and I used to always argue, a power struggle if you will, and the fact that I wanted to work hard and prove him wrong and graduate from college, was really a driving force.

These forces led me to sacrifice, and I do mean it when I say sacrifice because I was working fifty hours a week, on Friday, Saturday, and Sunday. In only three days I was putting in fifty hours at my dad's grocery store. My brothers were working Monday, Tuesday, Wednesday, and Thursday, and my dad was helping them. I was going to Oakland University on Monday, Tuesday, Wednesday, and Thursday, attending night classes and studying during the day. I didn't have a life and I didn't see anybody. I did not see my cousins. I did not socialize with any of my cousins. The reaction I was getting from people was, "What the hell are you going to do with the college degree?" Because most of my cousins who dropped out of high school, believe it or not, they were doing very well. Some of them were even millionaires. So sometimes I'd say to myself, "What's wrong with this picture here?"

NOTE

1. The largest Iraqi Chaldean diaspora is located in metropolitan Detroit, where there are an estimated 100,000 members in Detroit, Southfield, Sterling Heights, Oak Park, Troy, West Bloomfield, Farmington Hills, Ferndale, Warren, and Ann Arbor. As Chaldeans establish themselves financially, more move out of Detroit and into the other cities. Other large Chaldean communities in the United States are in California, Arizona, and Illinois.

We Belong to America Just as Much as America Belongs to Us

B eginning in 1932, political power in Lebanon was precariously balanced between Christian and Muslim factions. In 1975 sporadic violence between the factions escalated into civil war. Conflicts among Lebanon's neighbors—Israelis, Syrians, and the Palestinians—spilled over the border. The fighting lasted until 1989.

During the fifteen years of war, hundreds of thousands of Lebanese sought homes in safer countries, including the United States. Earlier, most Lebanese emigrants were Christian, but members of all religious groups left during the civil war.

Lara Hamza was born in Beirut, Lebanon, in 1974. When Lara was very little, her father, Wafic Hamza, worked in Libya as an architect. When her family was getting ready to move back to Lebanon, civil war broke out there. They could not return, so they decided to visit relatives in Dearborn, Michigan, in 1979. The Hamza family thought they would eventually go back to Lebanon. They did return for a short time, but fighting continued near their home and they came back to America.

Lara's father, could not get a job as an architect in the United States because he did not have a U.S. license to practice architecture. Instead, he found work cutting down trees for the Wayne County

Road Commission. He eventually designed and built his family's home in Dearborn, where they currently live.

They lived for several years in Florida, where Wafic opened an Arab restaurant. There, Lara felt very isolated because they were not living among other Arab immigrants. They returned to Dearborn, where many other Arab Americans live. Her parents made one more trip back to visit their home and friends in Lebanon in 2000.

Her father and two of her brothers, Toufic and Mahmoud, own and run two Italian Bellacino restaurants in the Dearborn area. Her oldest brother, Fadi, is a commercial airline captain. Her mother still manages the household.

Lara went to the University of Michigan. After she graduated, she earned her master of fine arts degree in creative nonfiction and poetry from Ohio State University, pursuing a career in English education and writing. She writes about the pressures of family life, discovering her voice and ultimately herself through teaching, and all the beauty and adventure of growing up as an Arab American girl.

This story is based on oral history interviews that Martha Aladjem (Climo) Bloomfield did with Lara Hamza, her mother, Insaf Hamza, and her father, Wafic Hamza, on May 21, 2000. It also includes material reprinted from Lara Hamza, "Coming Home," from *Arab Detroit: From Marqin to Mainstream*, Nabeel Abraham and Andrew Shyrock (copyright © 2000 Wayne State University Press, used with the permission of Wayne State University Press).

We Can't Go Home

My father, Wafic, and my mother, Insaf, married in 1969. He was twenty-seven, and my mother was twenty-three years old, acceptable ages for their generation. But my maternal grandmother was twenty-six years old when she got married. This was very uncommon back then—twenty-six was considered over the hill. But her father was wealthy. He owned lots of land and had many servants, so my grandmother didn't need marriage for economic reasons, as most women did back then. Her father didn't want to marry off

Lara at age five. She went to Henry Ford Elementary School in Dearborn.

Lara Hamza's parents, Insaf and Wafic Hamza. The photo was taken in Lebanon before they came to America.

This needlepoint picture is a scene of Lebanon. Lara Hamza's mother, Insaf Hamza, stitched it the year she got married, at age twenty-three. She brought the picture with her to Michigan to remember her home.

his daughters to anyone who just came along to ask for their hand. He wanted them to be willing. At that time, it was more common for a fifteen- or sixteen-year-old to marry, and very uncommon for a father to let it go that far. Many people asked for her hand, but she didn't want to be married until she met my grandfather, Mahmoud Berry.

The wedding arrangement works like this. The parents tell their daughter that a man is interested in her and is coming over to meet her. If she feels uncomfortable, she can end it right there, depending on how flexible the parents are. There's a lot of emphasis on what the parents want, and what the parents of the guys want. When my father came to ask for my mom's hand, if his parents weren't involved, her parents never would have agreed.

My mother says that what she likes most about her culture is that the parents' opinions are so important. The opinions of other people matter very much. You have to bring the whole clan to show that you are well respected when asking for a girl's hand in marriage. If you don't have a group of people coming along with you, it doesn't look good. So the people who come with you, they're a support system vouching for you, saying that yes you are a good person.

My mom knew my dad as her brother's good friend before he took an interest in her. She felt that something funny was going to happen because he started paying a lot more attention to her and he was always very respectful of her. He had a great sense of humor and made her laugh. She thought he was very handsome, always dressed well.

If my grandmother knew that he was going to leave the country and take her daughter with him, she would have said no. But before agreeing to marry him, my mom spoke with her dad: "I like him. Wafic is very, very good with his friends and family." He had been her brother's friend, and every time he went to Libya to work, he always sent a lot of support back to his family. She knew he was giving and kind-hearted, so when my dad said he wouldn't live his whole life in Libya and that he went there to save enough money to come back, her parents finally agreed.

They got married and eventually bought a home near my grandparents in Beirut to travel back to, as my father's work was still in Libya. They vacationed in Michigan and visited my mom's brothers, Abe, Ali, and Khalil Berry, who had immigrated there years prior. My older brother, Fadi, was actually born in Michigan on one of those trips.

While my father worked as an architect in Libya, my parents thought of Lebanon as their home. They planned to return there to live. When my mom got pregnant with me, she went home to Lebanon to be close to her family to give birth. Eventually, they sent my brother and me to school there when we were very young, and my grandmother took care of us. In 1979, after two more brothers were born, my parents decided it was time to return to Lebanon for a better education for all their kids. They packed up their things,

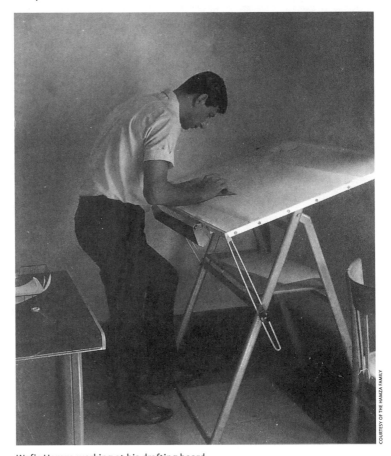

COURTESY OF THE HAMZA FAMILY

Wafic Hamza working at his drafting board.

sold their home in Libya, bought airplane tickets, and were ready to go. But then civil war broke out in Lebanon.

My father said, "I sold our house, sold our furniture. I packed everything. Then fighting broke out again. No airport, no plane, no flight. Nothing. Everything was closed. We didn't know what to do. My job in Libya was still available but we didn't have our home. All we had were our bags."

The civil war in Lebanon got worse. My father said that nobody knows why they were fighting. My parents were torn. They didn't know where to go or what to do. My father said, "All we had were our bags, waiting." Finally, my parents decided to visit my uncles in Michigan again—my mother's three older brothers. They went to the embassy to apply for a visa to the United States. My father needed some documents that he didn't have. But when they saw that my older brother, Fadi, was already a U.S. citizen, within two hours, Dad had the visa and passports. They still hoped to return to Lebanon after the fighting ended.

Early Ties to Michigan

My parents' ties to Michigan went even further back than my uncles. My maternal grandfather, Mahmoud Berry, had immigrated to Michigan in about 1913 when he was twelve years old. Actually, so did my paternal great-grandfather, Diab Salim Ghutaime. Mahmoud's mother had died and his father married a new wife who would never take the place of his mother. He felt like escaping. My father said that people went where their friends went at the time, and America must have appealed to them. He said that wherever someone has a friend, he goes—like okay, you want to go to McDonalds? Okay. You want to go to Burger King? Just like that. And travel was easier than after World War I—no visa, no security

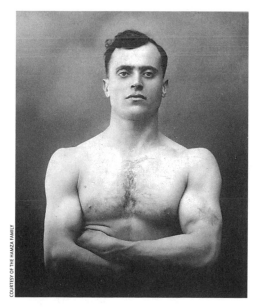

COURTESY OF THE HAMZA FAMILY

Lara Hamza's maternal grandfather, Mahmoud Berry, came to Michigan in 1913 when he was twelve years old. He was a stowaway on a ship from Beirut, Lebanon, to France and then to New York. He became a boxer in the United States, boxing with the great Jack Dempsey.

in 1913. You just jumped on a ship. So Mahmoud was a stowaway with his friends traveling from Beirut to France to New York, finally to Michigan. He had heard it was easy to find work here.

At first he lived on the street. He used to go fishing with a friend and ate the fish to live. Then he went to work at Henry Ford's River Rouge plant. My paternal great-grandfather also worked there. Mahmoud became a boxer and boxed with Jack Dempsey. Over the years, he gave most of the money he won from boxing to the Red Cross and other charities. Mahmoud returned to Lebanon years later—about 1930—where he met and married my grandmother, Jamila Saleh. He came back to Michigan a few times to visit, but considered Lebanon his home in the end.

My mom loves to tell and retell the story her father, Mahmoud, shared with her about meeting Henry Ford:

> Henry Ford came to the factory when my father was working. Henry Ford said to my dad, "Show me what you're having for lunch in your lunch box."
>
> My dad said, "Kibbe, wheat, chickpeas."
>
> Henry Ford said, "You're lucky. I wish I had good health like you. I wish I was a worker like you with good health rather than owning the factory with my health."

I guess his health was poor then. Many years later, after Mahmoud died in Lebanon, Jamila, his wife, my maternal grandmother, immigrated with her son, Hasan Berry, to Dearborn.

Coming to America

Leaving Libya instead of returning to Lebanon, my mom remembers crying. She said she felt she would never go back to Lebanon.

I could not understand why my mother was crying instead of rejoicing like my brothers and me. We were, after all, going to a new country. We were eager to meet old friends and relatives.

We came as tourists. But the fighting in Lebanon continued, so my father applied to become an immigrant and received a green card that would allow him to get a job. Usually you cannot

Lara's grandmother, Jamila Saleh, lived in Lebanon when this picture was taken in 1972. She is standing under a pomegranate tree. Eventually she also immigrated to Dearborn, Michigan.

change from a tourist visa to a green card. The immigration officials thought he was lying. My father said the fellow said, 'First you apply for a tourist visa. Then you are applying for an immigrant visa.'

My father told the officials, "Okay, listen guys. I came here as a tourist to wait here a little bit before I could go back to Lebanon. But the war is still going on in Lebanon. I have no place to go." The officials finally understood and gave him his card as a political refugee.

He could not get a job as an architect because he did not have a United States license to practice architecture. Instead he cut down trees for the Wayne County Road Commission.

Once we took a trip with our Uncle Ali and his family to the Kellogg Company for a tour. Frosted Flakes was my favorite cereal, so I was so excited when I saw the huge statue of Tony the Tiger. I

Uncle Ali took Lara and her brothers with his children to see Tony the Tiger at the Kellogg's cereal factory in Michigan. Frosted Flakes quickly became her favorite cereal in America.

remember standing next to his paws and staring up at him because I thought he could talk. It was interesting for me to see how Tony could be so lifelike. I thought of that factory as his home. We first tasted Frosted Flakes when we visited America, at my Uncle Ali and Jean's house, because they were not imported to Lebanon when we lived there. I had never tasted them before and I was hooked.

My family returned to Lebanon for a while. But the fighting came too close to their home.

We Move to Florida

We came back to the United States. This time we moved to Florida, where my father opened up a restaurant. Few other Muslim Arabs lived there.

When we moved to Florida, my mom told my dad that the house we owned in Dearborn was important to keep, even if we eventually went back to Lebanon. She had said it would be a great house if one of us wants to come back to study at the university.

Only when we moved to Florida did I become conscious of my differences. I never thought of myself as a foreigner in Dearborn because of the prominent Arab community into which we naturally blended.

My brothers and I met Muhammad Ali when he came to our father's restaurant, the Beirut Restaurant, in Florida. I remember feeling very lucky and star-struck because my parents had talked about Muhammad Ali to us many times before we even owned the restaurant. They told us he's not an Arab, but he chose to change his name and become a Muslim because he believes in the religion so strongly. When I saw him in real life, it was like seeing

Lara and her brothers met Muhammad Ali in her father's restaurant in Florida. Here Mahmoud is pictured with him.

COURTESY OF THE HAMZA FAMILY

a very important part of our identity in the flesh—another person in the middle of a town where we felt so alone and secluded as Muslim children. Yet there he was, the legend, the Muslim boxer Muhammad Ali, and all I could do was smile in awe at him! When we gathered for pictures, he put his arm around me and kissed my chubby cheek, and I remember blushing with embarrassment! It was exciting for all of us to meet him.

Growing up was a confusing time. That is a very good word to describe the whole thing. Because even when we came to America there was hardly any stability until that four-year period when we lived in Florida because then for four years we were in one place, the same elementary school. It was really nice. I had a nice group of friends. But my parents wouldn't have remembered that because during that time, they were losing their business, they were losing all their money. But for me, it was a very pleasant time because I had lots of friends. I enjoyed school very much.

I felt very American because I was the only Arab there, and I didn't even feel Arab, only at home. At home, I experienced everything Arabic, but there wasn't as much to experience because we weren't around even the food, as we are here in Michigan. Here you can just go down to Warren Avenue, which has many Arabic shops and bread with zatar (thyme mixed with sesame seeds and olive oil) on it, but in Florida we hardly had the common Lebanese foods like this.

My mom was always tired. She hardly had a social life because she didn't speak English very well at the time. She hardly went anywhere. She didn't know people. She felt very alone. Her entire family lived here in Dearborn. And over there in Florida she was alone. My dad ran the restaurant all day, early morning till all night, and all she had there was the house and us. My mom did most of the cooking for the restaurant that exhausted her, like the stuffed grape leaves. She would stay up all night long making them, and it was hard work. It must have been a horrible time for her. But of course, I couldn't see this because I was too young to see this, but I felt it. I could feel the tensions between my parents. It wasn't a very happy time for them. But like I said, that was the only time I felt

I had some stability since I was a kid because we were constantly moving.

My dad's restaurant business didn't work out. He said, "We lost every penny I brought with me."

My mom said, "Every time I think maybe we lost everything, I remember we still have the house in Dearborn, so it gave me hope. We would always have somewhere to return to."

And there were so many times in Florida when my dad wanted to sell the house, when he wanted to rebuild the business. And my mom said, "Don't touch that house. Don't sell that house." And we did lose everything. So we came back to Dearborn and moved into our old house.

I remember in 1982 when I was in second grade and still in Florida my mom asked me if I would write the president a letter. President Reagan wrote me back with a signed picture of him on a horse. I had asked if he could help us. Looking back on it, I see how useless that was. I guess my mom really thought the president could help. She thought the president would do more for struggling families in America. She said she thought the president might not be able to sleep knowing there were hungry families in the U.S.

I remember I was really embarrassed because well, we live in America. It's a huge place. The president, you know, it's not like he's your father. He's not going to loan you some money. I knew that it was really worthless to write it. Even as a kid I knew this, but I didn't want to hurt her feelings. I told her, "I don't know how to write the president a letter." So she walked me over to our neighbor's house. Our neighbor was a very old woman. She must have been about—maybe she was close to ninety. She was very, very old and we went into her home and I said, "My mom wants me to write the president a letter." She said, "Oh, okay" and helped me. She got me the address: 1600 Pennsylvania. I remember how long that was to write out on the envelope. And then my mom told me what she wanted me to write down, so the neighbor helped me write it as I tried to translate, and it was basically telling the president how we came from Lebanon, we lost all our money, and if he could please help us. And that's it. And I sent it.

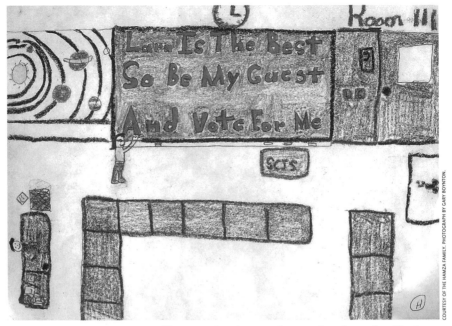

Lara Hamza created her campaign picture and poem when she ran for office in the fifth grade in elementary school in Michigan.

I included a school picture and a picture of my brothers. Reagan sent me back a big picture, an 8½ × 10½ of him on a horse saying that the economy is getting better and just to be more optimistic. I remember Mom said, "No bank will accept this picture!"

Back in Michigan

In 1984, after four years of detachment from our cultural roots in Florida, we returned to Dearborn to live among family and friends. Once more I felt awkward and displaced in school—only this time, I believed I had the upper hand. I spoke much better English than my classmates and it made me feel good knowing that I wasn't like them. I remember I sent the principal of my old elementary school, Hollywood Hills Elementary, a thank-you letter for the education I received there. He was very happy I wrote him and said he displayed my letter at the school.

By age ten, I was already plagued with misconceptions,

stereotypes, and ignorance about my Arab identity. My family seemed foreign to me. I felt awkward and displaced in school. I wanted to assimilate, to fit in with the majority.

Despite my confused feelings, I worked hard in my new school, Henry Ford Elementary, running for class office in fifth grade. I remember having fun working on my campaign; I drew a goofy poster I had grown so tall in fifth grade. I was ten years old and I was the tallest kid in my class. I was taller than my teacher, Mr. Hadous, who was pretty short. I felt so awkward. I remember the first day of class in my new school in Michigan with everyone checking me out. I was taller than all the boys and felt so embarrassed. But quickly I made friends here, too.

My dad helped my brothers with a newspaper route in the early mornings and worked in a gas station all day long. He said, "I worked all kinds of jobs. I didn't just sit at home and cry for my past. I started all over again. And someone gave me a job at the airport, driving a bus and I kept this job until now. We built this house and all four kids, everybody, is cooperating. We treat everyone the same. Anybody who needs something, the other one can help."

And my mom said, "And nobody in this house has something that another doesn't have. Everything in this home is for every body."

Back here, I began to learn more about what it meant to be more like an Arab. Almost everybody in my classroom was also an Arab. My cousins were here. The people I was friends with were Arab, whereas in Florida, all my friends were "just American."

Actually, it became harder for me because when I went over to my relatives' home and they talked to me in Arabic and I replied to them in English and they give me this strange look, "What's wrong with you? Have you forgotten how to speak Arabic?" And even though I know how to speak Arabic, I felt so much more comfortable speaking English. And I wanted to say, "So what if I want to speak English? So what if I don't want to respond to you in Arabic?" I found it a very difficult thing to balance. How much is being too much of one? What's being too little of the other? And where do you find the balance? I felt empowered when replying to my relatives in English instead of Arabic.

Even my looks helped set me a part from the rest. With my light brown hair and light complexion, I felt good when people told me: "You don't look Arabic." Such negative feelings about my heritage made adolescence all the harder to endure.

I had friends who were going through similar kinds of things as I was but never felt it to the same degree that I did because they had never been out of the community, as I had. Being born here in Dearborn is different than being born here and moving to Florida. Being in Dearborn is almost like being in—I don't want to say right back in Lebanon 'cause, I think, had I lived in Lebanon, it would have been very different all together. It's so hard to explain.

I really think that people living here in Dearborn try so hard to hold on to their values, their traditions they fear they're losing by moving away from Lebanon, so they go overboard to protect them. If you were to go back to Lebanon today, you would see that these people are living so freely, so casually. If you were to compare Lebanese society to the way people are living in Dearborn, you would be shocked at how free people are in Lebanon and how strict and traditional they still are here. And it's because they've separated themselves from the culture and they don't want to lose what they think they have lost by leaving it. They've psychologically boxed themselves in.

Like my cousins. They grew up in a very strict household. Their dad said, "I have to protect their innocence. I can't let them become Americanized." That word frightened them so much—being *American*—that they lose sight of just living, just being a human being. And if they lived in Lebanon, they could live, there's nothing wrong with living. And here, I think, they've lost it, they've lost it. A lot of families have. I'm fortunate that my parents weren't so strict.

My mom is very wise. She understands this, like when she let me go away to Ann Arbor by myself for four years. I'm sure other families would not agree. How could you let your daughter go away? But it opened up the doors. Right after I left, it started. My cousin started considering graduate school in a different state. She never even considered it until I went to Ann Arbor. Her dream had been to go to Michigan State for her undergrad but she went to the University of Michigan–Dearborn to stay home.

Lara Hamza graduated from the University of Michigan in 1999.

My mom and my dad paved the way. The night I said I wanted to go to Ann Arbor, I made up my mind and told my parents. I told my mom first and then we brought it up to my dad. And my dad's first reaction was, "What? What are you talking about? Away to school? Away?" And I knew I was going to get this lecture. But then I knew immediately right after a small talk with my mom, he would come around. So, like ten minutes later, he said, "Okay, when do you want to go?" You don't have to get wrapped up in the social pressure to do what everyone around you expects and remain boxed in.

Growing Proud of My Arab Heritage

Ironically, when I left home to study at the University of Michigan, I was driven to take courses about Arab culture and even to learn the Arabic language, something that my parents tried for years to get me to do.

I found that the more knowledge I gained about the culture I tried so desperately to evade during my youth, the more I hungered for clues and insights into my heritage. I even have closer Arab friends now than I ever had in the past. Only after separating from my home did I discover the importance of affirming my Arab identity, struggling to find a balance has made me find strengths in both of my cultures that I never knew existed.

This is part of what I wrote in an essay for the book *Arab Detroit.*

Although I grew up in an Arab home, learned Arab customs, spoke the Lebanese dialect, and was vaguely conscious of my Muslim religion, I received no reinforcement of my heritage outside the home. The only times . . . I experience[d] our "ethnicity" was when my dad took me to work with him. Our restaurant fascinated me, especially the mysterious music flowing from the band and the provocative moves of the belly dancers on stage. This was hardly the proper setting for a child to learn anything substantial about her heritage.

I vividly recall the time my younger brother bought my mother what he considered a "pretty necklace" from the school fund-raising sale. Although this gift was shimmering with gold, it instantly brought her to tears the moment she unwrapped it, because dangling from it was a crucifix. To my mother, the gift symbolized our growing detachment from our roots; to my brothers and me, it symbolized our growing confusion since we hardly knew what our "roots" were.

My emerging divided identity troubled and confused me. My family life increasingly appeared "foreign" to me, and I longed to fit in with the majority, to fully assimilate in the American life-style.

But I grew older, I learned more about my Arab heritage and grew proud of it. It took me many years to feel good about my Arab heritage. I learned to appreciate my mother praying daily.

While praying, my mother wears a special dress such as this blue-and-white one. She wears the matching head cover. Muslim women cover their hair as a sign of respect to God. She kneels on her many colored prayer rugs she brought from Lebanon to Michigan.

Insaf Hamza wears a blue-and-white Tyab-al-Sala't, a special prayer gown, when she prays. She also wears the matching head cover. Muslim women cover their hair as a sign of respect to God. Insaf brought the gown and head cover with her to America.

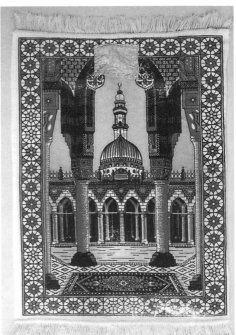

Top: Insaf Hamza's first woven prayer rug. Her father gave it to her in 1956, when she was ten years old. It has a pocket for prayer beads and a prayer stone. Her mother took the pocket from an old pair of her pajamas. The rug is very worn where she has knelt while praying. *Bottom:* This many-colored prayer rug belongs to Insaf Hamza. Prayer rugs were originally made in Mecca, Saudi Arabia, the birthplace of the Prophet, Muhammad. The picture is of a mosque in Mecca, the holiest site for the Muslim religion. When Muslims pray, they must face Mecca. Insaf brought both of these rugs with her to Michigan.

This book is a Ou'ran, the most holy book of Islam. It belongs to Insaf Hamza. She brought it from Lebanon in 1979.

She reads prayers from the Qu'ran, the most holy book of Muslim prayers. She touches her forehead to a prayer stone made from baked earth. The earthen stone symbolizes that people came from the earth and return to the earth. When she is not using a prayer stone, she places it in the little pocket she sewed at the top of the prayer rug. She also uses a strand of prayer beads while repeating her prayers.

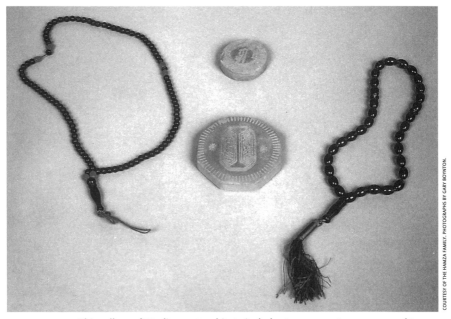

This collage of Muslim prayer objects includes two prayer stones, *qurs*, and two sets of prayer beads. Insaf Hamza brought them to America when she emigrated from Lebanon. The prayer stones are made of baked earth. When Muslims pray, they touch their foreheads to the stone to symbolize that they came from the earth and return to the earth. The round worn stone was Insaf Hamza's first, a gift from her mother. The longer string of prayer beads has ninety-nine beads. When Muslims pray, they repeat three prayers thirty-three times each. The shorter string has thirty-three beads. They are called *masbaha* in Arabic. Muslims, mostly elderly, slide them through their fingers to pass the time, saying "Alhamdullilah," meaning "Thank God."

This *quhwa arabiah*, Arabic coffee set, comes from Lebanon. The silver kettle is called a *raq-wa*. The small cups are *finjans*. Lara Hamza's family brought them to Michigan in 1979 when they emigrated from Lebanon. They still use them today.

Tawlet zaher, or backgammon, is a board game played in the Middle East. This game board is made from wood and mother of pearl. Insaf Hamza bought it as a gift for Lara's father in 1970. The Hamza family brought the game with them when they emigrated. Her mother jokes, "We thought we'd have time to play it."

I am fortunate that my parents gave me the chance to begin this precious journey toward self-discovery. Although I was excited once they agreed to let me transfer away to the University of Michigan, their decision did not surprise me. My father learned the hard way that without an education in America you were doomed for a life of hardship. He gave up his successful career as an architect and worked menial jobs in America to secure better opportunities for us than existed in war-torn Lebanon. This is why he encouraged my desire to further my studies, even if it meant parting with me.

My mother once said, "How can we forget the East when the sun rises in the east?" In translation, her sentiments may sound

This *breek-al-mai*, a glass bottle for drinking water, comes from Lebanon. Lara Hamza's maternal grandmother made the cloth cover, which is called a *gata*. Lara's family brought it with them to America.

COURTESY OF THE HAMZA FAMILY

awkward, but in Arabic her words jab at the core of anyone longing for their homelands in the East. My mother still looks to the East and I to the West, but all the while we are drawn to the center, continually pulled into compromise. We don't have to forget.

I can only imagine the anguish my parents felt eighteen years ago when they were forced to abandon their home in Lebanon. They weren't simply leaving behind friends and family, but a beautiful culture in a country brutally ravaged by war. Although they ache for the day they can go home again, still they know that America is now our home. It took my family a long time to accept this, but I think the only way for us to ultimately gain control of our lives and find comfort is by acknowledging that we belong to America just as much as America belongs to us. Like many Arabs here, my family continues struggling to strike that difficult balance between the two cultures. We continue to believe in our progression in America, despite the difficulties we faced searching for a place to call home.

"Even though we moved a lot from country to country," Lara's mother said, "I am happy that I was able to carry things that were important to me."

Minchuan Yang and His Daughter, Katie, from China

I Never Believed I
Would Stay in America

T he first wave of Chinese immigration to the United States
began in the early nineteenth century, when large numbers of Chinese came to work as laborers, particularly on
railroads and in mining.

While employers enjoyed the benefits of cheap labor, discrimination was rampant. Congress passed the Chinese Exclusion Act
in 1882 based on public outcry. Other laws followed that denied
citizenship and property ownership and prevented Asians from
marrying Caucasians. The Chinese were effectively barred from
immigration for over sixty years, until 1943.

After World War II, prejudice against Asians relaxed somewhat.
In 1965, Congress passed the Immigration Act, which removed
quotas based on national origin. The Chinese now make up the
largest group of Asian immigrants in the United States.

In 1966, Mao Zedong launched the Great Proletarian Cultural
Revolution and his policies of relocation, re-education, purging, and
genocide. The Cultural Revolution caused widespread panic and
upheaval in Chinese society. Unknown numbers of intellectuals,
educators, artists, writers, and religious leaders were persecuted,
imprisoned, or eliminated. While Mao declared the Cultural Revolution to be over in 1969, the after-effects lasted until his death in 1976.

COURTESY OF THE YANG FAMILY

Katie celebrates her birthday with her maternal grandparents in China. She lived with them while her parents studied in Michigan.

Under the guise of "re-education," the Chinese Communist government sent Minchuan Yang along with his classmates to work on a farm in a remote mountain village in central China. Yang lived in a cave there for two years. He and his friends nearly starved.

In 1976, Mao Zedong died, and the repressive policies of the Cultural Revolution eased. Minchuan was allowed to study at Sichuan University.

While at Sichuan he reunited with Jiajia Zheng, his former girlfriend from middle school in Beijing, and they were married.

Yang came alone to Michigan in 1983 to study anthropology at Michigan State University, where he eventually earned his Ph.D. At first, the Chinese government would not let him bring his wife to America. She was pregnant with their daughter, Katie, at the time. Eventually, his wife could come to the United States. Minchuan is currently a database administrator in the health care industry.

Katie Yang was born in Sichuan China in 1983. She lived with her grandparents for most of the first nine years of her life. She joined her parents in Michigan in 1992. Katie is currently a doctor in Kalamazoo.

Martha Aladjem (Climo) Bloomfield interviewed Minchuan Yang and his daughter, Katie, at their home in Okemos, Michigan, on May 20 and 28, 1999.

Minchuan Yang's Story

I grew up in Beijing, the capital city. When I was young I never thought about leaving China. I never thought about leaving my family to live in some other place. After I graduated from middle school the government sent us to the countryside, far away from my home in Beijing.

We were sent to a remote mountain area in central China in the Shaanxi Province.

China had a lot of turmoil in the 1960s and 1970s. The government criticized the Western cultural influence, and they believed that middle school and high school students needed to be re-educated by the working people. The working people had their practical knowledge and revolutionary spirit, so we were sent to a remote village in the mountainous area of Shaanxi Province. I was barely sixteen years old then.

We were supposed to live like the peasants. We were told that we had to be reunited with the working class and learn from the working class. That was a big change for me in my life.

I had mixed feelings. Certainly I had fears because I didn't know what the country life would be like. I didn't know the place because it was so remote and so poor. It was quite different from the urban life. At that time we were educated in the ideology of the government. We were called the "educated youth" when we went to the villages. We thought we could work for the peasants and we had some pride and some responsibility to go to the villages and help them.

Actually, we were kind of excited in a way. We thought we could do a lot of things for these people, but then we found out

As a teenager, Minchuan had to work in the remote village of Qujiagetai. They had to live in this cave where Minchuan (*middle*) stands with two friends.

that we had a lot of difficulties. The peasants were very poor and it was very hard work for us.

It was a very poor place. The peasants didn't have materials to build houses, so they lived in caves. A lot of them didn't have enough blanket or clothes. We lived in the caves with them.

They tried to help us at first. They assigned one person as a cook. We didn't know we had to learn how to cook. The first year we got grain from the government grain station. After the first year we had to earn our own living, so the villagers, under the Communist system, would distribute grain according to our labor contribution. We didn't have enough food, particularly in the first and second year. We experienced starvation, what hunger feels like when you are young and still growing. It was the kind of experience that you can never forget in your life.

I worked in the villages for about two years. The work was very hard. We had to work in the mountains, and a lot of those fields are sloped and far away. We had to walk about two or three miles to the fields and then back. We had no machines; we used manual labor to plow the fields. The villagers had some draft animals like oxen, but a lot of fields were plowed by human labor. At harvest time we had to carry grain back to the village from the fields.

Minchuan holding millet that he harvested.

In Qujiagetai, in the mountains of China, Minchuan herded goats.

Minchuan (*left*) and a friend hold goats.

In the winter it was very cold, but not much snow. The wintertime is not good for agriculture, and also it is the Chinese New Year and the spring festival. At that time we would be allowed to go back home for a visit. We had to pay for the trip.

I wrote letters to my family. I have one brother and two sisters. My brother was sent to northeast China under this policy. One of my sisters was sent to Inner Mongolia in the north. My youngest sister lived with my parents.

I worked in the village for two years, and then they gave me a job working for the local government. I had to go to the local villages to see if they worked appropriately, according to government plan. I had to talk to the peasants and give them the idea of what the government policies were at that time. I would make surveys and then report what kind of achievement they made. I had to survey their crops and make estimates about how much yield they would produce that year. Also I had the responsibility to organize the youth, to organize their activities as a youth leader.

In China, where you live and work is decided by the government. When I worked for the local government I lived in a government-owned house. The people there didn't have enough resources to make bricks, so they used stone.

The End of the Revolution

After Chairman Mao Zedong died in 1976 the Chinese government changed their policies. They wanted to open doors and start economic reconstruction and modernization. The so-called Cultural Revolution had ended.

China at that time had just opened up to the world. The Chinese people were just learning things about the Western world and Western culture. There was a great difference in a lot of things, like in politics and culture. The teachers at Sichuan University told us that you have to be aware of the Western influence. You have to maintain the Chinese culture and the Chinese ideology. Basically they said, "Don't lose faith in China."

The changes offered a lot of opportunities for people. Before 1978, universities in China didn't have an examination system.

They recruited based on recommendations given by local government officials. After 1978, universities were reopened to the public and now had an examination system. I got an opportunity to take the exam and I passed. I was lucky they accepted me.

I made the choice to go to Sichuan University in the southwest province. I wanted to go there at the time because of my girlfriend. Her family lived in Sichuan and I hoped we could be closer together. We were classmates in middle school. We were sent to different villages in different provinces, but we wrote letters to each other. She also took the exam and attended Sichuan University. It was lucky for both of us that we went to the same university. I was at the university for four years. My wife studied philosophy, and I studied history.

Studying Abroad

At the university I never had a thought about studying abroad. At that time China had no precedent for sending students abroad. One of my teachers had a very good English background. He told us to pay attention and learn English and maybe in the future you will have a chance to go to a foreign country to study.

China and the United States re-established their diplomatic relationship in 1979. China then gave back some of the money to the Christian Foundation for Higher Education that they had frozen for some years. When the opportunity came along, the foundation wanted to sponsor some students to come to the United States. They worked out the arrangements with Michigan State University. They found out that Michigan State University and the Sichuan University had just established this sister-state relationship, so they gave money to Michigan State University. Then Michigan State University sponsored us indirectly, acting as an intermediary. We took an exam and I scored higher in English than my classmates.

I came here in 1983 to start a master's degree program. At first I applied for it in history, but Michigan State University suggested that since the anthropology department had the funding directly from the foundation, they asked me if I would come to the anthropology department. History and anthropology are actually related, so I said okay, and I came to the anthropology department.

Marriage

At that time Sichuan University had a policy that students were not allowed to marry. You were not even allowed to date. We could meet but we couldn't let other people know that we were dating. In our senior year a lot of people found out. After I graduated we got married. Now there is no such rule.

It was a very simple wedding ceremony. We invited some friends and classmates and then they had a banquet in a restaurant. My parents work in Beijing and they couldn't come to Sichuan Province for the wedding.

When my wife got pregnant I had to leave her in China. There was a government policy at that time that students who were sent abroad to study were not allowed to bring their wives. It was very hard for me because I was worried about her. She had a hard time in China.

In China we had a simple one-room apartment. We had to share the restroom with a lot of other people. No kitchen, no bathroom, just one living room. She worked at the university and she was assigned a job there as a teacher teaching ethics because of her philosophy background.

She had our daughter Katie. I wrote letters because my family didn't have a telephone. It was very difficult to call China because the Chinese telecommunications system was very primitive at that time. The only thing I could do was to write letters to her. Sometimes she sent tapes of Katie's voice so I could listen to her sounds. My wife's parents sent tapes of my daughter playing the piano.

Return to China

When I came here to study for my master's degree I never believed I would stay in this country. I thought that I would have to go back. So I got my master's degree and then I went back. I arrived in Beijing and my wife came from Sichuan Province two days later. I

Five-year-old Katie at the piano. Katie's grandfather taught her to play the piano when she was very young in China. She still plays today.

met her and my daughter at the train station. It was the first time I saw my daughter.

I stayed in China two years teaching anthropology and history. I did fieldwork for a year. I focused on contemporary Chinese peasant society and culture. Also, the Chinese so-called economic reform started in the rural areas. The government had a new policy and had abandoned the commune system in 1985, so peasants had dramatic changes in their lives. I thought it was really fascinating. I knew they were very poor and now had a new system and new opportunities to work. I wanted to find out what cultural changes were effected by the new economic system, particularly the new market system in rural China. How do the peasants adjust to the market economy? How do they adjust to the new production system?

Immigration

My father is a history teacher in Beijing in a special adult training school.

He always encouraged me to study for my Ph.D. Then some funding became available for me to study abroad again. I thought it was a good opportunity. I applied for a passport and visa and came back to Michigan State University to study for my Ph.D.

My wife applied for a passport to come and visit me. The government had changed their policy and now allowed spouses to visit. But my daughter couldn't come here. For a lot of reasons it was very difficult to apply for a passport for both of them. I tried to persuade my in-laws to allow me to take my daughter to the United States. In China, parents and in-laws have a strong influence on your children. My in-laws were very reluctant to let my daughter go. They wanted to take care of my daughter and give her a special education, particularly my father -in-law. He was a musician and a conductor so he wanted to teach my daughter music. He had great hopes for her.

My wife got permission to visit me for about six months. She always wanted to study for a higher degree. She studied English and passed the exam, and then she applied to study at MSU. She came here in 1988 and studied communications. Then my daughter came in 1993. She was nine years old then.

Culture Shock

When I came here I had a lot of culture shock. People behave differently here. You watch TV and then you watch people on campus. People seem so free. Like in class for example, I saw that a student put her feet on the table and on the desk and nobody cared. The teacher didn't care and that really shocked me, because in China the teacher-student relationship is very rigid and stratified. You had to show respect, and certainly the teacher had the authority. You could never do that in China, putting your feet on the table or the chair. But here it seems that people do not have that sense of hierarchy that the Chinese have in the university and the workplace. There is always a sense of what is the proper behavior they are supposed to have.

In the early 1980s, before I came here, China had the kind of system where a lot of things are run by the government. We didn't have to take care of a lot of other things, like where you live or what job you want to do. The government arranged those things, so you didn't have to worry. You had no choice; you just did the work that the government assigned to you.

Here there are a lot of things you have to do on your own. You have to make a lot of decisions for yourself. We had to find an apartment; we had to do a lot of things on our own.

My daughter doesn't have a lot of basic skills. She doesn't know how to cook. She's not doing much in family chores. My wife and I often tell my daughter, "You are sixteen now, but when we were sixteen we worked as a peasant and had a very hard life."

They had a reunion last year in the Sichuan village, so my wife took my daughter back there to teach her about peasant life. Of course the village had dramatic changes and now was much better. They were glad to see the "educated youth" and talk about the old times and tell stories.

Katie Yang's Story

My real name is Que. It means "Little Sparrow" in Chinese.

I was born February 22, 1983. When I was four, my mother left China and came to MSU to study, so from age four to nine, I lived with my mother's parents.

For me, growing up was really fun. Even though I lived with my grandparents, they still knew how to have fun. My grandmother was an actress and she had a really powerful influence over me. She taught me how to act proper and be a little artistic. My grandfather also had an influence on me. He was a choir director. He gave me piano and singing lessons. There was always music around the house.

My grandparents' apartment was on the third floor of a big building. It was a building for people who had served in the Communist Party or the army, so that they had more benefits. It was three bedrooms; they divided up the dining room for the music room. That's where the piano was.

I always thought that I was one of the lucky ones. I didn't think that we really were low on money. Some of my friends weren't too

Katie posed for this picture under an umbrella in China when she was nine years old.

rich. A lot of them had just moved in from the country. They got some money and they just poured into the city.

School Days

School was harder in China. We had more homework, and the teachers expected more from you.

In first grade you had to be an exceptional student to get into the Little Soldiers. It's like preparing for the Communist Party. You had to do really well to be picked to get into the group. I was one of them. There was a ceremony out in the field. They give us each a red tie.

One day, some of my friends and me forgot to do our homework. The teacher started yelling at us and said, "You already got into the youth group. You're not doing your homework. That disappoints me because I expect more from you!" I felt really bad. I promised I'd do better.

In America all the students go to different rooms for classes, but in China all the students stay in one room and the teachers come there for one hour. So we didn't move around. Each class had about sixty students.

Here at Spartan Village School there were a lot of international students. I had taken some English in kindergarten, but I had forgotten everything. I had to take a lot of ESL [English as a second language], so that helped a lot. They taught you vocabulary. It was in an environment where not a lot of children spoke good English.

My classmates were pretty nice. They knew I didn't speak any English well, so they spoke really slowly and they tried to show me things so I would understand.

Piano Lessons

My grandfather taught me how to read music. Then he taught me how to play the piano, but he thought that I should have a more professional teacher. When I was five, he got me a teacher and I started going to piano lessons. In the summer when I wasn't so busy, my grandfather would make me practice about four hours.

At the beginning I was okay with it. My grandma would take me there on her bicycle, or sometimes my grandpa would take me there on his scooter. When I got to be around seven or eight, I started wanting to quit.

Coming to America

I don't really remember my mom leaving. I don't think I had a real hard time adjusting.

When I was around five or six, my grandma took me to the American Embassy and tried to get me get a visa, but we were rejected.

I remember the interview at the embassy. At the time, I didn't understand any English, so I don't know what they were asking. My grandma had taken some English in high school and college. She tried to say a few things in English to impress the person doing the interview, but I guess she didn't do a very good job.

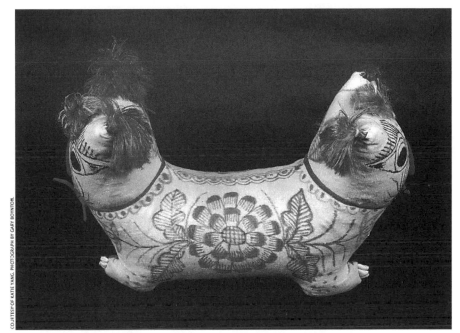

Katie brought this colorful two-faced dragon from China when she visited with her mother in 1997. In China, the dragon stands for prosperity and good fortune.

Afterwards, my grandmother said, "We will raise her." My parents thought my grandfather was just using that as an excuse for me not to come. "She needs to study piano in China. It's a better place to study." When I was about eight and a half years old, my grandparents decided that maybe I should join my parents. So in December 1991, we went to the embassy and this time they gave me a visa.

One of my parent's friends was in China at that time and he was going back to the U.S., so he took me with him. He and his wife brought me. They liked me. They said I wasn't much trouble.

We were one of the last to get off the plane at the airport. They were pretty strict about what's in your luggage. They would go through everyone's luggage. They opened my luggage and there were dolls and chocolate. They said, "What is all this?" I was just standing there waiting for them to be done.

Suddenly I heard my mom call out my name. I turned around

Katie brought this colorful slipper to Michigan after a visit to China with her mother. It is a Chinese equivalent of a bunny slipper.

and said, "Oh my gosh, It's my mom!" I ran to my mom and gave her a hug.

After we got home, Mom told me she wasn't sure it was me, but then she saw my sweater and she knew, because she bought me that sweater.

I was having fun, because it was a new environment. Everything was interesting. I met a girl across the street that was also Chinese. At that time, she had been living in the U.S. for maybe three years. We became really good friends. She taught me a lot. After a few months, her mom told my mom that her Chinese suddenly improved because we were speaking Chinese.

Return to China

When I went back the first time to my grandparents apartment I said, "Oh, this has changed. You moved this around. You got a new lamp." That was fun to discover.

My friends came over but we didn't really have a lot to talk about. Like, "How's school? What school do you go to now?" I didn't really know what was going on with them, and they didn't really understand what was going on in my life. That year was the World Cup, and we talked about some things going on in China. They were showing *Baywatch* on TV.

Reunion

We rode a train from Beijing to Shaanxi. That's the village she lived in. When we got to the village, the village leader came to greet us. My mother said, "Oh my gosh, when we were here, he was three years old. He was still wearing diapers!" That was kind of funny.

When I first saw my mom meet up with her friends from fifteen years ago, I had never seen that side of her. She just acted crazy like a teenager. She usually acts really serious all the time. With her friends, she was laughing. As they remembered all these things, they would laugh and cry at the same time. They were singing on

At age sixteen, Katie Yang's mother, Jiajia Zheng, had to go to work in Xisihou, a remote village in China. The government made the Chinese youth work on large farms. In 1997, Katie and her mother went to a thirtieth reunion for the people who worked on the farm. In this picture, the reunited farmworkers are having a feast.

COURTESY OF KATIE YANG

At the thirtieth reunion of the people who worked on the farm, Katie spun cotton at her mother's side.

the train like they did before, and they would try to remember all these things that happened to them when they were fifteen.

After we got off the train we got onto a bus. They drove us to the village. You can't get there any other way. As we drove through these villages, we'd see the markets, and there would be fresh meat lying right next to the road. And the road wasn't paved, it was just dirt. I was worried about the food not being clean. I'd see everything getting on the meat, and I thought, "Okay, I don't want to eat anything here." But the food there was really, really good!

The very first night we were all at somebody's house and there were three tables and on every table there were at least ten dishes. They killed chickens for us, but they looked different from the ones here. I guess store-bought chickens come from places where they feed them stuff to make them grow large really fast. But at the

On this trip back to China with her mother, Katie sits by a stove that uses wood and straw for fuel.

village, they just have chickens running around, so when there's a celebration, they kill one and the meat just tastes better.

It was different from what I expected. When I was little, I traveled around with my grandma because she was still acting. I went with her a lot. I had seen the countryside in Sichuan, and the land there was really fertile. I was expecting to see water buffalo and stuff like that. But when I got there, it was like dried up yellow dirt. I saw the fields with tiny little things growing out of it.

The one thing I really couldn't get used to there was the bathrooms. In the whole village, there was only one set of public bathrooms. They were outside behind a wall. You walk in and it's paved cement with a big hole, and you stand up on the cement. When we stayed with individual families, those bathrooms are just a hole in the ground. At night you can barely see where you're going.

What If . . . ?

I often wonder what my life would have been like if I had stayed in China. When I went back, my grandparents hadn't changed much, but my cousins, they changed a lot. My older cousin, the last time I saw him, he was ten. When I went back, he was fifteen. He changed a lot and I was surprised, and I wondered what my friends and me would be like if we had stayed.

I Can Almost Taste the Sweetness of Freedom

In 1975, after thirty years of nearly continuous warfare and two decades as a divided nation, the Communist government of North Vietnam conquered the South, reuniting the country. As South Vietnam fell, some 130,000 government and military officials fled, most taking refuge in the United States, the South's long standing ally.

More than 1.5 million refugees left Vietnam between 1978 and 1981. The government, focused on integrating the south ideologically into its Communist structure, had ordered many urban dwellers into rural work camps. The real work of rebuilding after the devastation of war was neglected. People became so desperate that they tried to escape in small open boats, risking storms and almost certain attack by Thai pirates. Crossing the Gulf of Thailand offered the shortest route, but many also braved the South China Sea to reach Malaysia, Indonesia, the Philippines, and Hong Kong. The United States accepted the largest number for resettlement.

Lance Truong was born in Hue, Vietnam, in 1970. His mother

I want to dedicate this story to my parents for being the greatest inspiration in my life. Thank you, Dad, for giving me a brighter future to become who I really want. Thank you, Mom, for all the years and the hardships trying to raise me. And most important, thank God for giving me so many blessings, especially a new beginning to be free and to be who I really am. —*Lance Truong*

COURTESY OF LANCE TRUONG

Lance Truong with his mother when he was a year old.

was a teacher; his father was in the army. When Lance was eleven years old, his father tried three times to smuggle him out of Vietnam and on to the United States. The third attempt succeeded but only after pirates attacked Lance and other escapees seven times in one week on the seas. The Thai navy picked them up and brought them to a refugee camp in Thailand. Lance lived there for two years.

In May of 1983, Lance came to America. A family in Gaylord, Michigan, who had adopted several other Vietnamese children, adopted Lance. After he completed high school in Gaylord, Lance went to Lansing Community College, where he studied computer science. Lance is a computer technician with the Michigan Department of Information Technology.

As an adult, Lance has gone back several times to visit his family in Vietnam. Lance has helped his family in Vietnam by sending his brothers money to buy the materials needed to build their mother a new house. When he was trying to escape from Vietnam to the United States, he never dreamt that one day he would return to his

In 1995, Lance happily jet skied in the waters near Vietnam where he had nearly drowned as a refugee when pirates attacked his boat.

Lance Truong returned to Vietnam to visit his family and friends in 2000. His father sent these pearl-inlaid panels back with him as a gift to Lance's supervisor, Robert Jackson, who worked for the Michigan Department of Environmental Quality. He generously shared these pearl inlaid panels for the Michigan Historical Museum exhibit. Lance has been back again to visit his family in Vietnam.

homeland to jet-ski in the waters close to where he had fought for his life and been marooned by pirates. He emailed photos of his brothers and himself in Vietnam to his friends in the United States.

Martha Aladjem (Climo) Bloomfield interviewed Lance Truong on May 21, 1999.

Life in Vietnam

My mom originally is from Hue—in the middle part of the country. My dad was in the army. My mom was a teacher. My dad and my mom met in Hue and apparently got married a few years later in the 1960s. I have four brothers and one sister. I am the oldest.

I don't remember a lot of things because I was so young. I remember we moved a lot. We moved from Hue to Da Nang. That is one of the locations that the American people were stationed in when they came over. They had many camps over there. The Communists took over several cities in the middle part of the country. April 30, 1975, is the date when the Communists took over Saigon. We had to move from Da Nang to Saigon, which is now called Ho Chi Minh City.

We had our house nearby the sea and there were a lot of soldiers, Vietnamese soldiers. On the other side of this fence, there were American people. Every time the American soldiers came in, I was at my house on the opposite side of the fence asking for gum. They came over and gave me a stick of gum and that is how I remember meeting the American soldiers. I remember when the Vietnamese people had a party and cooked for the American people, they liked the food. I know that every time they came over they gave us gum and hot dogs. The other thing was chocolate milk. When I came over here I kept trying to remember, what was the drink that was so good? It was chocolate milk!

Trying to escape took a lot of money and you need finance. You just can't say "I want to go" to get on a boat and go. You have to pay the people to set up the plan, and you have to pay them for food and water, and then the transportation, the gas and all that. We had no way to afford trying to escape out of the country.

Lance Truong (*far right*) escaped from Communist Vietnam in 1981, when he was eleven years old, shortly after this photo was taken with his mother, brothers, and sisters.

However, my dad knew a friend who planned the first escape. My family and I traveled down to the border and tried to escape to Thailand. During that time, the United Nations High Commissioner for Refugees set up a refugee camp there so we could eventually be accepted to the United States as refugees.

We didn't go as a whole family. My mom, my brothers and sisters, and I went on that trip. My dad didn't want to go with us. He wanted to make sure that, in case we got caught, he would be able to get us out. If he went with us and was caught, then the whole family had no one to bail us out. He would be the only hope, and maybe we would have another chance to go at it again. Otherwise we would be in big trouble.

Eventually, if we had made it to America, he would make another try to escape. He decided not to go because of the risk involved. If he got caught, he would be in jail a lot longer time. He probably would have had to spend at least ten years in jail or more for trying to escape. Eventually, if we had made it to America, he could make another try to escape.

The first escape didn't go well. Eventually we got caught. We ran out of money. We had to pay money so the organizers could plan the trip, buy fuel, food, water, and supplies. You have to pay something in any trip. Nothing is for free in life. Some of the money was used to bribe the navy police so they would let us pass the border.

Plotting to Escape

I can still remember a little bit when I was on a small boat. I didn't see any movement or anything. We just got stuck there for a few days without moving anywhere. It was on the river somewhere. I don't remember the exact location. I think it was a river that was nearby the border. From there, after you cross the border, you'll be free and then head for Thailand, Malaysia, or different countries that take refugees.

My family and I and the other people just sat there for a couple of days and finally we saw the police. They came over and pointed guns. I was looking up and they were screaming real loud and trying to help everyone get out of the boat. There were several shots fired. I was scared, not knowing what was going to happen. There were a lot of people there, about forty or fifty. I was nervous. I didn't know what was going on. They said, "Everybody get up and get out of the boat!" and they pretty much took everything we had. They made us leave everything. The only thing you had left was your clothes—that was about it.

After that, they took us to a jailhouse like a camp. It is made with bamboo trees and a few benches to sit around. The benches were our beds. They separated us into two different jail cells. One cell was for all the women and little children and the other cell was with the men and young kids like me. They let the women and little children go home.

It was really bad conditions. We didn't have enough food to eat. Water was very limited, and they won't let you out—only one time during the day they let you out. Going to the bathroom, you would have to hold it until they let you out at a certain time. I remember the food was rice and salt. We had some water there, but we had to wait for the rain to come, and we had to save water in there. They would let us out at a certain time of the day for us to take showers and wash our clothes in a very small pond. It was not even decent water. The water was very, very dirty. They didn't care who you were. You were treated as a criminal. That is what I remember. It wasn't a very pleasant time for me.

It was about four weeks. They were investigating me on all different questions. Since I was so little, they just figured that I had nothing to do with the political system whatsoever, so they let me go. Finally my family was united at home in Saigon.

The Second Attempt Fails

Then my dad figured I should be the only one going because he thought I had the ability to make it in America. He depended on me and he wanted me to become successful. He can see my future is very bright, so he planned the second trip for me to go. So I followed his directions. I was the oldest kid in my family and my dad figured that I would be able to escape. I think the main reason that he allowed me to go was that it was a risk if the whole family were to try again and get caught again.

I think the people that my father met—his friends—they were very generous to let me go without expecting me to pay anything. So that is why he wanted just me to go, thinking that I am the oldest in my family helped me out some. If I didn't go then, I would probably never have a chance to, so it happened at the right time to just go.

At the time, I was so little, I didn't know what it was all about. I just know he wanted me to go. I had no idea. If I come to America, what will I do? How will I survive? I don't know any people. I don't have any relatives. Not a penny in my pocket even. It was very hard for me thinking about how you should live in a completely different world with strangers.

He said I would be okay. There will be a lot of people there—people who had nowhere to go, no future. They came over there and they made it. I should be strong enough to make it through. He didn't say much, but I knew that he meant for me to go over here and have complete freedom of my future and myself—get myself educated and become whoever I want to be. He knows what kind of person I would turn out to be and he said, "It is time for you to go."

I had a lot of questions in my mind about being by myself over there. How would I be able to survive all that? He said, "When you get there you will get help. You can study a lot and become successful in the future." He was counting on me a lot, in the sense that I am going to be somebody in the future, instead of being there and going nowhere with the education system.

We didn't have a chance to move up in the society. It was very difficult. I would probably never become an engineer or have a chance to learn what I can be good at. Without money, I could not go to college at all. You have to have a certain amount of money to invest in an education. Over here when you fail, you still have a chance to go back to college. College is completely different in Vietnam. Once you fail to pass the test in university, they won't let you go back in. Even when you fail to pass high school, you are finished.

I followed the plan exactly as it was. I took a city bus to go to Vung Tau, a beach about an hour away from Saigon. After I got to the location, there were many people there waiting in the same house, in a living room. I waited and waited until late at night. Nobody came to take us out to the get-away boat. That night, my dad worried about my safety and wondered if anything happened to me. He took the bus down and went to the location to visit me. He had no intention to leave Vietnam.

Then I heard loud noises. The police arrived quickly and arrested all of the people in the house. It was so unfortunate that my dad was in there at the same time the police rushed in. They took him to one of the cells and started to investigate. They thought he was the leader of this escape. My dad kept saying that he doesn't know anything, but they insisted that he does. Even if he did, he would not admit it, because he would be in jail forever. I heard my dad was trying not to scream out his pain. They beat him up with gun barrels and kicked him with heavy boots to the head and stomach. Then everything went silent.

I talked to a lady that stayed in the same cell with me. We agreed on making up a story that I am her son, and she and I were just staying in the house as guests. A policewoman asked me a few questions about what I was doing in that house full of people. I told her, "I have no idea. My mom and I just don't know why so many people were in the house that night. I was just there with my mom." Realizing that I was such a young kid, she asked a few more questions and moved me to a different location. I had no idea what happened to my dad.

In the morning they let me go home. I took the bus and finally arrived home in the evening. To my surprise, my dad was resting upstairs! He was in a lot of pain. Later he told me that the police beat him almost to death. He passed out and thought life was over for him. The police didn't want to take the blame on killing an innocent man, so they sent my dad's lifeless body to the hospital. A doctor there brought him back to life and helped him return home.

Third Time Is the Charm

It was probably about a year later and things quieted down. We didn't want to take the risk of having the whole family caught again. Finally, my dad planned another trip for me. I never knew what it was like before I committed myself to try to get on a boat. It is all very simple—get on a boat, just let the people take you anywhere, take you to the land of refugees, and that is where you are going to stay. The idea sounds simple, but you don't know the real danger until you get on the boat.

I can remember that day. I packed a bag and just followed on the bus to the countryside where his friend was. His friend came to get me and I stayed at his friend's house for maybe that whole night, and I can remember his friend took me down to the boat. It was not like a boat, it was like a canoe, actually. We were sitting on the canoe and he was paddling until we got to one of the boats.

When I got on that boat, apparently there were a lot of people already on there. Later, I found out there were forty-nine people together on that same boat.

They were pretty much strangers to me. The only person I knew was my dad's friend.

You had no place to lie down. You sat right next to each other, so it was like being packed in a can of tuna. I didn't know what to think or what to do. I didn't know where I was heading. I didn't know who to talk to beside my dad's friend who was on the dock. He was a pretty good guy to me. He gave me food and water and all that, to make sure I am okay.

Once I got on the boat we started leaving, and after fifteen minutes the police were screaming. I could hear the noise like somebody was trying to stop the boat. I was hoping I wasn't going to get caught again. Then I thought they had some kind of agreement between the captain of the boat, and they just let the boat go.

Finally we got past the sea border between Vietnam and Thailand. We are now in a different country. Everyone was just screaming and they think they already have their freedom, because they are no longer afraid that the police can cross the border and bring them back to Vietnam. It took about a half a day to get to the border.

In the morning I woke up and looked around at the sea. There were just us in a small boat surrounded by blue seawater, the first time I have been out on the sea. It is pretty much an empty world. Now I can understand the true meaning of "I'm feeling blue." I didn't see a lot of things around like you see on land, just blue sky and water. It was an empty feeling, being stranded in the middle of nowhere. We just kept traveling. We were trying to head to one of the refugee camps in Thailand.

The first days were okay, and then we had a big storm come in and the boat was shaking so bad it tipped back and forth. The waves almost tipped the boat over. The water was running into the boat. I had no idea what was going to happen if the boat tipped over. I would probably be the first one to die. It was so dark, and I couldn't see anything. I sat there and prayed that everything will be calm. About two hours later the wind stopped blowing and the storm went away. I didn't know how to swim well, and if the boat tipped over, there was not even a small chance that I would survive that night. I had learned how to swim with my friends, but the best I could do was try to stay afloat.

In the morning we met a ship and it was a huge ship, one of the Thai ships. They came over and looked at the boat. They gave us some food and water. I thought they were friendly in a way, and never knew what was going to happen next.

Attacked by Pirates

Then about noontime we met another ship—a smaller ship, more like a fishing boat actually, but a little bit larger than that. They came over and they were very dark and their faces were all white from wearing sunblock. I looked at them and they were kind of scary. They jumped down on our boat with an ax. They were trying to rob everything that we had. I was so scared. The fear was even greater for the women and young girls. I didn't know what to do. I didn't have any money or jewelry. They came over and grabbed all the things—jewelry, watches, and money. They took away all that. I remember the girls were being dragged over to their ship and people were screaming and yelling. I didn't know what to say. I just sat there quietly. After a few hours, in the evening, they finally let everybody go. We got on the boat again. They took the women to the other boat. I was staying on my boat. Everybody got back on the boat.

Then we started going again and the next day the same thing happened. We met another ship and this time the pirates couldn't find anything much because the other ones took them all. They also brought the girls over to their ship and they were doing all different things. At that point I was too young to think about anything. I thought I would be safe on my boat. That was where I stayed. They were actually good with the kids. They didn't try to hurt them. They were giving us food and water. With the women and young girls they were very cruel. They raped all the women and the girls on their boat. I was glad that my family didn't go with me because I could not stand to see that situation happen to my family. In a way, I felt better that I went by myself.

Shipwrecked

We were on the seas for seven days. On those seven days we were robbed seven times. The women were being detained on the boats and the same thing happened to the women. On the seventh day, in the afternoon, another ship came in and tried to rob us. They couldn't find anything, so they ran their ship into our boat. They made a big hole in the middle of the boat with an ax and they chopped off things. Then the water came in. The captain of the boat had people try to pump it out. The water kept coming in. We had no choice but to leave the boat. I knew the boat was going to sink. I had no feeling whatsoever about dying—no worry about the boat sinking and that I was going to die. That wasn't even on my mind.

The pirates took all the young women and the girls over to their ship and they left. What we have left was all the men and little kids like me, and some older women. The pirates didn't like the old women, so they left them alone.

The captain of the boat broke down some pieces of wood and threw them out in the water. People jumped off the boat and hung on to them. I wouldn't jump down in the water because I knew I wouldn't make it. I was the only one left on the boat. I was looking around, wondering what I should do. Dying had not crossed my mind. I didn't panic or cry; I was calm but with a sense of hopelessness. I didn't want to say goodbye, or even scream for help. I just sat there silently in the boat. I looked down at the boat at this one big guy who did not know how to swim, and he was holding on to the boat. He was down in the water and trying to hang on for dear life. The water was starting to come in the boat. The next thing I knew, the water was all around my feet. By instinct I jumped off the boat into the water and swam like a dog. I didn't know how to swim well, I was just trying to stay alive. There is a limit to human strength. How much strength can you have? If you barely have any food and water for seven days, there is not much you can do. But when you are almost near death, your body and your mind are so strong trying to survive. You have extra strength inside of you.

When I looked up, I saw a piece of wood floating next to me. I grabbed the piece of wood because I knew my life depended on that. I held on to that piece of wood, trying to keep my head above the water. The waves kept rushing back and forth, and I swallowed a lot of seawater.

About eight or nine at night, it was starting to get dark. I didn't know if I was going to make it alive to the next morning. A lot of people were trying to swim to an island that we could see. I didn't know how far it was and besides, the waves were rushing backwards, so they couldn't even swim there. You pretty much hang on for your life and hope for the best.

Then someone started screaming, "The ship is coming back!" I was wondering who would come back and rescue us. They came back and they threw a rope down and pulled us up. When I got back on the boat, I laid down and I took a long nap—over three hours, trying to fight for my life, and when I got up, it was very dark.

Marooned

When I woke up I realized that I was on the same pirate ship that had sunk our boat and taken the young women away. I was puzzled as to why they would come back to rescue us. Usually the pirates would kill everyone and dump the bodies into the sea. They took us to the back of the island that we were trying to reach. They had a big long rope and brought it onto the shore and tied it to a tree. We all followed it up to the beach. I wanted to get myself on the shore. We finally got on the island, just rocks and trees all around us. I didn't know if we would be able to survive on the island, but I was glad to be out of the sea.

We were sleeping in the rain the whole night. The rain didn't bother me that much because I felt safer on land than in the sea. In the morning a Thai navy officer who was stationed there found us and took us to a camp on the island. There was another younger Thai navy officer there who wanted to sleep with the young women, but the older officer stopped him. We stayed there for a couple days until they brought us to the refugee camp in Thailand. Later I learned that it was illegal to bring refugees into Thailand. That's why the pirates left us on the island.

I asked the women why the pirates came back for us and the women told me that they gave them whatever they had left, like jewelry that was hidden inside their clothing. It was a miracle that they came back and rescued us and didn't kill us.

Some of those people were Catholic and some were Buddhist. The pirates were mostly Buddhist. The Catholic women took out their crosses. It was a symbol saying, "Have mercy on these people!" The Buddhist women showed the pirates their Buddha statue while begging for their mercy. I guess somehow the pirates had feelings for us people who were left behind. I think the women touched their hearts. We were all rescued except for one person, the one guy that I told you that was hanging on the boat. He was twenty-six or twenty-seven years old. He went down with the boat because he didn't know how to swim. When we got to the refugee camp, the camp manager separated us and set up a special place for the kids—like me—with food and water and a place to sleep. Living in the camp was very hard and the food was very minimal. There was no nutritional food. You depend on the support from outside. If you have relatives, you're very lucky because they can send you some money to survive. The conditions were terrible. You had to eat to survive. Still, it was a lot better than being stranded on the sea.

Sending Out an SOS

The Thai government was running the camps sponsored by the United Nations High Commissioner for Refugees. In Thailand they were looking for somebody in the United States to adopt children from Vietnam, so when I got to the interview, I passed the interview and they said they were going to send me to the United States.

They asked questions like "Why did you want to come to the United States?" That was probably one of the first questions. I remember I told them about my dad who had not been able to survive in Vietnam and about how he saw a future for me to come over here, because he didn't want me to end up being like him.

I remember they also asked me if I knew how to speak English, and I think I said, "A little," and that was enough for me to pass the interview. I was the first kid to pass the interview because they were very rough. Some other kids had relatives in the U.S. and they wouldn't even let them in.

When I left, and that was after August 1981, Thailand closed its refugee camps. They no longer accepted refugees at that point, so whoever came to Thailand after August 1981, they don't consider them being a refugee anymore. What happened was when they came over to Thailand they took us to a different camp where it was like a prison camp. They let you have some freedom, but just inside the camp.

I was in the first group in that camp, and I remember I lived in building number 1 and then we had more than ten buildings that were still empty. This building would probably take two or three hundred people. They were huge. It is like a two-story building. It has stairs and a balcony, with no beds or restrooms. Everyone had to sleep on the floor. The restrooms were located in the back of the building. I don't remember it exactly, how big it was, but it must have been very big because there were a lot of people in the building.

That one room is compared to, must be about eight or ten regular bedrooms that we have. So they have building number 1, and building number 2 is right behind that. At the time we came there was barely anybody there. We were the very first group.

Life in the camp was very difficult, especially for me as a little kid. I didn't have relatives there. Some people had support from their relatives from the United States or Canada, even different countries, and they sent them money, and then they would have the money to buy some food. I lived on the food that they provided me every day. I think it was just barely enough to eat. I had no nutrition at all. You just eat to stay alive. They would give you a little bit, but just one very small bowl of rice and then maybe a little bit of meat, maybe like four pieces or something like that, enough so you didn't stay hungry.

I see other people and they have their relatives and they could go out and buy food and bread and butter and enjoy all that. I had nothing like that. That was what was difficult for me.

I stayed there two years. At the time I was eleven but when I left I was thirteen. I came over here. I had no idea where I was going, but the only thing I knew was that I wanted to go to the United States where I had a lot of opportunity to be somebody. I had no idea what I was going to be or even if I get here what am I going to do

Lance Truong sent this aerogram letter to his parents in Vietnam while at a Thai refugee camp, letting them know that he had made it safely out of Vietnam.

without parents, without anybody. You don't know anybody else. What can you do? So at that point, I pretty much think in my mind that I am going to go to the United States. That is what I want to do.

People are allowed to send mail back and forth. Thailand and Vietnam, they are very close countries. When you send mail, it doesn't take that long compared to when it comes to the United States. The mail would usually get lost. I did write some letters, and my mom and dad did get them. They were very happy and knew that I had made it over here to Thailand.

It probably would have taken about a month before they heard the good news, because I was in the process of moving to a different camp, relocation and all.

There were other kids. After a few months, there were more people coming in. And soon, people filled up the buildings. A year later, building 7 and 8 started to fill up.

I was just by myself. I had no one looking out for me, but in Thailand they have the father, the Catholic priest. Thailand is also Christian people too, and Catholic people. The father over there set up a church. He raised money to help the young kids without parents and support, like me. He asked the other people from other countries to help. So what they did was take the pictures of all the little kids that had no parents and sent them out to other people in many different countries.

A very generous lady in France picked to sponsor me. She is the one who kind of adopted me in a way. She sent me money every month. The money is just enough to buy me some food and clothing. I sent her a picture of me and then I got her letters and usually, she would write in French, so I would have one of my friends translate them into English for me, and I could write her back. The first six months were very hard for us to communicate.

They started to build a little building on the other side, just for minors only. So the kids like me got a chance to go in and have a bed to sleep on. The bed they made out of bamboo trees, so it is not quite a comfortable bed, but at least you have a place to sleep on. Before that we pretty much slept on the floor.

So every day they had someone cooking for us. Then we all sat down at a long table and just had dinner and lunch, the same schedule every day. It was kind of nice to have somebody—finally not to worry about how to cook for yourself and then worry if today there is going to be food for you. I just felt like somebody is watching out for me.

During the day, there were classes. They taught English, so I went to study some English over there. I believe the teachers were some people who volunteered from England or Australia and maybe even the United States. They spoke with different accents than the American people do. I went to school to start learning English, because I knew I needed to speak it as well when I come to this country, the United States. During the night we would just hang out with friends.

I was such a little kid that I didn't know anybody, I just hung out. We did have a chance to watch some TV. They had one TV out in front of the building. I think it was little, like maybe fifteen inches, not even a seventeen-inch TV, small. But every kid was gathered around to watch cartoons. We didn't have a lot of time watching TV. It was seeing what cartoons from a different country were like. They just love it so much that they want to watch it every day.

We read comic books in Vietnam, but we never saw the cartoons on TV. We didn't see them until we got over to Thailand, that is a free country. They got all the Western society movies and cartoons from different countries. You can see Spiderman, Superman, and the Smurfs. Usually, I read it in the comic book. Then, in Thailand, we saw stuff like living animation. We saw the real thing instead of just reading it from the books. That opened my eyes.

I liked the Smurfs, my favorite characters. I am too old now, so I don't even read comics anymore. Sometimes I do watch some cartoons, just for fun.

The idea of finding me a family came when I lived in that building. There were a lot of little kids like me. At first, there were not too many, but when people started to come in, there must be at least twenty to forty kids without parents. The father—the priest—over there figured he was trying to help people like me. He would come out and do some asking for help from other people, and he raised money and then he gave to other people that needed help. He figured the little kids probably need the help most, like single kids that have no parent and no relatives. So they just asked all the little kids to come over and then he took pictures and then sent them out. And then whoever wanted to help these kids could donate some money. It must have been like ten, fifteen, or twenty dollars. That was to me huge money. I was able to have a good meal every day.

Going to Michigan

When I passed the interview, I let my parents know that I was going to go to the United States. I traveled by myself. When I left the camp, I had no idea who I was going to be with. They just tell you that they accepted you to the U.S. and then they will have somebody adopt you. I remember leaving in the airplane. We stopped at Tokyo, Japan, Hawaii, and then at another location—probably California—and then another stop somewhere in the United States, and then finally to Michigan. The first stop in Michigan was Detroit. When I arrived in Detroit, I stayed with a Vietnamese family there temporarily for about a week before they got ready to move me to Gaylord, where my foster parents lived.

When I came over here I started writing to my mom and dad. At that time, the relationship between Vietnam and the U.S. was very difficult. There was no trade between the two countries. When I would send stuff to my mom and dad, it would have to go through a

Frank and Agnes Moore of Gaylord, Michigan, adopted Lance. They adopted six children from Vietnam, giving them a chance for a better life.

lot of inspection to get to the house. When I sent the mail, I believe they were reading it at some point. They took a very close look at whatever you sent back to your relatives. The mail usually took a long time—at least a month to get from here to there, sometimes even more, that is, in the beginning when we didn't have any relationship with the United States.

When you want to talk to your mom and dad, you don't have that chance either. When I was a kid over there, they didn't have telephones. The Communists didn't allow people to have a decent job or have a telephone at home. Besides, they were trying to control everything, even your reading books if it has anything related to the U.S.—like a magazine with a bikini. They didn't want any exposure of the Western society. In a way, they were very strict in controlling the kind of material trying to flow into Vietnam.

So whenever I need to talk or write to my mom, what they used was a telegram. My mom was trying to send me one and it would be so difficult to send somebody information like that. That was very hard, trying to communicate when I was young and didn't have any money.

When I came over, I barely knew how to write English. I couldn't speak well enough for people to understand. My foster mom had some other Vietnamese kids, which she also adopted, so I had a chance to speak the same language. That is why I am still able to read and write Vietnamese fluently. I still have the accent, as you can tell. I talked Vietnamese all the time with all my friends so I didn't lose it. It is good in a way, that I still have my own language.

When you go back and see your mom and dad, you can't even speak the same language because at such a young age you start to forget things. I have seen that happened to a lot of kids that way. It is just fortunate that I have my foster mom, who likes the kids from Vietnam she happened to adopt. She actually adopted more than ten kids. She adopted like four or five kids, and they went to college and then they moved out and then she adopted some more.

When I came over, the family came out and greeted me and I can remember, it was kind of strange. I just looked at them a lot but didn't know how to speak English. I could understand a little, but not to a point where I could communicate fluently like I do now. I communicated just by "yes," "no." They took me home and they had some other Vietnamese there, so I felt welcome to have somebody from my country to speak with. In case you get stuck, you could ask them for help.

They had four kids, one son and three daughters. They all grew up and moved out of the house, so they were alone and they had a big house. They wanted somebody to fill the house. They figured that they wanted somebody from another country, and my mom was pretty much interested in Asian kids. So that is how they kept adopting kids from Vietnam. So I was staying with three other kids, a little bit older than me.

This was in the summer—May of 1983. I watched a lot of music videos. I remember Michael Jackson was very popular and we would go out swimming. There were lakes nearby and we probably went fishing, doing all the things we could think of. I think we played some basketball and soccer. It was a lot of activity to do because where I lived in Vietnam and Thailand I didn't have the opportunities.

My foster dad owned a carpet store. He would go and install carpet at people's houses and then sell carpet for a living. My foster mom worked there also. My dad would go out and install carpets and my mom was selling carpet and taking care of the store.

It made me feel like home because she allowed us to cook and talk in Vietnamese together. I believe one's own language is God's greatest gift ever. I didn't want to lose that because someday I wanted to be able to speak and write to my parents, to talk to my children, to tell my own people in the same language about my life. So we cooked a lot. Sometimes we like to eat noodles and she said, "Okay, go ahead and cook the noodles." She let us have a lot of freedom to do what we were used to over there, so I have to do a little cooking myself. We would eat a lot of rice, and sometimes they would eat the other food that we cooked too.

When I started school it was terrible because I didn't know English enough. On my report cards I kept getting an E. For the first six months I didn't even know what E stood for. I thought it stood for excellent, but my mom said, "No, it is not excellent. It is the worst grade you can get!" I remember this class, it was one of those science classes where they have to do with chemicals and you play with a lab and you have to get one of the exercises and the answers. I remember the teacher asking me questions that I didn't know how to answer. Six months later I started to catch on with the English words and then I started to understand the teacher when he asked me questions. I think from that point I started to get all A's and B's.

You can't go into somebody's country and expect to learn the language in a few months. That is an impossible thing, unless you learn in your country. You have the knowledge of talking to other people and you start understanding them. To me, it was very difficult to understand what they were talking about.

I was the only Vietnamese one in the school. The other kids were welcoming. I think there were a lot of people like me from a different country, but at the time I was a very shy little kid and didn't know much to talk. I felt that they were just fine. I was still trying to overcome the negative experience I had and because of that, sometimes I was afraid of people.

Of course there will always be prejudice. Some people don't like the way you are, the way you look or even where you come from. My uncle once said, "Life is like a cup of bitter wine. Think of each positive people you met is like a sugar cube that sweetens it. The more positive people, the sweeter the wine is." I pray that God can help me to see the goodness of all people, show me the positive and turn those negative people into positive people.

For whatever reason, I only see two types of people, those who are negative and those who are positive. I try to stay away from negative people as much as possible. Sometimes I put myself in their shoes, to see why some people act the way they are. Sometimes it was almost natural because the way we were brought up, our perceptions and the world around us.

The media makes it even worse. To me, it's so wonderful to know a positive person who is so different than I am. We have to communicate and interact with each other to find out the other side of the person. Sometimes we assume too much, I think. I felt comfortable being in a small town because there were many open-minded people.

There were a few people who didn't like me, but most of the

people there, I would have to say they were very, very helpful, even the teachers. They were very helpful and tried to encourage me to learn. They were very nice to me. I was very shy and afraid because I was not able to speak English, for one thing, and I was kind of afraid to get to know other people. In a way that affected me because the trip that I took to America made me want to stay in a corner by myself sometimes.

Back for a Visit

I first went back to Vietnam in 1995. I figured that it was fourteen years since I had seen my family. I needed to go see them and it didn't matter how much money it would take me to go. I had a job working with EDS [Electronic Data Systems], graduated from Lansing Community College, and had a degree in microcomputer systems. I knew I would get a good job with going into the computer field. After two years with EDS, I knew I could save enough money to go back to Vietnam, and if I didn't go and I didn't see them, what if one day something happens and I never get a chance to see my family again?

I went there for a month. It was completely different than I used to see. When I got to the airport, I went through a lot of trouble with the Communists. They have people who inspect and make sure you have the paperwork and everything before you can pass the gate, and they were trying to make it very difficult for you to get in. I had a U.S. passport. I became an American citizen right before I came back to Vietnam in 1995, a year before that.

They want to make money out of people. Some people gave me advice that I should pay—like five dollars—to get in just to make sure. I did get stuck there for two hours at the airport because they wanted me to pay the taxes on the things that I brought to my mom and dad. So finally we agree. My brother knew a guy that worked there and he came in and pulled me out and I finally got a chance to meet my parents.

My mom and two of my brothers came to pick me up, so it was kind of emotional to see my mom after like fourteen years. She looked a lot older than she used to and my brother grew up and he is mature. He is taller than me. We didn't have a lot of talk at the airport, but we just get in the car and the taxi took us home.

I went back to my little place where I used to live. The memories are still there; you just start refreshing your mind about where you used to come from. To look at the house, it was in bad condition. Everything looked old and crumbled down, so there were a lot of changes. I looked at the street, and so many cars now! They have so many motorcycles. It used to be crowded; now it is even more crowded than it was before.

They were still living in the same house in the same neighborhood. I just went in and I saw there were a lot of changes, but apparently my family couldn't afford—we just couldn't get—a better house. It was very hard for my brother and my sister to grow up, and they had to pay to learn English and that is what they learned in school.

My younger brothers and sisters are at the university. They passed and got a degree and then they went another two years. My brothers did pretty well. One got a job working for a tourist company, and now he is making decent money.

I was able to go see my dad. He had moved to a different location but my brother knew where he was. My parents were separated.

I went to see him and he was looking so old, just a completely different picture. He came out and gave me a hug. He cried a little bit. He looked at me, and one thing he noticed was how come I am still so small? He thought I was short; he was taller than my brothers and me. I was just a short guy, I don't know, because of the hard times that happened in the camp, and I didn't have enough nutrition to grow. Being the short guy that I am, I don't feel too bad when someone really tall hits his head on the top of the doorway—"Boy! I am glad I was short." I guess it's me and that is just the way it is.

So we sat down and talked for a while and he took me out to eat for dinner. I couldn't drink a lot of beer. I am almost allergic to alcohol because when I drink alcohol my whole face and my whole body turns red. It is good, in a way, because I never got into it. Otherwise, I would have come up here and, hanging around with friends up here, I would have been drinking a lot and that would have not been good for me. I didn't smoke and I didn't drink. When

I came back, my father was happy and surprised that I didn't do all these things.

We didn't have a lot of chances to go anywhere. I spent with him a couple of days, but the rest of the time I spent with my mom.

After the divorce, my mom was still very pained and she was very bitter about her life. At that point there was nothing I could do. My mom was trying to get me to choose where I should stay, by her or by my dad. I thought that would be wise to not stand on anybody's side. It was a difficult time for me because I couldn't say that I love my mom more or I love my dad more, but that is what it has come down to. You go home and get a chance to see them. You just don't worry about which side you are going to be on. I didn't tell my mom that it just doesn't matter what happened. I am still the oldest, my dad is still my dad, and she is still my mom.

My mom took my brother and me on tours. We went to different cities and to the beach to relax a little bit. My younger brother took me to a place called Cu Chi, where the Communists used to hide under the ground. They dug the tunnels under ground and they even have a hospital down there. People slept under there, too. They did that with the hand shovels, and when the Americans came over, they wouldn't be able to see where they were. They were hiding under the ground. That is why they won that part of the war, where they fought under the ground for so many days. You just couldn't kill the enemy that you cannot see.

I went back and saw a little history of Vietnam, things I had never seen before. And now I look back and say, "Wow, it took a lot for these people who tried to fight in the war." It took a lot of patience to do that. Because I was so young, I had no idea who was right and who was wrong in the war. All you knew, it was a piece of history, that is all. It made me feel lucky in a way that I didn't have to go to the war to witness all of these things happening. It was just amazing to see how the people have that much patience to fight in a war with somebody you barely knew.

It was very hot over there and humid, smoky, because they have a lot of motorcycles and there was that kind of pollution. I think that was the main problem. They don't have a lot of cars over there because the streets are crowded, like China. People travel with

Lance's mother stands by the stairs at the new home that her young adult children built for her in Vietnam.

bicycles and motorcycles. The roads are not big enough, and so it would take a long time to get from here to there.

Over here when I am traveling, I could get to the places that I went to in no time. When you have been to a different country, the condition over there is not going to allow you. The car that you have is not going to go that fast either.

My brother took me on the motorcycle. The first time I got on I was scared because I had to hold on to him because he would drive fast. I am used to driving a car and so it is kind of uncomfortable sitting on a motorcycle.

Coming back to see my mom and dad, I already saw a lot of changes over there. Finally I was able to help my mom and my brother. Two of my brothers got good jobs and they were able to rebuild our house. I am looking to go back next year to see our new house that we've built. They had to scrap the other house and start over with a brand new one. We have a two-and-a-half-story house. It is not really big because we live in the section where there is limited property that you don't really have a lot of room to expand on. They designed the house. The house looked probably one of the best in the neighborhood. They couldn't imagine—this was just like a dream. We were so poor. We didn't have money and we had the poorest house in the neighborhood. Then, ten years later, all of a sudden you were dreaming of having a nice house. Then, with the help of my brothers and me, we were able achieve the dream that my mom thought we never could.

Sometimes I wish that I had my parents here so they can give me the extra help and tender loving care. I don't have to come back home and worry about whether I have dinner tonight or maybe earning enough money to pay for school. It has been hard enough for me to do all that and at the same time supporting my family. But being independent taught me a lot of things. It made me stronger and more flexible to deal with situations in life.

I could probably go on and further my education some more because my family now has a decent house in which to live. A big dream finally came true for my family.

Everybody has his or her own destiny. Sometimes destiny finds its owner in some strange way. I finally found the love of my life and got married. I remember listening to the song "I Finally Found Someone" by Barbara Streisand and Bryan Adams, and that very much describes how I feel.

I still have dreams that I want to carry over to the next generation. I think that we all have them. I hope that if I have kids they will achieve their dreams. The way my life is turning out is giving me a hint. The road is already set for me. I just follow it and try my best. I will reach my goal. All my experiences I have learned in life, things I've seen from people, people I've met, teach me how to have a successful marriage. I can learn many things from people who walked that path ahead of me. I try not to fall in the wrong paths and prepare for problems that will happen. God gave me a second chance to live this life, and I cannot think of a better way than living this life to the fullest and happiest.

As I walk along the street looking at the big green trees and enjoying the cool breezes of the summer, I can almost taste the sweetness of freedom. As for me, I could never forget that event for the rest of my life. Whenever I think about it, I get very emotional. It helps me to overcome the troubles and the obstacles that I face every day.

Deo Ngonyani from Tanzania

Be Like the Bees—Make Plenty of Hives and Honey

In 1964, the newly independent African countries of Tanganyika and Zanzibar merged to become Tanzania. Only in the last decade has the country begun developing a multi-party democracy and a market economy. Tanzanians seeking economic and academic opportunities beyond those at home have settled, sometimes permanently, in other countries.

Deo Ngonyani came to study for his Ph.D. in linguistics at the University of California, Los Angeles in 1990. In 1999, he came to Michigan to teach at Michigan State University where he is currently an associate professor of linguistics and African languages.

After a long and hard struggle with illness, Deo's wife, Suma, passed away on March 24, 2008. Deo took her back to Tanzania for her final resting place.

Danielle Roth, an MSU James Madison College student intern at the Michigan Historical Museum, conducted an oral history with him on July 13, 2004. Danielle went on to earn a master's degree in history from Eastern Michigan University and a nursing degree from Michigan State University.

Deo with his siblings. From left to right, top: Kinanda, Deo, Grasia, Ado, Seth, Thecla. Front: Leah, Selina. They are in Mkongo Nakawale, Tanzania, shortly before Deo went to a seminary boarding school.

Under African Skies

My name is Deo Ngonyani. My full name is actually Deogratias, which is Latin for "Thanks be to God." I was born on the thirty-first of December, 1957, in a hospital in a small town called Peramiho. I grew up in the village of Mkongo Nakawale, near Songea in southern Tanzania near the border of Mozambique. My father, Stanislaus, is a retired schoolteacher. My mother, Rai, was a housewife. I have three sisters and two brothers. All of them are in Tanzania.

My father had a folktale, a fable, he would always tell us, to remind us about why he was being strict with us. The folktale went like this:

> There once lived two families: the bee family and the wasp family. They had a school in which the wasp was teaching. So the kids of the wasp were a very unruly crowd. They didn't pay attention. They didn't care. Why? Because their father was the teacher, and the teacher didn't care what the kids were doing.
>
> Now, the bee's kids were working very hard because their

father was very poor. So, unfortunately, the teacher met an untimely death, and the school didn't exist, and from then on, the two families went their two separate ways.

So you can see today, the bees make plenty of very nice hives, and plenty of honey. And the wasps never learned how to make hives and never learned how to make honey. So their hives are like small things like this, and there was no honey.

He would end it with, "I don't want you to be like the wasp, be like the bee."

I first came to the United States to go to school at the University of California, Los Angeles for my doctoral program in linguistics. I then got an opportunity to teach at Indiana University in Bloomington. From there, I was invited to come and teach here at Michigan State University.

I did my bachelor's and master's degrees in Tanzania. But it always helps to go and study elsewhere in Europe, Asia, or America. There are certain constraints if you are doing all your studies in places like Tanzania. There aren't many resources sometimes for things that you want to study.

UCLA has a big African studies program and they teach Swahili. In 1990, there was a professor who was in Tanzania while I was teaching there. He was actually looking for someone to come to assist him while doing graduate study in Swahili at UCLA. His name was Professor Tom Hinnebusch. He invited a few of us to apply. I got invited. He wanted someone who spoke Swahili.

Actually, my first language is Kindendeule, a very small language. Right now it is probably spoken by about close to 200,000, probably 150,000. If you grow up in Africa, most probably you're to be learning two or three languages. So, although that was the home language, once you left it and went to the marketplace, it was Swahili. Once you went to church it was Swahili. I picked up Swahili, I guess, from the age of four. I also speak another language that is called Chingoni or Kingoni.

There has never been a problem of food where I grew up. The southern highlands get plenty of rain for crops. That makes it appropriate for planting. The main staple is actually corn. There were some years that the harvests were not very good, but generally, all my years there, I never experienced hunger.

I remember, at one time, I was nine or ten; a good part of the country had a shortage of corn. People in Tanzania say there is a food shortage if there is no corn and there is no rice. At that time, there was plenty of corn in my region, but in many other regions there wasn't. But the roads to my region were so difficult that it was very hard for truckers to carry the corn to other parts of the country.

Generally everyone has to do some farming. You have to start farming maybe when you're ten years old in addition to going to school. You go to the farm with your whole family and with the other people because we don't have tractors. We don't have horses or cattle, so you have to hoe, dig up the plant, weed. Corn, bananas, peanuts, beans.

My father was a schoolteacher, but since we lived near the school, we actually did something on the farm very early in the morning. We had to go to the farm, wash, have breakfast, and then go on to school. And later, in the afternoon, when school is done, we went back to the garden and the farm.

My father hired some builders to build our house. Now it is an empty house, because my dad and mom stay with just a few grandchildren. It used to be a really good size, because several cousins lived with us. Their parents were in their villages.

When I was a kid, I loved dancing. I come from an area where there is a confluence of many small ethnic groups, and there were lots of different kinds of dancing.

Some other fun things were making toys. When you grew up in my village at that time, your parents never bought you a toy. There was no shop that sold toys except in the cities. So we had to make our own little cars out of wood and out of straws.

I remember when I was like five or six, sometimes we would go hunting for birds for fun and food. You don't hunt for things just to kill them. That almost never happens. Hunting is for food. We would go fishing or hunting birds or hunting grasshoppers. Oh, it's fun catching grasshoppers. That's food. These are a special delicacy. And as you grew up, you learn which ones you can eat, and which

Deo's father, Stanislaus, built this home in 1970 out of burnt brick and corrugated iron on a twenty-acre farm. Deo lived here when he was growing up. The house is surrounded by mango trees.

ones you cannot eat. You learn which ones are poisonous. The older kids show you: "Leave that alone!"

Worries about big animals were always there, although they are not a big problem. I saw my first big cat ever when I was eleven or so. It had been killed in a trap. It was actually about a mile from home. It had started catching goats, so it was captured. Every once in a while there would be a big campaign to go hunt down a lion.

People here think in terms of land that you have to own it. You have to sell. You buy yourself a title. Things are changing now, but when I was growing up there was no land to be bought. If you wanted to live with other people, you go to them if you are a newcomer and you say, "I would like a piece of land." They will show you, "From that little hill there all the way to the river, you can do whatever you want." That's no problem. You don't pay for it. You don't get a title for it. There is nothing to worry about. You just take a piece of land and work it.

You don't want to go just all the way out and live in the middle of nowhere. There is a saying in Swahili that goes, "He who doesn't want to live with other people is a witch"—a sorcerer or something like that. You have to live near some other people. In the middle of nowhere, your neighbors would just probably be elephants and lions. If you have a farm in the middle of nowhere, you share your crops with monkeys. That means you are not going to harvest anything. But if you are alone, you are going to be a victim. You want to be near a market, a hospital, schools, and so on. If you live in a village, usually the animals will stay away from you. They don't live nearby.

When I was a kid in the sixties, occasionally there would be animals coming pretty close to our house. Usually antelopes, and there was also wild dogs, which somehow later disappeared. There was an outbreak of rabies that caused the end of the wild dog. Some other animals like lions occasionally venture into the village. Usually the old lions that are too sick for hunting would come for easy prey like fenced-in goats. Usually they don't hunt children. Humans would be hunted by accident.

The district I come from is predominantly Muslim. My family became Christian only by accident, because the Muslims were the first to come to the area and brought their religion. When other young people were converting to Islam from traditional religions, my grandfather was not impressed, so he didn't convert at that time.

But unfortunately, when he got married he had a problem. They would have children, they would not get strong, and they would die very young. Remember, this was a time when we didn't have hospitals to take care of people. Someone told him, "You know, if you take your kids to the mission [which was some forty miles away] and have them baptized by those white missionaries, they will live." So this desperate man, who had had several kids die, decided to take the next child.

Now the story is not very clear, because this is how it was told to me. What I know is, that mission also had a hospital right there, and they probably took some of the kids to the hospital. But after they took the first child and converted, it lived, it didn't die. So they also baptized the next child. The third, that was my dad, the fourth,

Sixteen-year-old Deo Ngonyani (*first row, right*) In Likonde, Tanzania, at a seminary. When Deo was eleven, he left home to become a priest. However, he changed his mind, and soon after this picture was taken he left the seminary to go to public school.

and then two girls, they all lived. So, later in his life, he decided this is the religion he's going to adopt, because they made his kids live. He converted.

First a Student . . .

Schools were not available everywhere. My dad was a school-teacher, and therefore, by village standards, he was rich. People came from twenty or thirty miles to go to school. Many of them couldn't come every day and go back.

The government pays for the schooling. The Catholic Church ran most of the schools, so the Catholic Church hired my father. Then later, immediately after independence in 1961, the schools were taken over by the central government.

When Deo's parents came to visit him at the University of Dar es Salaam, they had this picture taken. Deo was studying English and education.

I spent five years going to school in my village. I started school when I was six. Then I went to a boarding school in the village of Likonde. It was a seminary. I was young, I was thinking of becoming a priest. My parents actually encouraged me to go wherever. I think probably my mother was very enthusiastic. But she is enthusiastic about everything. I was in the seminary from fifth grade, and I was there for four more years. I had never been away from my family before. I stopped wanting to become a priest because I just wasn't too impressed by it. I finished public school when I was nineteen.

Then I went through basic military training. I learned how to handle arms. I did some groundwork, some parades. We didn't have a war until towards the end of my contract. I had to go to war towards the end. There was a dictator, Idi Amin, in Uganda. In 1978, he sent troops to annex part of Tanzania, but Tanzania fought back, invaded Uganda, and helped unify the various anti-Amin rebel groups. The dictator was forced to flee and a new government formed, to the delight of the Ugandan people. He tried to say that a part of Tanzania was actually a part of Uganda, so we had to fight to get him out. We kicked him out.

Towards the end of my service, I went to the front for the last few months. I'm probably a pacifist. I don't particularly like war. For a year, you then also work in food production or in a factory. I worked on a rice farm. It was a huge rice farm and a huge poultry farm. After that I worked on a ranch.

. . . Then a Teacher

After I finished my training, I was in early secondary education. I taught ninth and tenth grade for two years. Then, I went to the University of Dar es Salaam and studied education and English. I spoke English because, actually by law, instruction in secondary schools is in English.

I trained as a teacher of geography and history. I went to teach in a technical school that was training people to be bricklayers and that type of thing. They were all very focused on their skills, and they paid no attention to anything like math or science, let alone things like history or English. So I was very, very disappointed.

I had been interested in language. I think that I had decided I wanted to teach when I was very young, maybe because I liked my dad's job. Three of my sisters are also teachers. My uncle was also a teacher. Two of my cousins are teachers. I became very much interested in linguistics. It was one of the required courses. I was recruited by the department to get my masters there. Because I

Deo married Suma in the church in his village in Tanzania on July 31, 1991.

liked it, I probably showed a lot of enthusiasm. So I stayed on for a master's degree.

Love and Marriage

I met my wife, who was my neighbor. I came down with malaria frequently. Sometimes I would get it every six weeks, which means I was never really cured of it. She was a nurse, so instead of going to the unhygienic hospitals, she would take care of me in my home. She would come and diagnose me, and give me medicine for the malaria. Eventually we started to date and four to five years later we wed in Tanzania. Quite often I wasn't too happy to go to the hospital. I was suspicious of the hospital, so she would come help me.

We got married in 1991 as single parents. We each had a son. People in the village expected me to get married sooner, but I would always say, "Ah! Well! I haven't met the right woman yet. I'm looking further ahead." That was very difficult for them to understand. It was only much later when I married my wife. That's when people understood. They said, "Now we understand what you were saying." I wasn't thinking in terms of living in the village with a wife who understands the ways of the village. I needed someone who understands the ways of the city or the country or somewhere else.

The scope of understanding of the other women I had met was very limited. I mean, if you grew up in a village, and you've never been outside the next bigger village, then you are missing a lot of things. You don't understand about people you don't know. So expectations and goals and all that are different. What would we talk about? What would we do? All those things got complicated. My relatives just thought I was being too choosy.

So my family had a lot of very good things to say to me on the wedding day. The only bad thing they said to me was, some of the relatives felt I didn't pay attention to them. We have extended family. You have to pay attention to everyone. When you go home for vacations, they want you to see everyone. When I say extended family, I mean, the cousins of my father do not consider themselves

Deo took this picture of his sons, Mike and Stanislaus, in Dar es Salaam, before he immigrated to the United States.

cousins of my father, they consider themselves brothers and sisters of my father. Therefore, they consider themselves my first uncles and aunts, and I have to pay attention to them, and all those that come from them. So, it's a very extensive kind of thing. I haven't been in the village for many years, so that's a problem.

They give lots of good advice. Everyone comes; everyone wants to say something: "You have a family now, you have to take care of them. You have a special kind of relationship to maintain with them."

Leaving Home

I came to America in 1991. It is very expensive to travel from Tanzania to here. The average price of a ticket from Tanzania to the United States is fifteen hundred dollars right now. That's for one ticket.

I guess I was used to leaving. I left when I was like ten or eleven years of age. I wouldn't see my family for four or five months. I wasn't sad, but I got lonely after a while. I had to get used to it. So my wife and kids joined me a year later. They are now big boys. The first year was really very bad.

I had a foggy picture about America. Rich, affluent, stuff like that. I wasn't as delusional as some other people. I had been on a study abroad trip in England, but when I came to Los Angeles, it was a big shock. I passed through some of the poor areas. I saw people living under bridges, stuff like that in the middle of a rich country. You know there is stuff like that, but you don't expect to see it.

My family came when I was in California. We decided to stay in America instead of going back. There were several considerations: One was the kids. We thought they had better chance of opportunity here. When I left Tanzania in 1991, a very small percentage of kids actually went on to secondary school. A majority of the kids did not go. When I went to high school, the percentage of primary school students that went to high school was around 6 percent.

We decided to stay here so that the kids could go to high school. That's how it started. Then, you stay somewhere, you get used to it. Then there was this position to teach and we thought, "Well, that's good." So we stayed here.

People were very helpful. The professor who recruited me was extremely helpful. He met me when I arrived before the start of the term, and I stayed with him for three weeks. He spoke Swahili, but I spoke English. It took me a month to be understood. I mean, if you come to a place like this, when you come from my background, the education system is a big, big shock. In terms of the first term of graduate school, it is generally really difficult. You speak English with a very heavy accent. You don't understand the pace of how things work in the class. It's fast, but also the culture is very different, because we are used to a very strict, rigid system. When you come here you find things are much, much more flexible. So it's difficult to adjust to all of it.

I'll give what might appear a very trivial example. I come to a classroom, and there is a student there having lunch. And the professor is teaching, and someone is chewing gum, and someone is asking a question before the professor allows them. I mean, this is all crazy. And then the amount of reading that I have to do. It is very, very weird. Add to that, my background was not in the same type of style or theoretical orientation. Every institution may have a slightly different orientation. My background in Tanzania was with professors who were European trained. Now it's a little different.

My department was very helpful, a lot of support. Without that, you drown.

People always think of me as African American as opposed to just African. The race issues are always going to be there. Before I came, I wasn't too aware of it. I was made very much aware. Suspicious eyes looking at me. In stores, even on the street, in the classroom . . .

I came to Michigan in 1999. I was forty-two. I liked America, but you do find lots of problems. For one thing, you find life here can be very fast paced. Life in Africa is very laid back. No rushing things. Take it easy. Do stuff, but don't worry and rush. There wasn't as much pressure. But I found there was a lot of pressure, academically as well as in life.

After I arrived in Michigan I decided I wanted to be a citizen in this country. Professionally, my life was going pretty well. I really don't feel like an American. I probably will. I don't know . . .

Going Home

I've been back to Tanzania three times. I first went back in 1999 to see my family—my brothers and sisters—and to pay respect to my ancestors. Eight years is a long time. You go to your parents, your relatives. You go to the gravesite. You do a ritual. It involves several things. It involves slaughtering an animal, saying some words, having someone else speak for you, giving some offering.

COURTESY OF DEO AGONYANI

When Deo and his wife, Suma, came back to Tanzania for a visit in 2001, they helped harvest the crops. In this picture, Suma carries some harvested plantains.

The gravestone is not very elaborate. Usually it's just a wooden or even metal or concrete cross with a name.

The flight from Michigan to Dar es Salaam is very long. From Detroit or Chicago, you have to go to Europe, which is six or seven hours. From there to Dar es Salaam it is like ten hours. There is no direct flight from here.

It's not an option for the village people to come here. Even if it is not a lot of money here [for airfare] it is a lot of money there. That's why I always send my parents money.

My parents work on the farm, but they are old now. They cannot do all the work they did when they were young. One of my brothers who lives there who does a lot of farming, he sometimes manages to hire farmers. It is customary for the sons and daughters to support their parents in old age. You don't have an old people's hospital or anything like that. No Social Security. Now they are trying to adopt it, but we don't have that. When you grew up, your parents take care of you. When they get old, they will always tell you that they have become children again. They have become your children.

I have two brothers now living, but I had another brother who died. He died of complications of malaria and typhoid. He left behind a son who is now fourteen and whom we adopted. I send money to support him. When my other brothers and sisters are in serious trouble, then I send them money. But usually not—they are supposed to be on their own.

No one in my family has ever been outside of Tanzania. Not even to the neighboring countries. Oh, now you can go to the cities and towns. No one leaves. Only crazy people like me—who like to go to different places.

If I had stayed in Tanzania, I probably would have been still at the University of Dar es Salaam, or maybe I would try to start my own school or something like that, a private school.

The first time I came I just had my clothes—one suitcase. When I went back, I began to collect things and brought some things back. I brought some art. There are a famous people in Tanzania called Makonde. They're actually from Tanzania and Mozambique. They are famous for this art. They make it out of a hardwood that is known as "ebony." It is a black wood used for decoration.

I think I was very happy as a child. The more I reflect on it, the more I realize we were a very happy home. That's probably why so many cousins stayed with us. There was a lot of very good food. My parents are big fans of really good food. Meat is not very abundant, but we had plenty. We had lots of goats and pigs, and

The Makonde people from Tanzania and Mozambique are famous for this type of carving, called a *kinyago*. They make it by hollowing out ebony, a black hardwood.

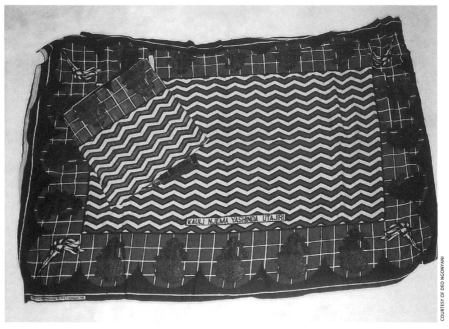

KAULI NJEMA YASHINDA UTAJIRI

A *kanga* is a rectangle of cotton cloth printed with a border around it, a colorful pattern in the middle, and a Swahili saying at the bottom.

lots of chickens. My father would go hunting sometimes. My father was not poor. And since my dad was a teacher, he always wanted to make sure that we were productive. It was a very happy home. After all, he said, "I don't want you to be like the wasp; be like the bee."

COURTESY OF DEO NGONYANI

Deo Ngonyani today. He wears a *kanzu*, the traditional Muslim dressing for men. Many Christians in Tanzania have adopted this style of dress. Behind him are many of the artifacts he brought with him from Tanzania.

Afterword

Thank you for traveling with us on our journeys with our immigrant friends and for joining us in discovering their stories. Perhaps their courage and tenacity and profound sense of adventure will inspire you to explore your own family history. Perhaps you will find some 'old things or stuff'—such as travel documents, journals, letters, diaries, drawings, photographs, films, or videos. Perhaps you will be motivated to record your family stories and preserve them for your children, grandchildren, and great grandchildren, so that they may value and cherish their family history and memories.

Discovering and understanding our own families histories can teach us to respect our ancestors' challenges and sacrifices, as well as those of others who might on the surface appear to have radically different customs and beliefs. Maybe you will ask more questions of the people you know—or don't know—as you encounter them on your life journey. Perhaps they will share their stories or be inspired to discover more about their own families histories. And one day maybe we will all strive to understand and respect other cultures, societies, and individuals. When we depersonalize people, it becomes easier to mistreat, harm, or even kill them. We need only to look at the Holocaust or the Armenian Massacre as examples.

Remember, everyone has a story. That's really what we all have in common with one another. Perhaps this will inspire us to realize that we have more in common with others than we think. Perhaps, that's a starting point.

The Sweetness of Freedom